Mrs. Naunakhte
& Family

Mrs. Naunakhte & Family

The Women of
Ramesside Deir al-Medina

Koenraad Donker van Heel

The American University in Cairo Press
Cairo New York

First published in 2016 by
The American University in Cairo Press
113 Sharia Kasr el Aini, Cairo, Egypt
420 Fifth Avenue, New York, NY 10018
www.aucpress.com

Exclusive distribution outside Egypt and North America by I.B.Tauris & Co Ltd., 6 Salem Road,
London, W2 4BU

Dar el Kutub No. 25735/15
ISBN 978 977 416 773 7

Dar el Kutub Cataloging-in-Publication Data

Donker van Heel, Koenraad
        Mrs. Naunakhte & Family: The Women of Ramesside Deir al-Medina / Koenraad Donker
    van Heel—Cairo: The American University in Cairo Press, 2016.
        p.   cm.
        ISBN 978 977 416 773 7
        1. Egypt—Antiquities
        2. Women—Egypt—History to 500 B.C.
        I. Title
        932

1 2 3 4 5   20 19 18 17 16

Designed by Amy Sidhom
Printed in the United States of America

Govert Bastiaan 'Bas' Donker van Heel
1958–2015

"I'm waiting for my man."
—The Velvet Underground

Contents

Illustrations

Note on Translation

The symbols used in the translations are as follows:

[...]	Papyrus is damaged or broken off
< ... >	Omission by the Egyptian scribe
{ ... }	Superfluous words
(...)	Translator's remark or irrelevant passage
...	Problematic word or passage

Preface

Once again, this book was not primarily written for my colleagues, even though Egyptologists, (legal) historians, and authors engaged in gender studies may think something of it and even use it to their advantage. But they are not the intended audience. I want this to be a book for everyone. It is flattering to see the titles from my non-technical books on ancient Egypt cited in the scientific literature from time to time, but that is precisely *not* why they were written. They were written to be read by people like you and me, because the people in these books—even if they are from ancient Egypt—were ordinary people like you and me, the ones that generally do not make the history books.

Now that I have finally (as of 2014) received a permanent position as part-time university lecturer in demotic at the University of Leiden, much of my time is spent teaching, mentoring, and working on Late Period sources (preferably archives) in abnormal hieratic and demotic, and ancient Egyptian law. I also still work as a professional copywriter for ministries, large organizations, and trade and industry, writing about defense technology, police issues, obstetric software, and anything my clients want me to write about. It is the perfect match.

After I had finished my second book for the American University in Cairo Press—*Mrs. Tsenhor: A Female Entrepreneur in Ancient Egypt* (2014); reprinted as a paperback in 2015—I kept thinking about one of the side figures appearing in it by the name of Naunakhte, who lived in the Ramesside period. She is a famous figure in Egyptology, sharing with Mrs. Tsenhor the fact that she was 'just' an ordinary woman from ancient

Egypt, but in many respects a remarkable person in her own right. I had just this one question: who was she?

In this third book we will therefore look at Mrs. Naunakhte's life and all the people who shaped it. This meant going over many hundreds of documents in my spare time, but fortunately Deir al-Medina studies have become less cumbersome in recent years thanks to various extremely handy tools, which saved me a great amount of time. Kenneth Kitchen (Liverpool) has made the study of primary sources from Deir al-Medina infinitely easier by making them available through his monumental *Ramesside Inscriptions*. The freely accessible online Leiden-based *Deir el-Medina Database*, which was initially designed (and filled) by Ben Haring (Leiden) and me—with the invaluable help of IT whiz kid Hans van den Berg—and finished with the help of Rob Demarée (Leiden) and Jaana Toivari (Helsinki), gives ready access to all the relevant data contained in thousands of documentary sources from the village, meaning that we can now search these sources for specific subjects within milliseconds, rather than the weeks it took before this database came online. *Deir el-Medine Online* by Günter Burkard, Stefan Wimmer, and Maren Goecke-Bauer (Munich) is a similar free database of the material from German collections. Special mention, however, should be made of the village 'telephone directory' by Benedict Davies (Liverpool), *Who's Who at Deir el-Medina: A Prosopographic Study of the Royal Workmen's Community* (1999), which has done much to bring order to the chaos of the hundreds of village workmen bearing the same names, but living in the village in different centuries. I am not afraid to admit that without these tools I would have been lost from the start.

So here she is, Mrs. Naunakhte. I have done my best to unravel parts of her long life—she may have been as old as eighty when she died—and I hope you will come to like her as much as I did. Way to go, girl!

Acknowledgments

A gain, colleagues and friends from all over the world helped make this book into what it is (any mistakes or inconsistencies left are my responsibility, of course), so the only reasonable way to go about it is to list them in alphabetical order. One exception should be made, however.

My friend Cary Martin (London) is a demotist working on the demotic material from the Saqqara excavations by the Egypt Exploration Society, and many other things. Still, he will invariably find the time to beat my English into shape. Although he keeps telling me it is actually very good, the subtle changes to any of my manuscripts proposed by him (and the accompanying dry remarks) invariably make them better. Much better. As a copywriter, I can tell. He also taught me a valuable lesson about artistic integrity taking precedence over the current trend to blot out anything that might be deemed slightly offensive.

These are the people who agreed to read (part of) my manuscript, saving me from many mistakes:

Rob Demarée is the Leiden Nestor of Deir al-Medina studies, training generations of students, including me, to become scholars in their own right. In the recent *Festschrift* dedicated to him I described his bi-weekly classes on Deir al-Medina in Leiden (started together with Jack Janssen) as a life-changing experience cleverly disguised as a normal class. Needless to say, he has made many contributions to this book by adducing numerous sources (some hitherto unknown), often giving very casually phrased tips where I should look next. If I have learned anything from him, it is that curiosity never kills the cat. It made this cat once again find out things beyond his expectations.

Chris Eyre (Liverpool)—whose dissertation on Deir al-Medina should be mandatory reading for all students aspiring to study the village—went through the first chapters. I think he is probably one of the sharpest thinkers in Egyptology. It will therefore be no surprise that he uncovered many inconsistencies and fantasies that could be grouped under his header 'flying pigs.' Well, of course—that is precisely the purpose of this book: seeing as many pigs as possible take off if that is what it takes to create a real image of Naunakhte, however imperfect that may be. But he made me think hard.

Maren Goecke-Bauer (Munich) is responsible for putting me onto the subject of Deir al-Medina once again, knowing full well that apart from demotic, abnormal hieratic, and ancient Egyptian law, Deir al-Medina is the subject closest to my heart. Apart from that, her meticulous reading of the manuscript uncovered scores of typos I had overlooked. I may eventually repay her by reviewing her dissertation on anonymous hieratic scribal hands from Deir al-Medina. This is not a threat.

Ben Haring, one of my dearest colleagues at Leiden University and a great Deir al-Medina specialist, unfortunately did not have the time to go through this manuscript before the deadline. But working with him on the *Deir el-Medina Database* and a book on the scribes from the village (2003) was always fun and a constant inspiration. So I thought I'd mention him just the same.

Janet Johnson (Chicago) is not only a demotist, but she also knows all there is to know about gender studies. Although this domain has a tendency to attract authors writing in a jargon that nobody understands, her own articles and books are always written in a totally accessible style that makes reading them fun and instructive, which is how it should be. She pointed out some serious flaws in my manuscript which I had completely overlooked. She has also agreed to help supervise one of my PhD students working on demotic marital property arrangements—a big relief for me, as a male.

Silvia Štubňová readily gave permission to use her MA thesis on the scribe Qenhirkhopshef, which saved me massive amounts of precious time. Although some of the conclusions I reached differ radically from hers, I need to say that it was her work that made it much easier for me to write the chapter dealing with this fascinating character. She also did very well in my beginners' class on demotic. She will get there.

Deborah Sweeney (Tel Aviv) is always special. When I think 'gender studies' (more or less the subject of this book) and Deir al-Medina, I think Sweeney. She has done so much for our understanding of the people in this village, and in so many original ways, that I needed to know if this manuscript would fit her bill. Unfortunately she was swamped with work, but the suggestions that she made were all right on the mark, leading to an improved text. I would not be surprised if one day there will be another—and better—book on women in Deir al-Medina by her.

Terry Wilfong (Ann Arbor) almost managed to convince me that some of the original passages in the manuscript on gender studies required some serious rewriting (well, I deleted some of my comments). So if the reader thinks my jabs at some of the authors active in this field at least look elegant, that is—again—entirely his work. Otherwise his comments were, as expected, totally *au point*, for instance the remark that nowadays students no longer understand the significance of Montaillou (the same was remarked by Deborah Sweeney). My second book for the AUCP took much of its inspiration from his *Women of Jeme: Lives in a Coptic Town in Late Antique Egypt* (2002). Time to meet this man and have a beer.

There were even more people helping me out with this project. Benedict Davies (Liverpool) gladly gave his permission to use his extended family tree of the Naunakhte family. Jan Geisbusch (*Journal of Egyptian Archaeology*) had no problem whatsoever with my use of material from what is now 'his' journal. Ilona Regulski (London) said "of course" when I asked her if I could use Stela BM EA 278, which became the cover of this book and a subject of its own in the chapter on one of Naunakhte's sons. Hans Schoens (Purmerend) responded promptly as ever (that is, within minutes) when asked if he had a good map of the site of Deir al-Medina. Lara Weiss (Leiden) kindly let me use a figure from her most recent book on everyday religion in Deir al-Medina.

Jody Baboukis did a wonderful job copyediting my manuscript. At AUC Press, Kevin Dean and Nadine El-Hadi turned the manuscript into a book with their usual and much-appreciated efficiency.

To all of you I am very grateful, and I extend my heartfelt thanks!

The next book may be even more fun. The Louvre keeps eight abnormal hieratic papyri under the inventory number E 3228. These are texts from the reigns of kings Shabaka and Taharqa (Dynasty 25), forming the archive of a Mr. Petebaste son of Peteamunip. The texts are extremely difficult, and thus right up my alley. It may therefore be time to try and write a scientific and a non-technical book about this archive at the same time. Can this be done? We can always try.

Chronology

Dynasty 19

Ramesses I	1292–1290 BCE
Sethy I	1290–1279/78
Ramesses II	1279/78–1213
Merenptah	1213–1203
Amunmessu	1203–1200/1199
Sethy II	1200/1199–1194/93
Siptah/Tawosret	1194/93–1186/85

Dynasty 20

Sethnakhte	1186/85–1183/82
Ramesses III	1183/82–1152/51
Ramesses IV	1152/51–1145/44
Ramesses V	1145/44–1142/40
Ramesses VI	1142/40–1134/32
Ramesses VII	1134/32–1126/23
Ramesses VIII	1126/23–1125/21
Ramesses IX	1125/21–1107/1103
Ramesses X	1107/1103–1103/1099
Ramesses XI	1103/1099–1070/69

1

A Walled Community

This is a book about Mrs. Naunakhte, an 'average' woman (but not really) from the New Kingdom village of Deir al-Medina. She has become a famous figure in Egyptology because of a statement about her inheritance she made in court in year 3 of Ramesses V (1145/44–1142/40 BCE) that robbed several of her eight surviving children of their maternal inheritance. By this time Naunakhte was very old and weak, and she must have died soon afterward. Her children were probably there to hear her speak (as would most of the villagers).

In her statement Naunakhte indicated precisely why these children would be disinherited. Two daughters had never bothered to care for her in her old age, whereas most of the other children had provided her with monthly rations. One of her sons was simply a bum who was always short of money, so that she had to look after him instead of the other way around; he is not even mentioned by name, because everybody knew who he was. But what would her life have been like?

For some reason Egyptologists have up till now never thought about trying to piece together the parts of Naunakhte's life, up to and including her kitchen-table conversations (yes, that can be done). Maybe because she was just an average woman. However, by retracing the steps of her children and her two husbands it should be possible to turn this mere name "Naunakhte" into a woman we can relate to. That has been more or less the ambition of this book. However, this quickly turned out to be problematic. Most of the sources from Deir al-Medina are about the workmen who lived there. Women appear much less often in these sources, so that the choice had to be made to also include texts about women who were not related to Naunakhte at all, but were—well—women, illustrating by proxy, so to speak, some of the experiences that Naunakhte and her daughters may also have gone through in their lives.

The facts are easily told. She was married (off) to the senior scribe of the village, a Mr. Qenhirkhopshef, somewhere toward the end of Dynasty 19, when she was about twelve (or slightly older, which was quite normal in a premodern society) and he was forty years her senior. They had no children that we are aware of. Qenhirkhopshef left her some real estate (which is difficult to explain from what we know about ancient Egyptian law, unless he decided to adopt her) and an extensive library. It is probably no coincidence that her four sons—most of whom were workmen moonlighting as carpenters—could read and write, which was a big thing in the village. It would not even be surprising if Naunakhte herself could read and write, and taught her sons.

After her first husband's death Naunakhte remarried, this time to a regular workman, Mr. Khaemnun, to whom she bore at least ten children, two of whom died before she appeared at the local court to make her famous statement (see chapter 7, "A Day in the Life of Menatnakhte"). Some of her other children probably did not even survive their childhood, as so often happened.

Apart from the court record of Naunakhte's statement and one related document, there are two texts recording the division of her household goods (P. DeM 23 and 25), but nothing is said about the real estate that she owned, some inherited from her father and some given to her by her first husband Qenhirkhopshef (see chapter 4, "Some Husband"). There is also no record of her allotting her extensive library—which included some literary gems—to her son Amunnakhte, so that one has to assume that most of the transactions involving her inheritance were concluded orally, and that her statement was only a general outline, unless of course we find new papyri that inform us otherwise. If these papyri pertained to ownership, they would have ended up in the archives of her children who did inherit.

So let us have a first look at the list of Naunakhte's children that was made on the basis of her statement in court (the names of the women are in italics):

Maaninakhtef
Qenhirkhopshef
Amunnakhte
Wasetnakhte
Menatnakhte
Neferhotep
Henutshenu
Khatanub

The five people mentioned first were actually the ones who would inherit and were therefore listed first in their mother's statement. Naunakhte's daughter Menatnakhte would inherit slightly less, maybe because she had been fooling around with another man (as will be seen below), but certainly also because she had not helped her siblings provide her mother with a monthly ration of grain and oil. For the sake of completeness, we will reproduce here the extended family tree as it was published in Davies, *Who's Who*, Chart 25 (figure 1).

Although the sources suggest that Deir al-Medina was a man's world, Naunakhte's daughters Menatnakhte, Henutshenu, and Khatanub (aka Khanub) occur in the sources more than once. And when they do, they make a real entrance. This is the story.

Women may actually have ruled in the ancient Egyptian village of Deir al-Medina, simply called *pa demy* ('the village') in everyday life—at least during the week, when most of the men had gone to work. The women would be responsible for everything that happened during the absence of their fathers, brothers, husbands, and sons. It is very difficult to imagine that they would be willing to step back completely the moment the men returned home for the weekend, which was generally on days 9 and 10 of the ten-day week. That is, if everything went according to schedule. There are many written sources showing that the workload of the men who built and decorated the royal tombs in the New Kingdom Valley of the Kings was at times not exactly very heavy, although one should probably not think too lightly about hacking away at the limestone cliff by the light of oil wicks without any protection. Not to mention the snakes and scorpions.

This is a book about Mrs. Naunakhte, her two husbands, and her sons and daughters, who lived, loved, and died in the walled community of New Kingdom Deir al-Medina, which acquired its modern name, the Monastery

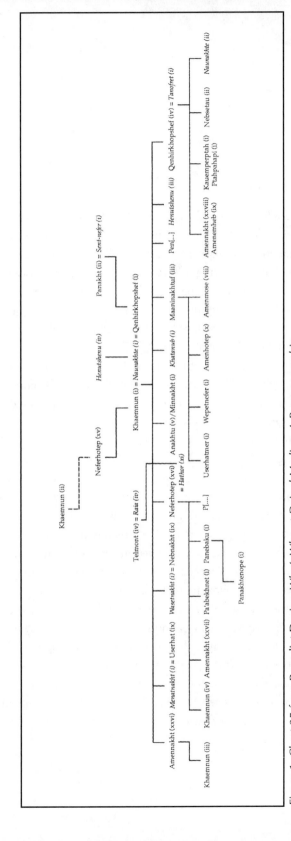

Figure 1. Chart 25 from Benedict Davies, *Who's Who at Deir el-Medina: A Prosopographic Study of the Royal Workmen's Community* (1999). The Roman numerals refer to the numbering that Davies uses in his study.

of the Town, after the Coptic settlement at nearby Djeme. The best—and no doubt the shortest—description of this unique community comes from the Dutch Deir al-Medina expert Rob Demarée, who dubbed it the "Montaillou" of ancient Egypt. Montaillou is a village in France where a man who would later become Pope Benedict XII conducted an inquisition against the heretic villagers between 1294 and 1324 AD. The records are now at the Vatican, forming the subject of an epic microhistory (1975) by Emmanuel Le Roy Ladurie.

What would the lives of these women have been like? For many of them it would probably have been short, but Naunakhte, her husbands, and eight of her children lived to be old, even by our own standards.

The site of Deir al-Medina has produced thousands of written sources on papyri and ostraca, ranging from accounts to letters and from court records to necropolis journals, covering several hundreds of years. And much more. These sources give us an intimate insight into life in this New Kingdom community, although most Egyptologists warn against viewing it as representative of ancient Egyptian village life in general, which makes sense. For one thing, literacy in the village was probably much higher than in the average community. Also, the workmen who lived there received a salary and housing from the state. Still, from the looks of it, the lives of the people there were pretty much the same as our lives today. So how should we picture Deir al-Medina?

In the Ramesside period (Dynasties 19–20) the village counted some sixty-eight houses within a roughly rectangular wall, covering approximately 5,600 square meters, but houses were also built outside the village wall (figure 2). Inside the village a narrow road—maybe covered to block out the sun—cut through the middle of the housing area. Near the northern entrance to the village there was a so-called *zir* area for the storage of water jars. We now know—or at least we think we know—that there was also a large administrative center right next to it. Deir al-Medina as it stands today is oriented from the southwest to the northeast, lying in a desert valley behind Qurnet Muraï. From the village two wadis in the north and south lead down to the fertile plain below.

The areas east and west of the village consist of cemeteries, and to the north we also find a temple of Amunhotep I (1525–1504 BCE) and his mother Nefertari (the village patron saints), a chapel of Hathor from the reign of Sethy I (1290–1279/78 BCE), and a small temple of Amun erected under Ramesses II (1279/78–1213 BCE). The Ptolemaic temple dedicated to Hathor in this area, which was later converted into a Coptic church, was built at a much later date. Slightly farther to the northwest are the tombs of a number of Saite princesses. And there were more chapels. This was clearly a sacred area where people wanted to be buried, because we also find tombs from the Middle Kingdom and the Roman and Coptic periods. One other conspicuous landmark is the so-called Grand Puits, or Great Pit, to the northeast of the chapel of Sethy I, a mysterious fifty-two-meter-deep pit which has yielded many of the written sources that make up the history of this settlement. Probably at one time in the history of Deir al-Medina the authorities tried to dig a well here. It would have made more sense to have done this in the plain below.

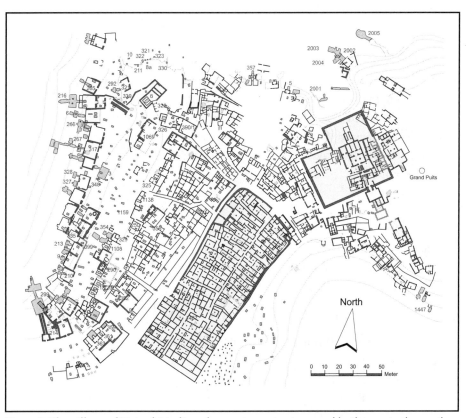

Figure 2. The village of Deir al-Medina, the western cemetery, and built area to the north (courtesy Hans Schoens)

According to a number of brick stamps in the encircling wall, the village itself dates back to the reign of Thutmose I (1504–1492 BCE), but in the early days the settlement was still much smaller compared to Ramesside Deir al-Medina, the houses being mostly confined to part of the enclosure, the remainder of which served as a parking lot for donkeys and other animals. It is uncertain whether the village was occupied under the heretic—but by many modern people still much revered—king Akhenaten (1351–1334 BCE). The village is even believed by some to have been destroyed by fire and abandoned in the Amarna Period.

For one thing, when Akhenaten built his new city Akhetaten, he would certainly have had a good use for the highly skilled workmen of the village, so that they may have been told to pack their belongings and move to the new residence. But if the village was really temporarily abandoned, this would make the theory of the British Egyptologist Nicholas Reeves all the more spicy: that Tutankhamun's tomb (KV 62) was actually originally carved out for Akhenaten's wife Nefertiti, who apparently ruled Egypt for some years after her husband's death and is believed by some to be hiding behind a wall in the young king's tomb. Who would have been there to prepare this tomb—or did the workmen make it before they were ordered to leave? Would the Egyptian authorities really have allowed the wife of the 'criminal of Akhetaten' (the new capital) to be buried in what was a most sacred place, namely the Valley of the Kings? One would expect the *damnatio memoriae* that was to become the fate of her husband to have extended to her as well, and in that case an anonymous pit somewhere in the desert would be a far more effective way to prevent her from enjoying a carefree afterlife than a secret burial in a hidden chamber in the Valley of the Kings. Unless of course some loyal retainers had moved her there and covered up a wall in Tutankhamun's tomb to eradicate any trace of a secret burial chamber (can you do this unnoticed?).

Archaeologists have also found magical birth bricks inscribed with Akhenaten's name, Neferkheperura Waenra, in KV 55, so the site may surprise us yet. Many even believe that the mummy found in this tomb is actually Akhenaten himself, which somehow is very hard to reconcile with the official policy of erasing his memory forever. But then, this is Egypt; things never go as they are planned.

Under Horemheb (1319–1292 BCE), who did much to restore the damage wrought by his predecessor, the number of houses in the village rose to about forty, and one can imagine that from time to time solutions had to be found to house more workmen and their families. In year 2 of Ramesses IV (1152/51–1145/44 BCE), for instance, the number of workmen was raised to 120 (P. Turin Cat. 1891) and, given that the village contained only sixty-eight houses, by that time it seems probable that many of them—and their wives and children—would have to have been living in houses near the village, and not inside. The opposite happened as well if there was not enough work to be done. In that case, would the authorities have forced people to leave the village? The lucky ones would have been demoted to the logistics crew (which paid less), but the workmen who were laid off would no longer receive any salary from the state.

Figure 3. Deir al-Medina in 1970 (photo by Rob Demarée)

During the reign of Ramesses XI (1103/1099–1070/69 BCE) the village was abandoned for good and the villagers went to live in nearby Medinet Habu. Some believe they did this because its walls offered more security against marauding bands roaming the countryside, although the fact that, with Ramesses XI, tomb-building in the Valley of the Kings and the

Valley of the Queens had come to an almost definite end (there were still some priestly clients left) may have helped as well. It could also be that many of the families moved to Thebes on the opposite bank of the Nile. One may, however, be sure that the people from Deir al-Medina regularly visited the nearby necropolis to bring offerings to their forefathers (and mothers). We also know that while they were in Medinet Habu they still received rations, suggesting that the authorities had found some new use for them (see chapter 15, "Protecting Your Daughter's Rights").

2

Where Was the Management Located?

The most important office for the administration of Deir al-Medina was the so-called *khetem en Pa Kher* 'enclosure of The Tomb,' often shortened to *pa khetem* 'the enclosure,' because everybody knew where that was. 'The Tomb' was the standard designation of the (work on) the royal tomb and the organization responsible for building and monitoring it. Although the translation 'enclosure' for *khetem* is correct, and people could actually be imprisoned there (such as the unfortunate Mrs. Ese from O. Turin N. 57556, whom we will meet later), 'main office' appears to be nearer the mark. This is somehow also in line with the notion that movements in this area—which housed the tombs of many kings and an unheard-of amount of treasure—may have been slightly restricted, which seems strange if the workmen had free access to the Valley of the Kings and the Valley of the Queens, at least when there was work to do. But the best craftsmen among them also did business with the people from Thebes, and beyond. So maybe the restrictions applied to women and children only.

O. Cairo CG 25831 (Dynasty 19) seems to suggest that women were not allowed to roam around, although as usual the source is ambiguous. It comes from a draft report to the vizier (the highest ranking official after the king himself):

> Also a daughter of a widow came out in regnal year 1, second month of the *akhet* season, day 30, and she [. . .].

11

Note how the scribe does not even bother to record her name. After a few unclear lines that suggest some action was taken, the letter continues on the verso of the ostracon:

> Then she reached the checkpoint [. . .]. May My [Lord] cause that his agents come [to] hear her.

The verb used is *sedjem* 'to hear,' not *semety* 'to interrogate.' The latter verb would probably also include a beating, as in the case of the unfortunate woman Herya, who may have been framed after all (O. Nash 1, for which see chapter 5, "Criminal Women"). But there is something about this checkpoint. The ostracon was published by the Czech Egyptologist Jaroslav Černý in the famous *Catalogue Général* of the Egyptian Museum in Cairo. By this time—the 1930s—his knowledge of New Kingdom administrative hieratic was unparalleled. He saw the sign for 'desert' right after the determinative of 'checkpoint.' So what is one to make of this, something like 'desert checkpoint'? And in that case, should this designate the desert itself or a necropolis (as in later times)? A useful explanation for this is still waiting to be found. Also note how the sender refers to the (probably) detained woman as 'a daughter of a widow,' but he wrote 'a widow' first and then only later added 'a daughter' above the line, almost as if this person were some *quantité négligeable*. For one thing, if the mother had fallen on hard times, she would not have been able to muster the proper dowry to make her daughter eligible for marriage. There are only a few mentions of widows in Deir al-Medina using the word *kharet* 'widow,' but there is one ostracon showing that a scribe allowed a widow to collect the paycheck of her husband for some time after his death, although this was later reclaimed by the authorities (see O. BM EA 66411 in chapter 4, "Some Husband").

There is also the curious case of eight menstruating women roaming about that is described in O. Oriental Institute Museum 13512, which may be construed as proof that the villagers were confined to a specific area. In this particular case it is likely that the problem was specifically that the women were menstruating, which prompted the scribe to make a note of it all:

> Year 9, fourth month of the *akhet* season, day 13. Leaving [the] place of women which these eight women did, while they were in *hesmen*. They came up to the rear of the house that [. . .] the three walls.

There are also multiple records showing that the workmen went down to the valley en masse to claim arrears in salaries, so it may be that their mobility was actually considerable (see chapter 3, "The Five Walls of Pharaoh"). Then again, people going on strike do weird things they are not supposed to do, so that is not really an argument. But they also had livestock, some of which would be grazing in the valley below. And fields, which would have to be located there as well.

We should probably envisage this main administrative building as some rectangular structure—or more probably structures—with a gate, offices, and maybe a stateroom for VIPs, grainhouses, and a courtyard large enough to accommodate the entire working crew. For this is where the workmen assembled on specific occasions, for instance when a special announcement was made by the authorities.

This is probably also where most of the sessions of the local court of law, the *qenbet*, were held. In a very thorough investigation of the rather ambiguous surviving evidence from 2006, the German Egyptologist Günter Burkard identified five separate functions of the main office. But we can actually narrow them down to three for the sake of convenience. It was the office where all administrative activities took place, ranging from official announcements by the vizier and the taking in of blunt chisels (these were made of copper, and copper was used as money, so the authorities were very keen on receiving it all back); the site of many, if not all, sessions of the *qenbet*; and finally, also the place where the workmen collected their monthly rations. In short, it was the main administrative office.

This would have been a place that bustled with activity every working day of the week, and we will come across it many times in the pages below. But what we are curious to know is whether this meant women could also walk in and out of this main office, where their husbands sometimes went to drink, just as easily as the men. In Late Period sources such as P. Rylands 9, 'a day of drinking' was actually the Egyptian way of saying 'to take a day off,' and one can imagine that the Deir al-Medina men who went for a drink there could have done so precisely because the women were not allowed to go there, except when they appeared in front of the *qenbet* or formed part of the audience (and in rare cases as part of the court itself) at a court session.

But this theory is directly undermined by O. DeM 570, in which several women are seen drinking at the *khetem* while the workmen's crew—

conveniently divided into a right side and a left side, just like the crew of a ship—was at work in one of the nearby valleys. They were sitting there with the coffin of a Mrs. Ta'anet (which may have been the custom). This interpretation has some shortcomings as well, however, because why would they be taking her coffin to the main administrative building to mourn over her when the place to do this would be at her own home? In any case, women were at times clearly admitted into the *khetem*.

The activities surrounding the death of a woman are more often a mystery (at least to me). When a woman named Neferet died, a number of workmen in O. Cairo CG 25746 from late Dynasty 19 went (probably) AWOL at 'the sacred place,' which may have been the hillside over Deir al-Bahari. Did they collectively decide to go to the Valley of the Kings because of it? But why? Were they related to her in some way (well, yes, otherwise why would they do this in the first place)? The term 'the sacred place' occurs also in O. Cairo CG 25518 from year 1 of Siptah (1194/93–1186/85 BCE), which was found in the Valley of the Kings, and there it suggests the Valley of the Kings may be meant. As any Egyptologist can tell you, the more we know, the less we know.

The exact location of this main administrative building has always been a matter of conjecture, albeit perhaps well-founded conjecture. An additional problem is that there appears to be more than just one *khetem*, namely a *khetem* of the village (but mentioned only once) and a *khetem* at the riverbank, which may or may not be the same as the main checkpoint we are dealing with.

Let us just run through some of the possible locations of our main checkpoint. The British Egyptologist Christopher Eyre—and this author—have always thought it could be near the village of Deir al-Medina itself, and most probably near or at the site of the Ptolemaic Hathor temple to the north of the village. Others think it was somewhere in the Valley of the Kings or in the vicinity of the nearby Ramesseum. In that case, why would so many texts that were clearly written at the main administrative office have been discarded in the Grand Puits, up the hill, and some way away from either location?

Some of these proposals were quickly demolished by Burkard, including the hypothesis that the *khetem* was in the Valley of the Kings. For instance, if the workmen had to collect their rations at this main checkpoint—and these rations could amount to about four hundred liters of grain per person per month and the crew consisted of, let's say, sixty men, meaning 24,000 liters or twelve tons—it would make very little sense to haul these all the way up to the Valley of the Kings for the workmen to haul them all the way back to the village again. Then again, from O. BM EA 50727 and the recently discovered O. KV (Kings' Valley) 18/3.584 it appears that sometimes rations were actually delivered to the workmen in the Valley of the Kings, and in sizable amounts as well. In the latter ostracon most of the workmen involved received one sack and one oipe of grain, about a hundred liters. This suggests that the authorities expected them to stay there for some time to come. Or they simply did not care, which seems improbable.

Likewise, there seem to be too many instances in which the main checkpoint is associated with the fertile plain below to locate it near the village; also, the Five Walls apparently screening the village were—at least in part—located between the village and the Ramesseum, suggesting that there was some space between the main checkpoint and the village itself. For reasons of logistics alone, therefore, this main checkpoint would have to be at walking distance from the village and at some vantage point where it was easy to monitor incoming and outgoing traffic.

Perhaps the decisive argument brought forward by Günter Burkard was found by him in P. Turin Cat. 1879 + 1899 + 1969 (it is a very complicated collection). There, mention is made of a half-finished statue that was supposed to go to somewhere near the Ramesseum, but was left at the main office, meaning that this would have been located somewhere between where the statue had been delivered by ship and the Ramesseum itself. Thus he was able to confirm the suggestion of the Israeli scholar Raphael Ventura that the main office was probably to be found to the southwest of the Ramesseum, near the entrance to the wadi that goes up to Deir al-Medina. This is exactly where the German Egyptologist Georg Möller found some traces of buildings, silos, and a number of administrative ostraca in 1911. One wonders whether this was not rather the site of the main administrative building at the riverbank.

Once on a visit to London, Jack Janssen—the famous Deir al-Medina specialist—told me that he had actually worked out the location of the main checkpoint of Deir al-Medina, and that it would be somewhere in his papers for us to find after he died. Janssen's papers are now at the Griffith Institute in Oxford. Perhaps the solution is simpler than that. There may have been more than one *khetem* after all, and one was probably right near the village. It appears it has now been located to the north of the village, exactly where Chris Eyre had predicted it would be. Someone took the trouble to go through the *Notebooks* of Bernard Bruyère, the French archaeologist who brought the village and its inhabitants to life through decades of digging, so it is not always enough to rely on the official publication of an excavation, and Egyptologists should also consult the original dig diaries (which was almost impossible before the Internet).

3

The Five Walls
of Pharaoh

Movement in the necropolis area was perhaps at least partially restricted, although the exact extent is unknown. One has to assume that the workmen usually had free access to the Valley of the Kings and the Valley of the Queens, and that their wives and children were allowed to bring them food and messages there. There would be checkpoints to monitor the incoming and outgoing traffic, probably also in the Valley of the Kings and the Valley of the Queens. These checkpoints in the necropolis area have always been associated with the Five Walls of Pharaoh, although sometimes mention is also made of a single wall, "walls," and "four walls."

In year 29 of Ramesses III (1183/82–1152/51 BCE)—the year of the strikes, as it is known in Egyptology—the workmen passed these checkpoints (rather than actual walls probably, because in that case the archaeologists should have found at least some traces) more than once in search of their rations (e.g., O. Berlin P 14689, O. Cairo CG 25530, and P. Turin Cat. 1880 or the Turin Strike Papyrus). O. Cairo CG 25530 reads:

> Year 29, second month of the *peret* season, day 10. On this day: passing the wall that the crew did on account of their rations. Day 11: idem. Second month of the *peret* season, day 13: the chief of police [. . .] supply your [. . .].

One of the first, and more persistent, Egyptologists who investigated the question of the location of the main office and the Five Walls—viewed as checkpoints rather than long walls—was the Israeli Egyptologist

Raphael Ventura, in his book *Living in a City of the Dead* (1986). He was very frank about how much leeway he had.

> Assuming that the watchposts were situated in the vicinity of the village, obviously on the path leading from it to the plain, and assuming further, with Edgerton and Thomas, that these were not massive walls encircling the village, one is still left wondering whether the five *inbwt* (i.e., walls) guarded the path leading northeast from the front of the village to the vicinity of the Ramesseum, or, alternatively, the one leading south and then east, starting from the back of the village and emerging near Medinet Habu. Since neither this example (i.e., the Turin Strike Papyrus), nor any other among those quoted above, provides an answer to this specific question, we can only resort to speculation.

In the end Ventura opted for five checkpoints in the southern wadi, but it is difficult to see why people would have five checkpoints on a single path if all you actually need is one, namely, precisely at the spot where people enter from the plain below. And even if the area to the north of the village was densely built, it would still be possible to go around it and walk to the plain through the northern wadi, so why not put a checkpoint there as well?

The Danish Egyptologist Paul John Frandsen arrived at a conclusion that was totally opposite to Ventura's, namely that there would have been a screen of checkpoints to the north of the village, and another one somewhere to the south. Although he, like most Egyptologists, stuck to the conviction that the original Five Walls had to be passed in succession (the mere thought of five checkpoints positioned in quick succession suggests one would want to keep terrorists out rather than mere workmen in, so that alone should be enough to reconsider the evidence), Frandsen appears to have been the first to have looked at the problem from a more practical point of view:

> In other words, a reconstruction that would account for all the data would place one guard-post near the causeway of Montuhotep III—presumably near its upper, western portion—with the remaining four either at Sheikh Abd el-Qurna or forming a series of which the southernmost one would be on the north side of Qurnet Mura'i, e.g., where the remains of the Monastery of St. Mark are still extant. As we have said before, this does not

rule out the existence of another set of—southern—guard-posts. (*Journal of Egyptian Archaeology* 75)

Frandsen's notion that these checkpoints would have been distributed intelligently across the necropolis area, occupying strategic vantage points from where the lines of sight would provide easy and effective surveillance, was elaborated by the Swiss Egyptologist Andreas Dorn, who envisaged checkpoints in the Valley of the Kings, the Valley of the Queens, and the northern and southern wadis leading from Deir al-Medina to the main office near the Ramesseum and Medinet Habu, respectively. From the perspective of security, this would also make the most sense. In his very careful review of the evidence quoted earlier, Günter Burkard concluded that Dorn had confused some of the mentions of "walls" and that some still had to be sought in the direct vicinity of the village, monitoring traffic between the village itself and the Ramesseum. If Dorn's proposal were followed, the many sources mentioning the workmen passing the Five Walls on their way to the plain below would then suggest that the workmen all came from various places on their way down, thus passing the checkpoints in the Valley of Kings, in the Valley of Queens, and in the northern and southern wadis, whereas the impression gained from the written sources is that they passed the Five Walls as a single organized group. However, the sources we have do sometimes refer to walls, for example in the Valley of the Kings.

Burkard made the very elegant and clever suggestion to connect the walls mentioned in the various sources with the roughly circular half-open structures made of rough stone up to 50 centimeters high found across the necropolis area. These structures may indeed have served as checkpoints or simply landmarks of some sort. In most of the cases he examined, he found that these 'cairns' were located at elevated spots offering an excellent view of either the Nile Valley itself or one of the many wadis where they are located, and that the actual Five Walls of Pharaoh were still located somewhere near the village itself. He did not, however, go into the question of whether these checkpoints between the village and the main office near the Ramesseum would have been shaped similarly to modern cairns.

Perhaps the 'Five Walls' simply referred to the entire surveillance system in place to monitor the necropolis, consisting originally of five checkpoints and extended in later years, but still referred to as the 'Five Walls of Pharaoh,' in much the same way as 'The Tomb' referred not just to the royal tomb, but also to the organization responsible for building (and guarding) it. Of course, the entire problem would probably be more quickly solved if someone asked a local officer from the present-day Egyptian security forces to pick what he thinks would be the best spots to secure the whole area if he had only five options at his disposal, including the entrances to the Valley of the Kings and the Valley of the Queens. One assumes there may have been at least one checkpoint near the village itself, and maybe the question of there sometimes only being four walls (as in O. DeM 571) should in the end be connected with this village checkpoint. Four plus one is still five. Problem unsolved? In the end it may be just a question of village lingo.

4

Some Husband

B ut this is a book about Naunakhte. One way to learn more about
her is by taking a closer look at her husbands, who are both known:
the famous scribe Qenhirkhopshef and the workman Khaemnun.
Apart from being a prominent Deir al-Medina scribe who remained
in office for approximately forty years (or more)—with only about
thirty texts that we can assign to him with some certainty from just two
find spots in the Valley of the Kings, so that somewhere around Deir
al-Medina there must be an enormous hoard of ostraca written by him
waiting to be found—Qenhirkhopshef was also to become Naunakhte's
(presumably) first husband when he was fifty-something years of age and
she was twelve (or slightly older).

The reason for trying to piece together parts of his life—most of
which was spent *before* he married Naunakhte—is that we should at least
have some idea of what he was like, because even after his death he would
shape the lives of the sons and daughters of Naunakhte and her second
husband Khaemnun. And then we have to try to imagine a twelve-year-old
girl running the household of this senior scribe of the village who was far
too old to change his ways, and most certainly not because his child-wife
wanted him to do so. Did he read to her from his library or even teach her
to read and write? Did she tend to his sore feet when he came home, and
then cook for him? Did they have sex? If we want people from antiquity to
become people again we have to think about things such as these, even if
this involves a good measure of speculation here and there (but since this
is a book for the general reader, and not addressed to my learned confrères,
we can speculate at will). The fact that Naunakhte's sons—known to be

workmen and carpenters—could read and write is undisputed (some called themselves *sesh* 'scribe'), and one should really not be too surprised if Qenhirkhopshef had indeed taught Naunakhte to read and write as well, after which she taught her children or had some scribe do this, having understood what this did to your status in the village. O. Turin N. 57431 is a student copy of The Teaching of Amenemhat, a popular piece, and some authors believe that this was actually written by the woman Henutnefer who is mentioned in what appears to be the colophon. Some women in the village could read and write.

According to the literature Qenhirkhopshef came from outside the village—although it is unknown why and how he ended up there—and was then adopted by the senior village scribe Ramose and his wife Mutemwia (or Wia for short). As a senior scribe during several decades in the reign of Ramesses II, Ramose had been doing very well for himself. He was able to construct—some people are always overdoing things—no fewer than three tombs (TT (Theban Tomb) 7, 212, and 250), whereas Qenhirkhopshef's own tomb has not been found to this day. Yes, TT 1126 has been ascribed to him by none other than the Czech Deir al-Medina specialist Jaroslav Černý (whose talent for reading administrative hieratic and understanding of the people of Deir al-Medina are unsurpassed to this day), because it contained the remains of a statue of Qenhirkhopshef and his (probably first or perhaps second) wife. Husbands would be used to seeing their wives die in childbirth. But these may be simply stray finds and there are good reasons to think that it was actually built for someone else, or a shared tomb, which in the case of Qenhirkhopshef sounds very improbable, as will be seen below. This was not a man who liked to stand in the shadow of others, at least not in the village.

There are other finds that can be connected with his tomb, such as an alabaster headrest (BM EA 63783), some doorjambs, and a beautiful *ushabti* of royal quality (BM EA 33940). But the claim that TT 1126 is really Qenhirkhopshef's tomb is not very solid, as can be read in the excavation report by Bernard Bruyère, *Rapport sur les fouilles de Deir el Médineh* (1928). Qenhirkhopshef's tomb is actually mentioned once in a papyrus dating to year 18 of Ramesses IX (1125/21–1107/1103 BCE), when apparently some trees were cut down in front of it, but after that he vanishes from the stage for good. So he did not share a tomb after all.

Ramose and Mutemwia were apparently desperate for a son of their own and they were not afraid to show this to the world. In the Deir al-Medina collection of the Museo Egizio in Turin there is one small limestone stela of 45 × 30 cm depicting the couple (inv. no. N. 50066). Some of the delicate color is still mostly preserved. They are shown praying before the Asiatic goddess of love Qadesh (quite an exotic choice, but the ancient Egyptians were not very particular, as long as a deity did what he or she had to do), her husband Reshep (equally foreign), and the Egyptian ithyphallic (with erect penis) god Min. The latter gods are both associated with fertility. There are more images showing them praying for a child. It is probably not a coincidence either that Ramose dedicated an ex voto to Hathor in the shape of a 50 cm phallus, which was found by Bruyère in 1926. Fit for a goddess, one might say. The Turin stela is just a little snapshot in time, but the fact that both Ramose and Mutemwia are shown prostrating themselves before these specific gods suggests that the subject of (not) having children would have been regularly discussed at home. One may even assume that Mutemwia did shed a tear or two at night or when Ramose was on his daily tour.

Or did she pray in front of her house altar, to Bes and Taweret, for instance? The dwarfish demon Bes protected the household, and especially women and children, particularly at childbirth. The big-bellied hippopotamus goddess Taweret influenced fertility and childbirth as well. Although they were relegated to the lower regions of the Egyptian pantheon, they played a very important role in daily life.

In the first room of about twenty of the houses in the village there was this structure that is often referred to as a *lit clos* or 'box bed.' It is a mud-brick platform about 75 cm high and measuring about 170 × 80 cm. These platforms have often been associated with what went on in the 'women's quarters,' and indeed one author even proposed that it could be a "ritual place for sexual intercourse and/or conception," which would be highly impractical, because this was also the place where people could enter from the street. (Their relatively modest size would also seem to make them impractical for sex.) It is now believed that instead of a bed or bench this could actually be an altar, in spite of the fact that these platforms—if they are decorated—show pictures of women or Bes, or both. According to the German Egyptologist Lara Weiss (who studied popular religious culture in Deir al-Medina), this platform could very well be connected with a house cult, which would include fertility and regeneration rituals. In other houses this room seems to have had a connection with the ancestor cult, and maybe we should even connect the two.

In any case, nothing came of her prayers, and Mutemwia remained a childless woman in a village where children were born almost every week. Women giving birth were not just women giving birth. They made a statement to all about their fertility, showing that they enjoyed the favor of the gods. Men could divorce their wives over barrenness and nobody would find fault with it. Surely the neighbors would talk behind Mutemwia's back, believing that the gods were clearly not favoring her, even if she was the wife of the senior scribe.

Mutemwia's barrenness may be the reason why the couple adopted a son called Qenhirkhopshef, who received his formal training from Ramose and then worked as a junior scribe for a number of years. We may perhaps likewise assume that Qenhirkhopshef—who himself later composed model letters and word lists—in turn selected some talented students to assist him and learn the ropes. And married or adopted Naunakhte along the way.

But actually this adoption of Qenhirkhopshef by Ramose and Mutemwia is all just theory. The fact that he sometimes referred to himself as the son of Ramose and subsequently may have become the next most senior scribe actually tells us nothing. In ancient Egypt the word 'son' had the extended meaning 'behaving like a son toward' or 'being very close to someone who acts as a father figure' (a teacher, for instance). Qenhirkhopshef could even be Ramose's son-in-law (but that is really just a theory). My own children refer to my best friends as 'uncle,' because they are more like brothers than friends to me.

It often happens that if a famous Egyptologist launches a brilliant theory (such as the one above), most colleagues tend to repeat it without bothering to check the evidence. Perhaps people should check evidence more often, however. In her MA thesis about Qenhirkhopshef (2013) the Slovak Egyptologist Silvia Štubňová investigated the evidence to see whether this whole adoption theory held. She pointed out the existence of an ordinary but otherwise rather elusive workman Qenhirkhopshef who lived in Deir al-Medina during the middle of the reign of Ramesses II, which would make him a contemporary of the scribe Ramose. He is mentioned in O. Ashmolean Museum 219 (actually O. Ashmolean

Museum 219 + O. BM EA 25289), O. Cairo CG 25573, and O. DeM 698, which are all firmly dated to Dynasty 19 or Ramesses II. One author even managed to date O. Cairo CG 25573 to year 40 of Ramesses II—the year in which the famous work roster (or rather absence record) O. BM EA 5634 was written—but the Qenhirkhopshef mentioned in the BM text, even if he does not bear a title, is not the workman Qenhirkhopshef but the senior scribe himself (so this author probably confused the evidence or had his own different view of things). The entries above the line (in red), listing why the individual workmen in the line below (in black) were absent, include "Carrying stones for Qenhirkhopshef," "Likewise," "With the scribe," and "Carrying stones for the scribe."

Now if this elusive workman Qenhirkhopshef, who may have become the scribe Qenhirkhopshef according to some authors, is actually the same as the man who is mentioned on Stela BM EA 144—which was commissioned by the chief workman Qaha, who was active in the reign of Ramesses II—it may be that he really was an exceptional young man who was simply noticed by his superiors as having management potential. If this is indeed the case, we now—for the first time—know the name of Qenhirkhopshef's first wife: Tanehsyt 'the Nubian,' which may mean that she had a rather dark complexion. (On the other hand, the surname of one of my great-grandmothers was Turk, and she comes from the white bloodline in my family.) Still, one wonders if all this can be correct. In year 1 of Siptah, when the scribe Qenhirkhopshef wrote down his Graffito no. 551 recording the death of Sethy II (and died soon afterward), Naunakhte's second husband Khaemnun may have already been part of the workmen's crew, and in that case he was still working together with a workman called Qenhirkhopshef (e.g., O. Cairo CG 25521 from years 1–2 of Siptah), whereas it is believed by some that 'a' workman Qenhirkhopshef had become the scribe Qenhirkhopshef by year 40 of Ramesses II. This does not add up, but as long as these workmen are not listed with the names of their fathers, it will remain a bit of a mystery.

But we have to get back to the scribe Qenhirkhopshef. The three ostraca mentioning him when he was still a workman during the reign of Ramesses II are all lists or accounts mentioning workmen, but without any filiation. (This assumes that the Qenhirkhopshef of the ostraca was indeed the workman and not the Qenhirkhopshef from, for example, O. Cairo CG 25521; the latter is all the more likely because the father of the scribe Qenhirkhopshef was rather high up in the administration.) They only mention the name of the father if two workmen bear the same name. So if by this time there was apparently a workman in the crew who was called Qenhirkhopshef, and if this is our man, did he perhaps show an interest in writing and history—as is shown by his later track record—and is this the precise reason why Ramose chose him as an apprentice scribe? As a senior scribe Ramose would have been in a position to select apprentices and bend some rules if need be. Although it is impossible to prove or disprove this alternative theory, it is at least corroborated by the fact that the workman Qenhirkhopshef disappears from the official record at the precise moment the scribe Qenhirkhopshef makes an entrance, or so they say. We have already seen that a workman Qenhirkhopshef was still part of the crew in years 1–2 of Siptah (e.g., O. Cairo CG 25521), thus much later in Dynasty 19. So this could either be the workman who was contemporary with the scribe Ramose who became scribe, or—and this sounds like too much of a coincidence to be true—a namesake (the name is very, very rare in Deir al-Medina) who became part of the crew after this.

We do not really know whether Qenhirkhopshef was ever part of the crew. Why could Ramose not simply have looked for a successor elsewhere, outside the village, where he found a young man called Qenhirkhopshef son of Panakhte? Qenhirkhopshef's father was sufficiently high up in the local administration to have been in contact with Ramose.

In the absence record O. BM EA 5634 from year 40 of Ramesses II we see some workmen carrying stones for the scribe and Qenhirkhopshef, separately. It makes perfect sense to connect this event with our Qenhirkhopshef being the scribe of that name, especially in view of his later exploits. He had workmen carrying stones for him more often during business hours, and one assumes that these men had been put to work on his own tomb rather than the king's. On one occasion he even had them—as the record drily notes—carry stones at midday (O. DeM 389). Since Qenhirkhopshef's many graffiti in the Theban hills were mostly written while he was comfortably sitting in the shade, one wonders what he was thinking at the time. In ancient Egypt exposure to the sun was actually used as a punitive measure, as is shown by the Late Period P. Rylands 9 from the reign of Darius I—probably a real petition to the Persian satrap—which describes how the authorities put an old man in the sun for a few hours to improve his cooperative skills. So ordering workmen to carry stones at midday seems more like a punishment of some sort. In any case, by year 40 of Ramesses II Qenhirkhopshef had apparently taken Ramose's place as the senior scribe.

But if we assume that Ramose did adopt Qenhirkhopshef, then where did Ramose's property go when he died? If he and Mutemwia had no children and Qenhirkhopshef had not been adopted by him, it would have gone to Ramose's siblings, even if we do not know whether he had any outside Deir al-Medina (although he probably did). If there were any, they would have a legitimate claim to his estate that would probably be more valid than any claim by Ramose's wife Mutemwia, unless Ramose had made some special arrangements.

As the famous Adoption Papyrus (Ramesses XI) shows, however, there were indeed ways to get around this. So, in theory, if Ramose had not made his wife Mutemwia co-owner of his property in some way—he could even have adopted her as his daughter and made her the rightful heir—she would be in some trouble. Or did Ramose strike a deal with Qenhirkhopshef that as his successor he would also become his rightful heir if he were to take care of his wife and the couple's mortuary cult (both very important to the ancient Egyptians)? This was the sacred duty of the eldest son, which the couple did not have, so in a sense their immortal life was in danger. It is something we may never know. In a previous study about the mortuary cult in Deir al-Medina, it was seen that professional choachytes (water-pourers for the dead) were only active outside the village. The villagers performed the mortuary cult for their deceased relatives themselves, although this observation may now have to be revised. O. Louvre E 27679 was acquired by the Louvre in 1994. It is a short letter from the reign of Ramesses II:

> To the scribe Khay. Pay attention and (go and) find an oipe of beans. Find
> it for the choachyte of my mother right now. I will give you its price, really.

The first editor thought the ritual itself (the pouring of water for the dead) was meant, but there is no reason to assume that this could not be a reference to a special funerary priest looking after the needs of a deceased mother.

Then again, who else could have inherited Ramose's property other than his successor and self-appointed 'son'? A famous court case is described in P. Bulaq 10 (for which see also O. Petrie 16, now O. UC 39617), which cites a law issued by the king stating that the person who buries a person is the one who inherits. There is, for instance, some evidence that Qenhirkhopshef lived in House N.E. VIII in the village, which was previously inhabited by Ramose. If that is correct, this would mean that this would also have been the house where Naunakhte lived, at least until the death of her first husband.

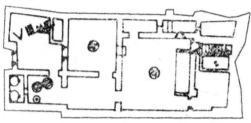

Figure 4. House N.E. VIII in Deir al-Medina (courtesy Lara Weiss)

Qenhirkhopshef's biological parents are known by name from other sources. His father, Panakhte, is mentioned in several of the many, many graffiti left by Qenhirkhopshef during his walks in the Theban hills. In fact, whereas Ramose has left only one graffito that we know of—along with a number of stelae and statues—Qenhirkhopshef accounts for no fewer than 239 (although a very recent publication mentions only 226), and new ones may come to light any day. This is by far the highest number of graffiti left by any ancient Egyptian scribe. This was a man who liked to leave his mark.

Interestingly, many of these graffiti are found in the eastern part of the Valley of the Kings (with only one in the western part)—the same location where Ramose wrote his on the cliff above the tomb of Merenptah (1213–1203 BCE), and on the path to, and in the immediate environment of, the workmen's settlement on the col, halfway to the Valley of the Kings where the workmen slept during the working week (they also had huts in the Valley of the Kings).

Qenhirkhopshef son of Naunakhte—the eldest son that the scribe Qenhirkhopshef never had?—and other 'relatives' often added their own graffiti right next to his (and in one case even carved right over it), as did other senior scribes who came after him. Whether we should interpret this as a token of a personal bond, or—in the case of the scribes—professional pride, is unknown, although Qenhirkhopshef son of Naunakhte clearly felt a relationship with the man who had apparently treated his mother right, made her rich in the process, and gave him his name (and probably the ability to write).

Not a single graffito by the scribe Qenhirkhopshef has been found in the Valley of the Queens. One has the impression that the work over there was often supervised by junior scribes, which may or may not be telling us something about the way the Egyptians looked at the world: the junior scribes learned the ropes working on the tombs of queens and lesser royals, and then moved on to the real thing, the Valley of the Kings.

Qenhirkhopshef's mother Senetneferet is mentioned in a prophylactic charm against headaches (P. BM EA 10731, for which see below), which in those days were evidently the work of demons. Was she perhaps the same as the woman Senetneferet who may have lived in Deir al-Medina? She is not mentioned very often in the sources, only in O. Berlin P 14256, in which she—a woman—commissioned several stelae and doorjambs for the temples of Hathor and Amun on her own. Then there are O. DeM 209 and O. Varille 26. All sources are from Dynasty 19, or more specifically, from the reign of Amunmessu (1203–1200/1199 BCE). O. DeM 209 is a simple account listing dates, absences of workmen, and the reason why. But on the recto (front side) in *ll.* 3–4 the scribe makes an unexpected entry. These absence and work records seldom mention women, but in this case the scribe thought this was an important event.

Senetneferet has become ill.

O. Varille 26 is even more interesting. It is very brief (it was not written by Qenhirkhopshef):

Year 2, first month of the *akhet* season, day 6, day 7. Not working by the crew on this day in order to bury Senetneferet.

Right. The entire crew takes two days off to see a woman called Senetneferet to her last resting place? Although the verb *qeres* has a wide variety of meanings, which include 'to embalm, to wrap up, to bury,' one has to assume that the latter is meant here, but still, why would the entire king's business be put to a stop for two days to bury a woman? This could only be because she was a woman of very high standing—in other words, the mother of someone who carried much weight in the village. Someone like Qenhirkhopshef, for instance. Now this is of course all speculation. But it is a strange coincidence that Qenhirkhopshef's mother was called

Senetneferet, a name that is extremely rare in Deir al-Medina sources, and that the crew—most likely including their families—turned out en masse to bury a woman called Senetneferet. And if she was Qenhirkhopshef's mother, does this mean she actually lived in the village after all and in that case most likely in Qenhirkhopshef's own household, looked after by his first or second wife (if he had two wives before he married Naunakhte)? The evidence we have does not contradict it, but then the evidence from Deir al-Medina always allows multiple explanations (which is why it is so much fun).

How differently things went for the unfortunate woman Taheny. O. Cairo CG 25554 was written in year 6 of Siptah:

Year 6, second month of the *akhet* season, day 15. Taheny died. Her burial was on day 17.

No extensive ritual there. Taheny died, the relatives had one day to mourn her when she was still above ground, and then she was stored away in a tomb (to decompose) or buried in a poor person's grave, which may have been a hole in the sand. Either that, or *qeres* actually means 'the embalming process' here. Still, someone noted it down. A woman Taheny is mentioned in several sources from this period, such as the fragmentary O. DeM 676, in which a woman asks her to send some items, and in TT 210 of Raweben, who may have been her father.

When checking the sources from Deir al-Medina for the burials of women, strange things happen. There is, for instance, O. Černý 19, which is a letter about the funeral of someone's wife:

The draftsman Pay says to his son, the draftsman Paraemheb. Make a point of looking for the two heart amulets of faience of which I told you that I gave (the) price to its owner, wherever he is, because he will long for their price (he only promised to pay, and then the son had to buy these amulets?). You must (also) make a point of looking for this incense of which I told you (to use it) to treat the coffin of your mother with oil (. . .).

It is in a way a sad message. But the photocopy of O. Černý 19 from Oxford also shows the transcription into hieroglyphs of O. Catholic University of America no. 148 (listed as Černý MSS 1.793) dated to year 28 of

Ramesses III. It mentions a *menet* jar of beer and some loaves (another party ostracon?) and several people, among them a woman called Naunakhte, who could of course be anyone, herself or one of her granddaughters.

But we really have to get back to P. BM EA 10731. Since nobody would think of wearing a charm against headaches if these only came about every now and then, one is severely tempted to suspect that Qenhirkhopshef may have suffered from bouts of migraine, which would not come as a surprise in view of some of the things he did, apart from the huge responsibilities carried by the senior scribe of Deir al-Medina and having a pretty twelve-year-old wife called Naunakhte (we do not know how she looked, but olive skin and black hair is probably not too far off the mark). Senior scribes reported directly to the vizier, also meaning that during inspection visits by the administration they would be held directly accountable to him. One likes to think (although this is conjecture) that when the vizier visited the village for some official business he also brought scribes along to go through the books, so the village scribes really did have huge responsibilities. Battling at home with a twelve-year-old wife who was no doubt coveted by some of the workmen would not have improved things either. Migraines would also help to explain Qenhirkhopshef's handwriting, which is probably the most atrocious New Kingdom hieratic ever seen. Qenhirkhopshef did sometimes report ill, but not very often. There are only eight ostraca that record him reporting ill (in a career that spanned decades), and six of these were only for a day.

In O. Ashmolean Museum 167 (reign of Amunmessu) he was absent from day 14 of the third month of the *shemu* season up to and including day 7 of the next month. In each entry his name directly follows the day date. It precedes any other name that may follow, reflecting his status in the village. But maybe he was elsewhere on business, or maybe someone had become ill in the family? Who knows?

In the Egyptological literature Qenhirkhopshef has received mostly negative comments, and indeed there are sources indicating that Naunakhte's first husband was not always acting in line with his position.

P. Salt 124 is nowadays referred to as P. BM EA 10055. It is dated to the end of Dynasty 19 (or the reign of Siptah). It contains a long list of allegations made by the workman Amunnakhte against the chief workman Paneb, who was not only something of a sex maniac forcing himself onto many women in Deir al-Medina but also a thief who was not averse to issuing death threats to others (including his adoptive father Neferhotep) or beating them up if things did not go entirely his way. On one occasion he was reported throwing stones at people. On another he seems to have offered some stolen goods to the goddess Hathor, with Qenhirkhopshef knowing, but doing nothing to stop it.

Figure 5. Qenhirkhopshef's handwriting on a good day (Černý, *Ostraca Hiératiques* (1930–35))

If all these allegations made by Amunnakhte had been true—they included theft of royal mortuary and divine property—one wonders why the authorities did not have Paneb executed on the spot, but nothing of the sort happened. There are several intriguing lines in the deposition by Amunnakhte—made directly to the vizier or his deputy—that also heavily implicate Qenhirkhopshef. It would have required some guts from any simple workman of the crew to raise allegations against both a chief workman and the senior scribe and expect to keep one's job. Or live, for that matter. But this time Paneb had crossed the line.

The workman Amunnakhte was, however, not a complete nobody. He was the son of the late chief workman Nebnefer. When he died, Amunnakhte's brother Neferhotep was promoted in his place, but he was apparently killed by 'the enemy.' Now Paneb had been adopted as a son by his brother Neferhotep and what he did next was outrageous. Now that Neferhotep was dead, one of the obvious candidates for the position of chief workman would probably have been Amunnakhte himself. Instead, Paneb took five slaves from the possessions of Amunnakhte's father— Paneb's adoptive grandfather—and gave these to the vizier Paraemheb to be promoted to this position himself. This essentially means that by now Amunnakhte was taking on a chief workman, the senior village scribe, and a former vizier at the same time, something he would never have done if he did not have some substantial backing that we are no longer aware of.

In the statement made by Amunnakhte, Qenhirkhopshef is mentioned twice explicitly, and in one case it seems clear that he had been bribed by Paneb to cover up some crime committed by the latter. Paneb and Qenhirkhopshef are also mentioned together in O. Ashmolean Museum 197, in which another allusion is made to a cover-up, this time involving the workman Rahotep, who for some reason had been cutting the scribe's hair (maybe he was simply the village barber). In the lines that follow, someone pays something for hiding crimes, meaning that Qenhirkhopshef either bribed Rahotep or was bribed by him (which appears to be the more likely option). This would be embarrassing, because as senior scribe Qenhirkhopshef was also a member of the *qenbet*, the local court of law, which could also be described as the plaything of the village elite (who mostly acted as members of this court). The sources indicating this are few (e.g., O. DeM 918 and possibly also O. IFAO 1079), but if we compare it to the numerous times the senior scribe Amunnakhte son of Ipuy was a member of the court, it seems that much of the written evidence from Deir al-Medina is still lying about somewhere, waiting to be found.

We do not know how this story ended, but we do know that on several occasions Qenhirkhopshef pressed workmen into doing work for him during their regular office hours. The same seems to apply to O. DeM 534, for example, which describes how the workman Neferhotep was absent from work because he was painting the funerary equipment of the chief workman Paneb. One should, however, be cautious. The line between official and private business seems to have been very thin in ancient Egypt to start with and a senior scribe or a chief workman would have had prerogatives. These may very well have included the right to recruit workmen to do private work for them as long as it would not interfere with the regular work, meaning that taking two men out of a workforce of thirty may have been standard and accepted practice. There are various sources reporting that workmen were absent because they had been taken by Qenhirkhopshef to carry stones (e.g., O. BM EA 5634 from year 40 of Ramesses II), but if this were really illegal, one would not have expected a junior scribe to have reported it in an absence roster in the first place.

Or one could of course try some bookkeeping trick. We may be on to the latter in the case of some texts from Cairo. In the spring of 1922 Howard Carter found a number of limestone ostraca near KV 47 (Siptah). They were rolled up in a mat and placed on a shelf in what appears to have been a shelter of some sort. Since two limestone desks were found nearby, one may surmise that in antiquity this had been the mobile work office of a scribe. This junior scribe was a contemporary of Qenhirkhopshef, and the latter actually occurs in a number of the texts written by him. The ostraca now carry the inventory numbers O. Cairo CG 25779–25785. They all date to the same reign, which was probably that of Amunmessu. What is striking about these ostraca is that they are unusually large, one even measuring 52 × 15.5 cm (a very weird format). They are straightforward work journals (or absence records) in a neat but not very elegant handwriting. Four of the ostraca—O. Cairo CG 25780, 25782, 25783, and 25784—list consecutive working days between the fourth month of the *peret* season, day 2 of year 3, and the third month of the *shemu* season, day 29 of year 4. This is not to say that we are missing an entire year in the accounts here. Day 18 of the third month of the *shemu* season was actually Amunmessu's accession day, meaning that the new year of the civil calendar would start on that day. Not very surprisingly, the first entry in O. Cairo CG 25784 on day 18 of the third month of the *shemu* season lists quite a number of workmen reporting ill, either as the result of heavy partying the night before to celebrate Amunmessu's upcoming accession day or because they were planning to do so on the day itself and to enjoy a long weekend (the regular weekend was days 9–10 of the ten-day week) to recover. It so happens that both O. Cairo CG 25780 and 25782 contain entries for days 27–28 of the fourth month of the *peret* season in year 3. Since the header of O. Cairo CG 25780 states that it refers to the fourth month of the *peret* season, we may be sure that all the dates on the ostraca refer to this month. And maybe—just maybe—these dates were redone by the scribe of O. Cairo CG 25782 to cover up some of Qenhirkhopshef's allegedly illicit exploits. After all, this was a junior scribe who would have to answer to him. But then why keep the ostracon that seemingly implicated Qenhirkhopshef and not simply throw it away or, better still, destroy it?

These are some of the entries:

O. Cairo CG 25780	O. Cairo CG 25782
(Fourth month of the *peret* season), day 27	Year 3, fourth month of the *peret* season, day 27
Rahotep, Kasa: likewise	Chief workman Neferhotep: ill Nebnefer son of Wadjmose: ill Nebnefer son of Nakhy: ill Amenemope: brewing for Hathor Rahotep: ill
(Fourth month of the *peret* season), day 28 Chief workman Neferhotep: inactive Rahotep, Kasa: with likewise Amenemope: offering to Hathor Pendua: ill Qaha: inactive	Fourth month of the *peret* season, day 28 Chief workman Neferhotep: ill Nebnefer, both: ill Rahotep: ill Pendua: offering to the Mistress of the Northern Wind (Hathor) Amenemope: likewise The draftsman Neferhotep: at his feast Qaha

Since the entry for day 25 dealing with the workmen Rahotep and Kasa states that they were with the scribe Qenhirkhopshef, we can safely assume that the entries for days 27 and 28 ("Rahotep, Kasa: with likewise") refer to the same, even if we do not know what exactly they were doing there. So when our junior scribe started on O. Cairo CG 25782 it appears he may have glanced over O. Cairo CG 25780 once more and then decided that it might be advisable to slightly alter the data. This way the workman Kasa—who had been requisitioned by Qenhirkhopshef—vanished from the books altogether, whereas Rahotep was now suddenly listed as ill instead of working on some private exploit by Qenhirkhopshef. Then the scribe decided to stash the ostraca together in a safe place, which worked, because they were only found in 1922 during the Carter–Carnarvon excavations.

As we saw earlier, in O. Ashmolean Museum 197 the same workman Rahotep is mentioned. This text also mentions Paneb, while suggesting that some irregularity had taken place involving Qenhirkhopshef and Rahotep, namely a bribe to keep silent.

It is somehow easy to see why Qenhirkhopshef always gets such a bad press in the literature and some of the evidence does indeed appear incriminating, but—it is useful to stress this once again—one has to bear in mind that in ancient Egypt the public and private spheres were not distinguished in the way they are today. Why would the chief workman Neferhotep have depicted Qenhirkhopshef on one of the walls of his tomb chapel if he had been all bad? There he is shown with several of Neferhotep's relatives, including the latter's brother Amunnakhte (not to be confused with Naunakhte's sons Neferhotep and Amunnakhte), the same man who made some very serious allegations against him in P. Salt 124. On the other hand, until recently this was just about the only depiction of Qenhirkhopshef in any Deir al-Medina tomb, other than his 'adoptive father' Ramose, who appears in other people's tombs multiple times. But could this really be an indication of his unpopularity in the village? One wonders.

In 2014 the American Egyptologist Emily Teeter published a stela—inscribed on all four sides—that is now in the Oriental Institute in Chicago (Stela Oriental Institute Museum 14315). It was found at Medinet Habu in 1928. The stela was commissioned or possibly even made by the workman Khaemtir (the owner of TT 220) around year 40 of Ramesses II. The three 'lesser' sides depict several generations of his family and were probably made a generation or so after the main depiction on the recto. The most prominent picture on the frontal side is actually none other than the scribe Qenhirkhopshef, which suggests that Khaemtir may have been very much indebted to him, probably meaning that the former helped him to get a job as a workman. The stela shows Qenhirkhopshef—in the typical Egyptian way, so that he could be anyone—but there is also an inscription:

> Giving adorations to Amun-Ra Lord of the Thrones of the Two Lands, kissing the earth for Ptah Lord of Truth, King of the Two Lands, so that he may cause that my name lasts in his temple, for the *ka* of the royal scribe in the Place of Truth Qenhirkhopshef, true of voice.

If this side of the stela only contained this text, one could surmise it had actually been commissioned by Qenhirkhopshef himself, but it also mentions Khaemtir (as its maker) and several others. But if the other three sides were indeed done much later, the stela could then actually have been placed with Qenhirkhopshef's image facing a blind wall, giving him something to think about in the afterlife. This would not be a good thing, because nobody entering the chapel would have seen his picture and said a prayer for him, thus consigning him to oblivion forever, at least in this particular tomb chapel.

In any case, Qenhirkhopshef was obviously an important man in the village, even if he may at times have come across in a way that prompted Černý's quote: "We cannot escape a suspicion that he was rather a vain man." As if that would be a bad thing. One could also say that maybe he understood his role in the village better than most.

In the halfway camp between the village and the Valley of the Kings on the col overlooking the valley below, where the workmen stayed when working in the royal tomb, for instance, he occupied the largest and most luxurious hut (house R in the eastern group), which he may have inherited from his 'adoptive father' Ramose. Here he proudly noted on the seat on which he would relax after a long day of sitting in the shade, while the workmen hacked out, stuccoed, or painted the royal tomb by the light of oil lamps:

> The scribe of Pharaoh in the Place of Truth Ramose. His son, who makes his name live, Qenhirkhopshef.

Ramose and Qenhirkhopshef together even had a beautiful (expensive) offering table made that mentions both their names (Louvre inv. no. E 13998), and the latter is likewise named on one of the statues of Ramose (which may go a long way to explain why previous authors thought he was adopted by Ramose). He even had his own reserved business seat in the Valley of the Kings, in a shadowy spot near KV 8 (Merenptah), where he could supervise the work (in a way). Graffito no. 1400 is in bold hieratic. The workmen would all know it was his seat, so to whom did he address this message?

> The sitting place of the scribe Qenhirkhopshef.

One has to suppose this was to deter people (those that could read his handwriting) from taking his seat when he was absent, but absent is absent, so that one should probably not be surprised if some of the workmen would use it when he was out of the way—or worse, that someone might have peed on it and told his friends about it, so that the next time Qenhirkhopshef sat there they would have a good laugh together.

Qenhirkhopshef did own an extensive library and he copied texts, showing a distinct interest in lexicography and history. He compiled correct or almost correct kings' lists. It is easy to see him instructing his young wife Naunakhte about the things he knew, proud to display his knowledge (again speculation, but still). An offering table now in Marseille mentions no fewer than thirty-four royals, including Seqenenra Taâ (who was the first to launch a military campaign against the so-called Hyksos in the north and was killed in the process) and his wife, although one should note that the compilation of kings' lists happened more often in Deir al-Medina. On O. Cairo JdE 72503 (O. Carnarvon 301) Qenhirkhopshef jotted down the names of sixteen princes, all sons of Ramesses II, but there would of course have been many more of these by the end of his long reign. In a list covering Dynasty 18 (O. Cairo CG 25646) he skipped Hatshepsut—a woman—and the Amarna kings, which was surely not by accident. On the verso of the text Qenhirkhopshef wrote the names of both Montuhotep II and Horemheb. The first king founded the Middle Kingdom, thus ending a period of serious unrest (which took him thirty years or so), while the second restored order after the Amarna heresy, clearly a traumatic period for many. Yes, Qenhirkhopshef was interested in history, and one assumes that he may have used these texts to teach new students.

He probably regularly consulted his Dream Book (P. Chester Beatty III) and used the back of it to copy the famous story of the Battle of Qadesh by Ramesses II (obviously a ruler he was interested in), in which the king—in his own words—practically annihilated the Hittites. By some strange quirk of fate, however, Ramesses II was then still forced to conclude a peace treaty with them, suggesting that this battle (and who knows how many skirmishes before and after that) had actually ended in a stalemate in which neither side could claim victory. Since Qenhirkhopshef's Dream Book was mostly concerned with men's issues—for instance, what does it mean when you have an erection in your dream?—one can imagine that on specific days he may have felt slightly troubled. Omens were a big thing in ancient Egypt and the events that occurred in people's dreams could be either good or bad omens.

One text from his library—presumably worn folded up as a charm or amulet around his neck—really stands out. P. BM EA 10731 is a prophylactic charm against headaches. It came from the personal archive of the British Egyptologist Percy Newberry. According to its editor, I.E.S. Edwards, who is mostly known as the author of *The Pyramids of Egypt* (1946 and 1986), but also revered by his colleagues for his many outstanding purely scientific publications, the charm consists of numerous fragments written on the back of a draft letter (or possibly the other way around). Edwards had a penchant for attacking grueling hieratic—he published the *Oracular Decrees* from the Late Period, which until then had been almost illegible—and according to him, this charm was clearly ("beyond reasonable doubt") written by Qenhirkhopshef himself. The text preserved on the papyrus is also known from O. Ashmolean Museum 300 (O. Gardiner 300) and O. Leipzig 42 (or 5152), demonstrating that there were other people in ancient Egypt who were interested in a spell protecting them from headaches. It was supposed to repel a demon called Sehaqeq, who is depicted as a young man covering his face with his arm. This suggests he was either a migraine case himself or was shielding other people from his *malocchio*. The notion that someone's evil eye can give you terrible headaches, by the way, is an Italian superstition that has survived to this day. This would help to explain why Qenhirkhopshef may have had a bad temper in daily life.

Since the edition by Edwards is nothing short of brilliant as it is, even if some may find it slightly outdated, I include here his own translation from the *Journal of Egyptian Archaeology* 54, with some minor adjustments for the reader's convenience. It shows nicely how difficult the first edition of an ancient Egyptian text can really be, especially when the hieratic writing is poor.

> [Get back,] you, Sehaqeq, who came forth from heaven and earth, whose eyes are in his head and whose tongue is in his jaws. He feeds on excrements. His right arm is outstretched. His face discerns (?) the stars beholding them (?). He lives on dung, lord of what is hidden [in] the southern [heaven]. He who is in the netherworld fears [him]. Nedjerhesemem is the name of thy mother, Djubeshet is the name of [thy father. If] you come (against) the scribe Qenhirkhopshef son of Senetneferet I shall come forth (to) (?) . . . you (?), your arms being far [from] you, [you] shall not fall upon me. I am Terus-behind-his-shrine. To be recited four times over a (stem of) flax (?),

the stalk (?) of which is made into an arrow, tie [it] to it. The . . . of the arrow shall be outwards.

If this would not scare off Sehaqeq, what would? It is unclear whether it was actually this spell itself that was to be tied to an arrow (and then shot away?) or if it was always worn around the neck. If the text was to be shot away tied to an arrow, the owner of the spell would have to retrieve it each time, or have the same spell written all over again each time, which seems slightly difficult to believe. But we can now picture the people of Deir al-Medina—or at least some of them—sitting on their roofs at night (where much of their lives were spent, sleeping for instance) talking to each other, with the neighbors sitting within immediate earshot, or catching up on the spells that needed to be spoken to keep their children safe at night or to ensnare that handsome guy or girl next door. The example written on O. DeM 1057 is given here in the (slightly altered) translation by the Dutch Egyptologist Joris Borghouts, *Ancient Egyptian Magical Texts* (1978):

> Hail to you Rahorakhty, Father of the Gods. Hail to you Seven Hathors, dressed in wrappings of red linen. Hail to you Gods, Lords of Heaven and Earth. Let (the woman) N.N. born of N.N. come after me like a cow after grass, like a maidservant after her children, like a herdsman after his cattle. If they fail to make her come after me I will set <fire to> Busiris and burn <Osiris>!

How the writer of this love spell intended to burn down these two very sacred icons and get away with it is not known. The tone of voice in the communication with the gods is often quite frank. The much later love spells in demotic and Greek mostly seem to be aimed at breaking up an existing relationship (or marriage) so that the supplicant could take the vacant position, and this may well also be the case here. But these were often young men and women packed together in a small community. Of course their hormones would bother them from time to time.

When trying to pinpoint Qenhirkhopshef in time—meaning the time he was in office, the age at which he married Naunakhte, who could hardly have been his first wife, and the age at which he died—things start to become confused. There is some evidence that he did have one or perhaps even more wives before Naunakhte. In O. BM EA 5634 from year 40 of Ramesses II—an absence record—the workman Paherypedjet seems to be absent relatively often, as Štubňová noted. But that was probably because he also moonlighted as the village doctor. On day 25 of the first month of the *shemu* season he was absent "to make medicine for the scribe's wife." The two days after that he was again absent, as well as on days 2–8 of the next month. If all this was because of the scribe's wife—the scribe in this case can hardly have been anyone else but Qenhirkhopshef—she must have been very ill indeed, or delivering a baby, and may have died soon afterward, although the record does not mention any death in this case, whereas it does in the case of some of the workmen. (Then again, the text deals with the workmen, not with the scribe.) Janssen was the first to show that even these boring absence records contained much useful information about the daily lives of the workmen, and of their wives and daughters. O. Ashmolean Museum 563 and 679 are two very fragmentary records providing such information. Both were only very recently published in the *Zeitschrift für Ägyptische Sprache und Altertumskunde*, the German scientific journal. O. Ashmolean Museum 563 (Ramesses IV or V) reads:

[...] Nebnefer: ill, deceased. [...] Hormin: ill, deceased. (...)

These men may be the same who attended a party somewhere in Dynasty 20 (Ramesses VI, 1142/40–1134/32 BCE) together with Naunakhte's sons Amunnakhte, Neferhotep, and Maaninakhtef in O. Berlin P 14328 (see chapter 11, "Women Can Party Too"), in which case we would have to redate the text. O. Ashmolean Museum 563 is just a list of workmen, presumably, and in a few dry words it summarizes two households immersed in tragedy overnight. The death of the man in the house also meant that the wife would have to leave the house and also the village at some point, unless relatives were willing to take her in. One rather hopes that some of Naunakhte's sons who had been at the party offered some assistance to the widows of their deceased friends, as happened in the case of a Mrs. Hutya (O. BM EA 66411), where we see several men—including Qenhirkhopshef—chipping in to pay off her debt to the state.

But on the upside, there would also be the birth of a baby girl, as in O. Ashmolean Museum 679 *ll.* 4–5, another absence record:

[. . .] the birth of his daughter. [. . .] for his daughter.

One assumes that the new father was absent because he was throwing a party to celebrate this happy event, but of course we do not know. The villagers were very well aware of the precariousness of newborn life, and O. DeM 952 (dating unknown) gives us some small hints of this:

[. . .] given to him at the birth of his daughter: wooden bed 1, installed in her sleeping room. Basket of food 1. What is in it: *akek* loaf 1, *djeses* fish 1, meat dish 1, [be]er 10 jars. Barley [loaves] 9, [ointment (?) . . .] hin.

It almost looks like proud grandparents coming to their children's house to celebrate the birth of one of their new grandchildren, at the same time carefully noting down what they had brought. The bed for the little girl was probably their birthday gift. Gift-giving was a thing in Deir al-Medina (see chapter 11, "Women Can Party Too"). But the next sections of this text are actually more interesting. On the verso there is a new entry showing that more food and some rosebuds were brought on account of the fact that the girl was alive after three days. The same happened when fourteen days had passed and the baby was still there. The last entry refers to food for a "great drinking party," and maybe this was done to celebrate the girl having lived through the first critical days of her life. We do not know.

Childbirth would each time have been a life-threatening situation for mother and child, and workmen probably often had to bury their wives after all. But we want to return to Naunakhte's first husband, Qenhirkhopshef.

According to the British Egyptologist Morris Bierbrier, he stayed in office till the end of the reign of Sethy II (1200/1199–1194/93 BCE), which would be approximately forty-three years. But he lived slightly longer. In Graffito no. 551 from year 1 of Siptah—by which time he must have been very, very old—he records the death of Sethy II. In view of his age by this time, the mere fact that he left the village (probably supported or carried by some workmen) and wrote this graffito is a feat in itself. By now he was far too old to be the acting senior scribe of the village. He died in his late sixties, if not much older. Naunakhte is believed to have survived him by some fifty years, which sounds almost impossible.

Černý agreed with Qenhirkhopshef's accession date, but hesitated between year 4 of Amunmessu or year 6 of Sethy II for the termination of his office, meaning that he did work as a scribe between forty-six and fifty-four years, which—again—seems impossible. There would have come a time when he could no longer manage things, so that he must have had a so-called 'staff of old age,' someone assisting him, a human cane so to speak. And it gets more impossible still. The age difference between Qenhirkhopshef and Naunakhte was forty-two years according to Černý, so that he was fifty-four and she was twelve when they married.

This raises a number of questions. As the most probable heir to the senior scribe Ramose and being a senior scribe of Deir al-Medina himself, Qenhirkhopshef would have been the prize marriage catch of the century. Yet, apart from the enigmatic entries in the absence journal O. BM EA 5634 from year 40 of Ramesses II and the broken statue from TT 1126, nothing is known about any wife (except possibly Stela BM EA 144, although this is probably another person) or children in his entire life before Naunakhte. This is difficult to believe. It may merely be due to chance finds, of course, but most Egyptians would have been dead well before they even reached the age at which he married Naunakhte. There has been some speculation that he and Naunakhte stayed married for about thirty years. And still no children? Simple mathematics rule out this scenario. If Qenhirkhopshef died at the age of seventy or eighty, Naunakhte would have been in her forties. But we know that she raised at least eight (or even ten) children to adulthood, and some more that died along the way. Egyptologists generally assume that these children—including a son called Qenhirkhopshef—were by her second husband Khaemnun. The latter was just a workman and not the richest person in the village (which may be exactly why Naunakhte decided to marry him, so she could keep her economic independence), whereas she would have been well off after Qenhirkhopshef's death, presumably having inherited from him. This makes no sense.

So could it be that some of these eight children were actually Qenhirkhopshef's? But that would also be strange because, if Qenhirkhopshef and Naunakhte did stay married for thirty years or so, the age difference between the children she had with Qenhirkhopshef and those from her marriage with Khaemnun would have been almost too vast to bridge. It may sound strange, but could Qenhirkhopshef not simply have been infertile or no longer interested in sex (or homosexual)? Not having children was not the thing to do in the village, especially since he appears to have had at least one wife before Naunakhte.

Perhaps the most direct insight into Qenhirkhopshef's character can be gained from the letters he wrote and those that were written to him. O. Cairo CG 25832 was probably written in the reign of Ramesses II. Although it is presented as one single letter in the very handy volume *Letters from Ancient Egypt* (1990) by the American Egyptologist Edward Wente, it more probably consists of two separate draft letters. The recto is a letter to the vizier and the verso is addressed to two junior scribes. The two letters look as if they were written in a single session. Since the text on the verso strongly contradicts the content of the recto, we may be sure that these are indeed two separate letters. In the letter on the recto Qenhirkhopshef assures the vizier that all is going well (the official communication with the vizier went through the senior scribe), but on the verso he takes apart two junior scribes, who were only *semdet*. So no flowery introductory letter formulas there.

The *semdet* was a separate crew looking after the logistics of the village, supplying the workmen with all sorts of commodities, such as food, water, wood, and plaster. But somehow it is not very realistic to imagine that plaster had not been brought to the royal tomb under construction for some time without Qenhirkhopshef doing something about it, so let us just hope that this was indeed a private doodle that was written to let off some steam (the migraine again?).

> [To the scribe] Meryra and the scribe Penta[weret . . .]. To wit: what [about] our telling you: "Let plaster be brought to the construction site of Pharaoh, life, prosperity, health?" You have not let (it) be brought for seven months [. . .]. Send us plaster [. . .] say it [. . .] hear. What about [. . .] Pharaoh is lacking plaster? [As soon as this] letter [reaches] you, let [. . .] plaster ASAP, this minute. [. . .] Good is my [. . .].

If O. Cairo CG 25832 were indeed a single letter, it would mean that Qenhirkhopshef in his letter to the vizier was actually quoting this message by him to Meryra (or Ramery) and Pentaweret, thus exposing both junior scribes to severe repercussions from the vizier's office (but also himself, because he had let it happen). If we are dealing with two separate letters, things immediately start to make more sense, but it does illustrate rather well how Qenhirkhopshef could deal with junior scribes.

O. DeM 303 is a letter to Qenhirkhopshef by the draftsman Parahotep, again telling us something about the way he could treat other people. At the same time, however, it shows that Parahotep was not in the least afraid to reproach the senior scribe. But then, he may have been rather desperate. Parahotep was out of beer.

> The draftsman Parahotep informs his superior, the scribe of the Place of Truth Qenhirkhopshef. In life, prosperity, health. What about this bad attitude of yours toward me? For you I am like a donkey. If there is work to do, bring the donkey. If there is food, bring the ox. If there is beer, you do not look for me, but if there is work to do, you look for me. But if—on our head—I am a man of bad behavior with beer, do not look for me. It is good to listen to yourself (?) in the temple of Amunrasonter, life, prosperity, health.
> (PS) I am a man without beer in his house. I am looking to fill my belly (?) by my sending (a letter) to you.

The letters sent to people in Deir al-Medina are generally great fun because they are frank. O. DeM 562, which is probably from Dynasty 19, is from a Mrs. Kher to a Mr. Minmose, who was either her husband or her son. And she was ill. There is no other way to explain her tone of voice.

> From (the woman) Kher to Minmose. What is this your taking away the pair of sandals and my [...] and not bringing the [...] I told you about? See to it personally and bring a [...] and also the jar of milk and anything else you have. Do not abandon me now that I am [in] such a sorry state. It will be good for you to take note.

Apart from not drinking beer with his friends, did Qenhirkhopshef have any religious beliefs? Of course he would have. If we look at the decoration of his alabaster headrest BM EA 63783, there are depictions of the demon Bes, although this is a rather common motif. In itself this raises some more questions, because this headrest was clearly designed for use in the afterlife. Still, the use of such a motif on a headrest seems to hint at Qenhirkhopshef longing for some offspring of his own. We simply do not know whether he did have any other children from an earlier marriage but, if he did, there would have been a fierce fight over his inheritance, and we do know that Naunakhte inherited some real estate from him, as well as his library, which according to Černý may well have been the most valuable item of the lot.

Women and real estate. It happened all the time. There is one shred of a papyrus (P. DeM 30) that tells us that women could inherit part of the real estate owned by their husbands. But as usual, the source is totally inconclusive.

> Year 6, fourth month of the *peret* season. Dividing the places (the real estate) of Parahotep for (the woman) Tawerethetep and the female citizen Mut and Nesamun. Given (to) the female citizen Mut [. . .].

Since the papyrus is broken here, we do not have any information about what Mut got out of it. The break suggests that there would have been a list of the items she inherited. But there is also O. DeM 586 (Ramesses III or IV), telling us that Tawerethetep and Mut owned several buildings together, including storehouses and—surprisingly—a pyramid-shaped tomb chapel, probably to the west of the village.

Qenhirkhopshef would undoubtedly have brought regular tribute to the village patron god Amunhotep I—like any figure of authority, he would have realized this had to be done in public to keep the population at ease—and the usual Theban gods. But there is also the lintel Cairo JdE 33848. Its format is apparently too small for the entrance to a tomb (so say the archaeologists), and thus it probably comes from a little chapel. It shows Qenhirkhopshef adoring the god Sobek-Ra, a crocodile god that was not really from the Theban region. One could speculate about this forever, or simply concede that each Egyptian had his own personal preferences, apart from the state gods everyone was supposed to worship. Qenhirkhopshef probably revered countless other personal gods too. There were enough gods for everyone.

This whole package of a man would in the end become Naunakhte's first husband, but the picture remains blurred. Was he really the corrupt villain some make him out to be? A friend of mine once bought a house and some land in Portugal. His future neighbors urgently advised him to bring a sheep to the notary's office, because this would definitely speed up things. Just a little gift to get things done. So in order to rectify the image one may have of Qenhirkhopshef, we can adduce one more source that sheds a more positive light on him.

In O. BM EA 66411 he occurs only as a side figure, but even this is not unimportant. The ostracon deals with the woman Hutya who had to pay back a large amount of grain after her husband, the workman Samut, had died. In view of the amounts requisitioned from Hutya it seems she had been collecting her late husband's salary for some months after his death (meaning that the women were actually collecting their husbands' wages from time to time), but this could only have happened if the scribe who was responsible for these payments—a man who would know the situation in every household in the village—had agreed to do so.

> Year 9, third month of the *shemu* season, day 18. On this day the scribe [. . .] came to appear at the *qenbet*, saying: "Let the grain be exacted from the workman Samut, who is deceased." The attendant Penpamer (or Penpaiu) was sent after his wife Hutya and twelve sacks were requisitioned as well as six sacks of barley.

One would have expected the payments to the workman Samut to have stopped right after he died. Yet somehow his widow Hutya had managed to collect his wages for some time after that. Or did she borrow it from relatives and neighbors? If we assess the evidence correctly, the same Hutya may be mentioned in O. Turin N. 57062 from year 47 of Ramesses II, in which several people make pledges to the goddess Anuqet, suggesting that these people were members of a cult guild of some sort that was dedicated to her. Others believe that these people were all ill, and promised her things if only she would heal them. In any case, Hutya's promise sounds at least ambiguous: "I will do a day of drinking." This would be the normal way to say "I will take a day off," but in this case she probably meant that she would organize a day devoted to Anuqet. With drinks. But now she had fallen on hard times, with a bailiff knocking at the door to get the state's money back.

The verso of the text only mentions names and amounts of grain, evidently in connection with the case of Hutya mentioned on the recto:

Specification to inform you of the cost that the draftsman Neferhotep made: 3 sacks. Ipuy: 3 sacks. [. . .]: 1 sack. Iyerniutef: 1 sack. Pa[. . .]: 1 sack. Sem: 1 sack. Given [. . .] Hutya [. . .] barley: 6 sacks. Hay: 2 sacks. Qenhirkhopshef: 2 sacks. Nakhy: 1 sack. Huy: 1 sack.

As is so often the case, the amounts mentioned do not match the expected totals. It is somehow difficult to believe that these men, who had apparently given grain to Hutya in her period of grief, would have asked the *qenbet* to reclaim it (it was actually a scribe from the outside administration who did this). How was this woman with no income ever going to repay this? So the more humane—or perhaps more unrealistic—explanation would be to suppose that in fact these men all chipped in for a deceased friend's widow to cancel the debt owed to the authorities by Hutya. Including Qenhirkhopshef—unless of course this was the workman of that name.

The totally inconclusive evidence suggests that the young Naunakhte may actually have led some kind of a happy or at least comfortable life after all, living in a relatively spacious house (see figure 4), receiving instruction from her first husband. In the end she would inherit from him (which generally does not occur if people hate each other). The question is, simply, exactly what did she inherit from him and take into the marriage with her second husband Khaemnun? All of it or just one-third of the joint property from her first marriage? We do not know, but the fact that she also received Qenhirkhopshef's library and named one of her sons after him may be telling.

5

Criminal Women

Women did appear before the local court when they had done something wrong and, somewhat surprisingly, sometimes also as actual members of this court. O. Ashmolean Museum 150 from year 28 of Ramesses III lists two women, [. . .]pet and Merutmut, in the lineup for the day. Merutmut is otherwise only known from several party accounts (e.g., O. DeM 643, for which see chapter 11, "Women Can Party Too"). This, however, is no proof that women were regular members of the court, just that it may have happened occasionally, and perhaps only because there was a special reason for it, meaning that they were involved in a case in some way.

Women acting as official witnesses to an Oath of the Lord do occur, for example in O. Prague H 10 (O. Náprstek Museum P 3809, dated to Ramesses III), in which a draftsman Hor takes an oath and most of the witnesses are from the family of a Parahotep, including his wife and two daughters. The fact that the wife and daughters of Parahotep acted as witnesses means they were seen as valid legal persons. Compare, for instance, the Adoption Papyrus, in which the husband adopts his wife so that she can inherit his property after his death instead of his siblings, which was witnessed (and approved) by one of his sisters.

The women from Naunakhte's family are not mentioned in connection with any court case except the division of her will, so that once again we will have to make do with what we have. However, it may be that the adultery between Naunakhte's daughter Menatnakhte and the workman Weserhat (see chapter 7, "A Day in the Life of Menatnakhte"), although she was married to the workman Qenna, did involve the court, and there may have been other scandals in the family.

The divine played a role in legal cases more often than we think. There was the oracle of Amunhotep I that could be consulted to decide any legal issue. It was, however, operated by priests, meaning that the answers by the oracle were prone to manipulation. Its answers could also be rather brief, as is seen, for example, in an ostracon said to be O. IFAO 1005 (there is another O. IFAO 1005 that is now known as O. DeM 642): "No," in reply to a straightforward question (see below).

Dreams played a role, too. Of course they came from the other world, so people could always hide behind the fact that they were just the bringer of a divine message in case they had made an accusation which was later proved to be wrong. There is the famous case of O. Nash 1, in which the accused Mrs. Herya—whose crime of stealing state property and some item from the temple of Amun was deemed worthy of death—was tried after someone had seen her steal one of the tools of a workman in a dream. The villagers called these inspirations *bau* 'divine manifestation,' but unless we want to assume that people went around the village dropping to the floor having visions all the time, the safest thing is to assume that they had these manifestations in their dreams (we only need to recall that Qenhirkhopshef had a Dream Book in his library to explain what his and probably other people's dreams meant), as may be the case in O. Ashmolean Museum 166 (Dynasty 19):

> Statement by (the workman) Nakhtmin to the court: "Now I was sitting in my chapel <during the feast of> the Birth of Taweret and Tanehsyt stole a cake from me, but ten days later she came to tell me: 'A divine manifestation has happened.'"

After this statement the text continues with a seemingly unconnected account, but still it may be useful to look into this short statement a little further. Although one author believed that the chapel was actually called 'the Birth of Taweret,' it seems more likely that Nakhtmin was visiting his own chapel during one of the many religious festivals in the village to make an offering to one of the goddesses who oversaw the fate of newborn babies. This may be exactly why the woman Tanehsyt ('the Nubian') did have an uneasy dream or two, because the cake she stole may have been Nakhtmin's offering for the hippopotamus goddess Taweret, who could influence a woman's child-bearing capacity. This may also be why Nakhtmin chose to make a public statement in court, just so that everybody in the village—and in the divine world—knew that he had really set out to do his religious duty (with just one cake?), but had been prevented from doing so because of this horrible theft. Or, if one of our assumptions is correct, that Tanehsyt was the first wife of Qenhirkhopshef, this all may have had something to do with Qenhirkhopshef and Tanehsyt not being able to have children. She may have sought other ways to get to the goddess (by stealing her offering, which is not a clever thing to do), but this is unlikely. Besides, Stela BM EA 144, which mentions Tanehsyt, may be about a different Qenhirkhopshef. Nakhtmin may have felt inhibited about pressing charges against her in the first place, but he did in the end, and one may well wonder to whom his charge was addressed: Qenhirkhopshef's wife (if she indeed was his wife) or the goddess Taweret after all?

It would be something of a coincidence if this Tanehsyt were the same woman as the one mentioned in another court case, although by this time she was already long dead. O. UC 39617 (O. Petrie 16) was presumably written at the beginning of Dynasty 20, which would fit chronologically. It is a court case between an anonymous speaker and a daughter of the deceased called Wabet. The speaker's father had made a coffin for her—and, so one assumes, also his mother—which entitled him to her original share in the mother's storehouse. As happens so often, the moment there is something to be gained other people step forward to claim their share, and this is exactly what Wabet did. So the speaker asked the divine oracle to judge between him and her.

The ostracon then lists a precedent—and the same precedent is actually mentioned in P. Bulaq 10, about a similar case—in which the workman Sawadjet had done the same for his mother Tanehsyt, and asked the oracle to exclude other claimants (brothers and sisters) from the inheritance, because they had not helped to bury her, or perhaps rather to finance her burial.

Court cases are always great fun, because they show us by proxy what went wrong in the daily human interactions in the village, although O. BM EA 66411, for example, in which the widow Hutya was requisitioned to return the rations she had collected after her husband's death (see chapter 4, "Some Husband"), can hardly be described as funny.

Perhaps equally tragic is the case described in O. Cairo CG 25227 of a workman whose wife refused him sex, so that he had to make a public statement in court about it, no doubt watched and laughed at by most of the villagers.

Naturally—and this was seen more often in Deir al-Medina—it was not much use appealing to the court if some influential person was implicated, and this may be the case in O. Ashmolean Museum 4, where the divine oracle is consulted about some stolen clothes. These turn out to be in the house of the scribe Amunnakhte. Since this ostracon is dated to year 5 of Ramesses IV, this could very well be the scribe Amunnakhte son of Ipuy, but the source does not say so explicitly. Perhaps it was the carpenter Amunnakhte son of Khaemnun and Naunakhte after all, who did like to refer to himself as "scribe."

> Year 5, third month of the *akhet* season, day 28. Calling out by the sculptor Qaha to (the divine oracle) King Amunhotep, life, prosperity, health, saying: "My Good Lord, come out today, (because) my two clothes have been stolen." He (the oracle) brought the scorpion expert Amunmose, saying: "Call out the houses of the village." They were called out and when they reached the house of the scribe Amunnakhte he nodded to say: "They are with his daughter."

Amunnakhte was then summoned to face the oracle himself in front of many witnesses, where the issue reached a boiling point before the text breaks off. The obvious question is why he was asked to do this instead of his daughter, although in Deir al-Medina we do see fathers fending for their daughters in public more often (see chapter 15, "Protecting Your Daughter's Rights"). Was this really a case of ordinary theft or just a transaction—like a marriage—gone wrong?

There is, for instance, the Ptolemaic demotic O. BM EA 31940 from 117 or 100 BCE, in which a Mrs. Tamen daughter of Kallias took an oath at the dromos of the temple in Djeme (Medinet Habu). This oath was imposed on her by her husband Patem son of Amunhotep, who had also accused her of stealing. The husband's name looks Egyptian, but his wife seems to have been at least half Greek, which may not have helped to make this marriage a success.

As Amun of the Holy Eight lives, who resides here, and equally all gods who reside here with him. From the moment of sitting (in the) house that I have done with you (marrying you) until today, I have not stolen from you, I have not robbed you, I have not done anything against you in stealth for more than twenty deben. I have not slept with a man when I was with you.

There is nothing belonging to you in my hand, except for the (household) goods that I had brought to you.

This was clearly a clever ploy by what was most certainly her ex-husband, first spreading the rumor that she had slept with another man—which would free him from the obligation to give her one-third of the jointly acquired marital property he was expected to give her upon divorce—and then accusing her of stealing from him, which was, in fact, the property his ex-wife saw as her rightful share to take, and indeed had taken.

In other words, even little texts such as O. Ashmolean Museum 4 about a scorpion expert in Deir al-Medina being asked by the divine oracle to point out the house where the stolen items were may hide a world of intrigue that is not visible from the dry records.

Somehow it is also very difficult to see that this could be the scribe Amunnakhte son of Ipuy, although the fact that this was an oracle instead of a regular court case may again be telling. A court case against the senior scribe of the village would have been lost before it even started. Then again, the scribe Amunnakhte is often listed in the sources without his father's name. One would, however, have to keep in mind that the woman in question could equally well have been one of Naunakhte's granddaughters, because her son Amunnakhte also referred to himself as "the scribe Amunnakhte." Another of these dilemmas that are so typical for Deir al-Medina.

A most curious oracle procedure, which may have been preceded by a court case, is O. Cairo CG 25555 + O. DeM 999 from years 13 and 14 of Ramesses III. The conflict was about the right of access to the property of the workman Hay son of Huy, which is contested by his colleague Pentaweret, who then consults the oracle. But the oracle is clear, saying that Pentaweret cannot stake any claim, because Hay had been given the property by a Mr. Kel. But then the procedure continues with Hay asking another question of the oracle, namely whether the woman Hutiy should be allowed to take several wooden items (probably parts of a shed) that were on his property. So either Kel had allowed her to build it, or she had inherited it from a relative.

It is easy to see what would happen next. Owning a shed almost automatically implies that one is allowed to enter and leave (although there are some nasty disputes about the right of way in Deir al-Medina), but what if the new owner (Hay) had different ideas about this, and—this is not inconceivable—actually claimed that the shed was his, because it was standing on his property? This may also be why Pentaweret entered the discussion. Instead of being a party staking an unfounded claim, he may actually have been trying to help out Mrs. Hutiy. This is what happened next:

> After this (the denial of Pentaweret's claim) the workman Hay called out to him (the oracle), saying: "My Light, as for the things of this place, namely boards, beams, and a door, do you [. . .] agree that the female citizen Hutiy takes them?" The god agreed vehemently, saying: "She will (be able to) take her things."

It so happens that a similar case is described in the legal manual P. Mattha, from around 250 BCE (col. VI *ll.* 4 and following). Whether this is a code of law going back to a decree by Darius I, the Persian king of Egypt, to collect all the indigenous laws in place up to and including year 44 of Amasis and write them down, or a manual of customary law describing cases often treated in court, is still a matter of debate. But one can see a parallel:

> If someone files suit against someone, saying: "Mr. So-and-so son of Mr. So-and-so has built [on a plot for a house, but] the plot involved belongs to me, it belonged to my father and he made a contract about it for me," and if the person against whom suit is filed says: "It belongs to me, [it is] the plot [of my father and he has made a contract about it for me," the judges] will say to the person against whom a suit is filed: "Can you prove that the plot is yours, that it was your father's [and that he made a contract about it for you, or should one let the person] who filed suit against you furnish proof that <the plot> belongs to him, that it belonged to his father, and that he made a contract for him about it?"
>
> What the person against whom a suit is filed [wants will be done . . .]. If he (the accused) says: "I will furnish proof," and he does not furnish proof,

the house will be given to the person who filed suit against him, and he (the accused) will write for him (the complainant) [a quitclaim . . .].

If the person (who lost the case) says: "Allow me to take my construction material of this house," they will allow him to take them, and they [. . .]. If the person who filed suit does not furnish proof about the house, the house will be given to the person who built it and they will oblige him (the complainant) to write a quitclaim for [him (the accused)].

Some may argue that demotic texts written many centuries after the people from Deir al-Medina had long gone should really not be used to explain this conflict between Hay and Pentaweret and Mrs. Hutiy, but they do at least point to a possible scenario that most people looking at these sources are no longer aware of. One of the first things a papyrologist should learn is to look beyond the source, not just at it.

What is actually most striking about women and court cases is that there are so few, but this may also be explained by the fact that women were not always allowed to file suit in court about trifles and that, when there was a male head of the house, only the man could file suit. One author suggested that this may have been because women were "involved in fewer substantial economic transactions," which were indeed a major source of complaints in court. Some court cases in which women appear are about domestic violence (e.g., O. DeM 919), so that one has to assume that women could file suit if the case was serious enough, but we do not even know whether the Egyptians saw beating one's wife as a crime.

But then why did Naunakhte settle her last will in public? Because she was the former wife of the scribe Qenhirkhopshef? To make sure there were sufficient witnesses? The mere fact that she did suggests that she wanted to be absolutely sure that things would be done the way she wanted them done. Why do we not have other last wills made by women in court? Is this just a question of chance finds? It would not be surprising if this were so. There must have been other rich women in the village without husbands (such as Mutemwia, the wife of the scribe Ramose, who took Qenhirkhopshef into their own home as a 'son') who were free to decide where the inheritance would go, as was the female testator in the Adoption Papyrus.

O. Nash 1 (O. BM EA 65930) from year 6 of Sethy II records the court case about a Mrs. Herya, who apparently faced a death sentence. She appears only once in the sources from Deir al-Medina, which may be telling. A Herya is depicted on Stela Turin N. 50050, but this is dated to Dynasty 18, which seems too early to fit.

There are many strange and inexplicable events surrounding her indictment, and one does sometimes wonder if women were taken to court for entirely different motives from the reasons stated in the record. One needs only to recall the witchcraft trials from Salem starting in 1692, costing the lives of at least twenty-four innocent people.

The situation is as follows: the workman Nebnefer had accused her of stealing his chisel, which was state property. How she intended to use this chisel the story does not say. Apparently he had gone around the village questioning people (so evidently the police did not), but nobody knew anything, or at least said they knew nothing. But then Nebnefer received word from a Mrs. Nebuemnebehet, who had seen in a dream (divine manifestation) what had happened. Poor Herya swears that she is innocent, but the court has her house searched and there they find the chisel and some item belonging to a temple. Just imagine how easy it would have been to plant it there while Herya was detained, probably at the main administrative building. But her oath apparently makes no great impression on the court, and for one hour the authorities have her tortured. The record then states that this case is so serious that it will require the attention of the vizier. It is noted, however, that this crime is punishable by death, adducing a similar case from the past, involving a Mrs. Tanedjemethemes, the wife of a Pashed, who likewise appears only once in the sources from Deir al-Medina (another bad sign?). Since theft alone was not a capital crime in the village (the court could simply order people to compensate the aggrieved party, with interest), it may be that the death sentence hinted at by the official record has something to do with the fact that she had sworn a false oath, but that must have happened on more than just this one occasion. Somehow one gets the impression that Herya may have been framed by someone else, such as Mrs. Nebuemnebehet. Perhaps the latter thought that Herya was interested in her husband. Love magic was part of everyday life in the village, and there would always be women trying to remove a rival in love from the scene at any cost.

This is the record. The war referred to is most probably the one between Sethy II and the rebel king Amunmessu, who had seized control of part of southern Egypt.

Year 6, third month of the *shemu* season, day 10. On this day the workman Nebnefer son of Nakhy came to court to accuse Mrs. Herya. The workman Nebnefer said: "As for me, after the war I hid one of my chisels in my house, but it was stolen. I let everyone in the village take an oath that they had nothing to do with my chisel. And after many days Mrs. Nebuemnebehet approached me and said: 'A divine manifestation has occurred. I saw Herya steal your chisel.'" So he said.

The court then said to Herya: "So are you the person who stole Nebnefer's chisel or not?" Herya said: "No, I am not the person who stole it." Then the court said to her: "Are you prepared to take a Great Oath of the Lord, life, prosperity, health, about this chisel, saying: 'I am not the person who stole it?'" And Herya said: "As Amun endures, as the Ruler endures, life, prosperity, health, the one whose power is greater than death, Pharaoh, life, prosperity, health, if it is found that I am the one who stole this chisel . . ."

The rest of the oath spoken by Herya was never recorded, but it was clearly a moment of truth, because the scribe started to make mistakes in the protocol here. When he resumed the protocol one hour later, he left one line blank, almost as if he did not want to record what happened next. Things were not looking well for Herya:

An hour later the court questioned her. The servant Pashed was sent together with her (to her house) and she returned with the chisel. It was hidden in her things, together with a copper . . . of Amun of the Good Encounter. She had hidden these in her house, after she had stolen the copper . . . of the . . . of Amun. Yet she had taken a Great Oath of the Lord, life, prosperity, health, saying: "I am not the person who stole the chisel."

So the court stated: "Mrs. Herya is a great criminal who deserves death. The workman Nebnefer is in the right." Her case was postponed until the arrival of the vizier.

The record then lists the composition of the court: the two chief workmen (including Paneb), three scribes, a chief of police, and a guardian. The entire gang was watching what was happening. One wonders whether Herya's children were there too.

To make sure the authorities would take the proper measures, the anonymous scribe reminded them in a separate note of a similar case of a woman who had stolen some copper:

Indeed, here in this village stealing copper is a big crime. As far as the case of the widow is concerned, (I wish) to report to My Lord on the local custom. In the past Mrs. Tanedjemethemes stole a small cup of a half deben in this village, in the time of vizier Neferhotep, while she was the wife of Pashed son of Heh. Then the vizier sent the scribe Hatiay, who had her taken to the riverbank. May My Lord cause that the woman who stole this chisel and the . . . receives punishment (to make sure) that no other woman like her will ever do the same again. Now, I have reported to My Lord and the vizier is the person who knows (what to do). Let him carry out any procedure that he prefers. So that one will take notice.

Although nothing is said about the fate of Mrs. Tanedjemethemes, being taken to the riverbank—where there was another administrative building—was probably not a good thing, because it may well be that from there she would have been taken to the residence to be executed. How the case of Herya ended is unknown, but even after many thousands of years one has the impression she may not have been guilty after all. Anyone could have planted the evidence in her home.

It may be worthwhile to dwell on the workman Nebnefer a while longer, because he seems to have been a little paranoid about chisels. In O. Nash 2 (now O. BM EA 65956) he accuses the workman Huy of stealing no fewer than three chisels. The ostracon was acquired by the British Museum in 1959 from the same collection that housed O. Nash 1, so one assumes that both records had been kept together since antiquity (they were written by the same scribe and probably filed by him under 'chisel cases'). What is even more remarkable is the possible date of O. Nash 2, year 6 of Sethy II, although the alternative datings vary between Siptah and Sethy II at the end of Dynasty 19. If this dating to year 6 of Sethy II is correct, it would mean that Nebnefer in this year had been on some stolen-tool retrieval quest of his own, interrogating the entire population of the village.

In view of the serious accusation the court then summoned the two witnesses adduced by Nebnefer. They swore that they had seen two chisels in Huy's hut, but that this was all they knew. So in theory these chisels could actually have been left there by Huy's colleagues after a heavy night of drinking beer.

The court then ordered Nebnefer to take an Oath of the Lord, which he did, stating that these chisels were state property and that Huy wanted them to be converted into a cauldron, which he then sold for two donkeys.

Huy was clearly not impressed, saying that the chisels were his to begin with. The difference in outcome (which in this case is unknown, by the way, but the relaxed response of Huy is revealing) may therefore also reflect the impact such a court case had on a 'mere' woman accused of the same crime, unless of course Huy was in the end also taken to the riverbank.

[Dating broken away]. On this day the workman Nebnefer son of Nakhy came to [the court] and accused the workman Huy son of Huynefer, saying: "The workman Huy son of Huynefer stole the three chisels of Pharaoh, life, prosperity, health. I found them in his hut in the valley." So he said.

The scribe Pentaweret then said to him: "As far as these chisels of Pharaoh, life, prosperity, health, are concerned, of which you state that Huy stole them from the Place of Pharaoh, life, prosperity, health, can you produce any witnesses against him or not?" Nebnefer said: "I do have witnesses (to state that) he stole the chisels of Pharaoh, life, prosperity, health, together with Huy son of Kha and the stoneworker Kham."

The workman Huy son of Kha and the stoneworker Kham were taken before the court, and they took an Oath of the Lord, life, prosperity, health, saying: "As Amun endures, as Pharaoh endures, life, prosperity, health, we will speak the truth of Pharaoh and we will not tell a lie. If we tell a lie, we will receive a hundred strokes of the stick and the chisels will be demanded from their (our) households, to be given to Pharaoh, life, prosperity, health." So they said, and they also stated: "It is true that after the war we saw two chisels in the hut of Huy son of Huynefer in the valley, but we do not know [if they were the property of Pharaoh, life, prosperity, health]." So they said about the two chisels. [...]

[Then the scribe] Pentaweret [said] to the workman Nebnefer: "[As far as these chisels are concerned about] which you stated that Huy son of Huynefer had stolen them, are they the property of Pharaoh, life, prosperity, health, or his own property?" And Nebnefer son of Nakhy said: "They are the property of Pharaoh, life, prosperity, health."

The Oath of the Lord, life, prosperity, health, that he took, Nebnefer: "As Amun endures, as Pharaoh endures, life, prosperity, health, whose might is greater than death, namely Pharaoh, life, prosperity, health. Look, these chisels that Huy son of Huynefer has stolen are the property of Pharaoh, life, prosperity, health. If at some later date it is found that they are not the property of Pharaoh, life, prosperity, health, I will be ... [a totally unclear expression, although the determinatives of the words involved—a spitting mouth and fire—are an indication] because of it and be deprived of (?) my house, which will be returned to Pharaoh, life, prosperity, health (the state). Now see, he also had 28 deben of copper made into a cooking pot for himself, and he sold it for two she-donkeys."

Oath of the Lord, life, prosperity, health, taken by Huy son of Huynefer: "As Amun endures, as the Ruler endures, whose might is greater than death, namely Pharaoh, life, prosperity, health. If I am to be interrogated and they will find that these chisels are not my own property, and were (already) the property of my father Huynefer, he (I) will be thrown [. . .]."

One wonders what the court—partly consisting of the same men who tried Mrs. Herya—did next, watched by the entire crew (and their wives?). Perhaps Nebnefer was right after all, namely that Huy had indeed stolen these chisels, but then this would imply that these two chisels had been spotted at a place where they should not have been and also identified as state property. This can only mean that at that moment the chisels should have been in the possession of the authorities, who would occasionally take in blunt chisels for repairs (e.g., O. Varille 26) or remelting. It is difficult to believe that the scribe would have overlooked the missing chisels. Still, this case would be the talk of the town for some time to come. The same case seems to be recorded in the rather fragmentary O. Cairo JdE 72465, although this text also mentions some people who are absent from O. Nash 2.

The chief workman Hay, who was a member of the court in both O. Nash 1 and 2, had found himself in court only the previous year, when some people—among whom was a Mrs. Taweseret ('the strong one')— had been spreading a vicious rumor about him. O. Cairo CG 25556 is a rather sizable limestone ostracon describing how Hay took them to court:

Year 5, third month of the *shemu* season, day 2. The court on this day. The chief workman Hay arrived in court with Penamun, Ptahshed, Wennefer, and (the woman) Taweseret, before the magistrates of the court, that is, the chief workman Paneb, Nebsemen, Amunnakhte, Nekhemmut, Hy, Pashednakhte, Rahotep, Nebnefer son of Pennub, Nebnefer son of Wadjmose, Huy son of Inherkha, Ramery (or Meryra), Ipu, and the entire crew. What the chief workman Hay said: "As far as I am concerned, I was sleeping in my hut when Penamun came out with his people. And they said: 'They mentioned an accusation in connection with the greatness of Pharaoh, life, prosperity, health, that Hay would have said, which is greater than Sethy.'"

The court said to them: "Tell us what you heard." But they went back on their statement, while starting an argument (between themselves), and said: "We did not hear a thing." Then the court said to them, namely Penamun, Ptahshed, Wennefer, and Taweseret: "Say: 'As Amun endures, as the Ruler endures, there is no accusation against <him> as far as Pharaoh, life, prosperity, health, is concerned. If you (we) hide it today and bring it up tomorrow, then let his (our) nose and ears be cut off [. . .] evil.'" They received a hundred strokes of the stick each.

One assumes that these punishments were applied right after the court case and in full view of the entire crew. This included Mrs. Taweseret (a Taweseret occurs in one other source, O. DeM 567, but this could also be a namesake), so that we know that women were treated equally by the law—that is, the court, often mostly consisting of the elite of the village— all the way, even when it came to imprisonment and corporal punishment. But we do not see women in prison (or detained at some official place) very often in Deir al-Medina. One such case is described in O. Turin N. 57556 from year 25 of Ramesses III:

Year 25, first month of the *peret* season, day 25. On this day, taking Nekhemmut son of Khonsu up together with (the woman) Ese, the wife of Anynakhte, who were detained in the place of investigation on account of [the . . .] of The Tomb.

(Verso) [Year 2]5, first month of the *peret* season, day 15: [ta]ken to the riverbank.

If the 'day 15' on the verso is not a writing mistake for 'day 25' on the recto, which is easily done in hieratic, this procedure took up at least ten days. Also, in that case the verso was actually the recto, because it was written ten days earlier. From O. Gardiner AG 19 we know that many years earlier a workman Nekhemmut had divorced his wife Ese, and, if these are indeed the same people, Ese will have had some explaining to do at home afterward. Apparently this was a noteworthy event, because the scribe of the work journal O. Turin N. 57031, which he started to write on the same day, opens with the note that Nekhemmut was being questioned (being a woman, Mrs. Ese is once again ignored in this entry), whereas the rest of the text deals with lamps used and the work done in the period after that. In mid-Dynasty 20 there was a Nekhemmut living in the village who had a son called Anynakhte. Anynakhte married a Mrs. Ese, which would make her Nekhemmut's daughter-in-law (one hesitates to imagine that Ese first married the father and then the son). On one occasion the three of them seem to have attended a gift-giving party together (O. Berlin P 14328). The case therefore looks decidedly more complicated than initially thought, and we also do not know what Nekhemmut and Ese had been doing wrong in the first place.

The fact that women had to appear in court did not necessarily mean that they were criminals. Not paying the bills also meant that she could be sued. There is the case of an anonymous woman (the text is broken off where her name was written), who was not only sentenced by the village court but, when this did not have any effect, she was also brought before the court in the Ramesseum. O. Berlin P 14214 is dated to the reign of Ramesses III:

> [. . .] the water carrier Para[hotep] took her to court before [. . . Iuem]-iteru. She was sentenced to (pay) twenty deben for the chair and the footstool. Again he came to the court of the temple of Wesermâ'atra (Ramesses II) in the estate of Amun, before the temple scribe Pyay. The doorkeeper Khaemwaset of The Tomb went with her. She was sentenced to (pay) thirty copper deben and took an Oath of the Lord, life, prosperity, health, saying: "As Amun endures, as the Ruler, life, prosperity, health, endures. If I allow the Khoiak Festival to arrive and still have not given the thirty copper deben [. . .] the court of the exterior (?)."

She did pay two goats, but this was nowhere near enough to cover the cost. The text then switches to the first person singular ('I'), so it seems that the scribe Pyay recorded the action that he took, sending several water carriers to demand the rest. Whether the woman wanted to pay or not the story does not say, but they returned with all kinds of items taken from her house, including baskets, a mat, and several wooden chests.

Looking at the evidence at hand, it seems that the women of Deir al-Medina were generally law-abiding, albeit sometimes hot-blooded, people. Adultery and theft seem to have been the worst crimes they committed, but this is due to the sources that we have. The strange absence of rape, robbery, or murder cases (except some muddled sources) from Deir al-Medina is puzzling, to say the least. It is very difficult to believe that during the centuries the village was in business, not a single woman had plotted to have someone murdered. Then again, this would not have been a case for the local court (although one would have expected the scribe to have recorded the incident).

If we look, for instance, at O. Nash 1, there remains a nagging suspicion that the unfortunate Mrs. Herya may in the end have been eliminated by some rival in love. After all, the women of Deir al-Medina were just like women today. Not all of them were nice. One needs only to think of the so-called harem conspiracy directed at Ramesses III (the Turin Judiciary Papyrus), in which many courtiers and high officials made common cause with some of the wives and female relatives of Ramesses III in an attempt to assassinate him. Or the incriminating letters sent by General Payankh, now kept in Berlin, in which he ordered some people—including a Mrs. Nedjemet ('the sweet one'), who was his mother or his wife—to murder two policemen.

We can't leave this dossier without mentioning P. Berlin P 10487 (LRL 21), 10488 (LRL 34), and 10489 (LRL 35), which are all part of the so-called Late Ramesside Letters (LRL), a corpus of texts centering around the scribes Djehutymose (aka Tjaroy) and his son Butehamun, who were among the last scribes to manage Deir al-Medina's affairs under Ramesses XI, including the aftermath of the famous tomb robberies that took place in his reign. This is part of P. Berlin P 10487:

> The general of Pharaoh, life, prosperity, health, to the scribe of The Tomb Tjaroy. To wit: I have taken note of all the issues about which you have written to me. Regarding your mention of these two policemen going around, saying: "They have made these accusations." Team up with (the woman) Nedjemet and Payshuweben. They will send word and cause that these two policemen are taken to this house. Sort out their accusations as quickly as possible. If it is found that they are valid, put them in two baskets and have them thrown [into] the water at night. Do not let anyone on earth find out, however. (. . .)

Since the policemen involved would not be prepared to step into the baskets by themselves, this implied that Djehutymose would have to have them clubbed first. In the letter to Nedjemet, Payankh was faster in getting to the point, or maybe thought it best not to tell her how these men should be killed (see below).

After some derogatory statements about the power of the present king, Payankh asks for money to be sent, but not very much—a deben (about

90 grams) of gold and a deben of silver—which must therefore have been for personal expenses. The letter also tells us that, being an army man, Payankh had the nerve to speak about his king like that. He could easily have ordered the scribe who wrote this letter not to mention his name, but instead he boldly states that the letter was really from him. He also clearly trusted the scribe Djehutymose not to give his plans away. Perhaps just to make sure that the letter would not fall into the wrong hands, Payankh may have had it sent to his personal assistant Payshuweben, who then only showed it to Djehutymose for him to read. But why was the letter never destroyed?

In any case, part of this instruction was copied (or written beforehand) and also sent to Payshuweben, maybe telling him to team up with Mrs. Nedjemet and the scribe Djehutymose (LRL 34). This leads us to suspect that the courier who brought these letters—this was a trusted person— also had oral instructions from Payankh to Payshuweben, namely, to read one letter and show the other to Djehutymose. This same courier carried yet a third letter that was probably delivered personally to Mrs. Nedjemet (LRL 35):

> The general of Pharaoh, life, prosperity, health, to the head of the harem of Amunrasonter, the noble lady Nedjemet. In life, prosperity, health and in the favor of Amunrasonter. To wit: each day I call upon every god and goddess that I encounter to keep you alive and healthy, so that I can see [you] upon my return and fill my eyes [with your] image. I have noted all the issues that you wrote to me about. Regarding this issue of these two policemen of whom you have said they had spoken about, team up with Payshuweben and the scribe Tjaroy. Have these two policemen brought to my house and sort out their accusations as quickly as possible. Then have [them] killed and thrown [into] the river at night. Write me how you are doing. Greetings.

Note how Payankh this time does include a flowery introduction to his letter, which was not his habit. He also does not tell the addressee—his mother or his wife—to keep the matter secret. The latter two letters are concise and crisp. This is a man used to issuing orders and being obeyed. Even in translation the fact that Payankh was a military man shines through. Still, Payankh was taking a big risk here. We may summarize by saying that he wanted the two policemen silenced for good, after they had told what they really knew (so they would have had to be tortured). Still, these three incriminating letters were never destroyed, so that one wonders why these men had to be killed and whether Mrs. Nedjemet—a woman—would have to be there to watch this. To report back?

There is one other thing that sends a chill up one's spine, namely that the addressees of these letters probably had done this kind of thing before. One thing we can say about Mrs. Nedjemet is that she could be ruthless if need be. And we cannot look at the scribe Djehutymose again with the same reverence some Egyptologists have shown in the past.

6

Was Husband Number
Two a Demotion?

This is a book about Mrs. Naunakhte. But we know next to nothing about her apart from her famous will. Still, we also want to get closer to the people who shaped her life. So we will have to talk men, again.

It is not known when Naunakhte's second husband, Khaemnun, was born. There is some speculation that he was already active as a workman at the end of Dynasty 19, and more specifically in year 4 of either Amunmessu (1199 BCE), Sethy II (1196 BCE), or Siptah (1190 BCE). There is not much one can argue with here, because this was about the time he would have married Naunakhte. He presumably died around year 4 of Ramesses V or even later.

So let us calculate for a moment. If he were active in year 4 of Amunmessu (1199 BCE)—being somewhere between fourteen and sixteen years of age—and died in year 4 of Ramesses V (1141 BCE), he would have died in his seventies. This is not impossible, but it would be very old. In the Naunakhte files people tend to have become quite old, because even the eight surviving children of Naunakhte and Khaemnun would have been in their late forties or early fifties when she made her statement in court. A healthy family indeed.

Khaemnun is without doubt listed as an active workman in, for example, O. DeM 40 + O. Strasbourg H. 42 from year 1 of Ramesses IV (1152 BCE). At this time he would have been sixty years of age, and, in view of what we know about old age in ancient Egypt, it is very difficult to imagine him still chiseling away in the royal tomb. But then, there may have been some social scheme that relegated the older members of the crew to easier tasks, while the hard work was done by their sons, although this is speculation. So, as in the case of the generally accepted age—namely twelve—at which Naunakhte would have married the scribe Qenhirkhopshef in around 1210 BCE (see chapter 11, "Women Can Party Too"), the mathematics simply do not seem to add up, and it is perhaps worth investigating whether it is really possible to identify the Khaemnun from Dynasty 19 with his namesake of Dynasty 20, who was still active on guard duty in the main administrative building in the reign of Ramesses IV (O. DeM 32–47). From a whole series of ostraca (O. Turin N. 57026ff.), all written by the same scribe (although not the senior scribe) that were found by the Italian archaeologist Ernesto Schiaparelli in the Valley of the Queens, it is clear that during the last ten years of the reign of Ramesses III Khaemnun was working there on some secondary royal tombs.

At regular intervals—and just like the other workmen—Khaemnun would have to do guard duty, and the most probable location for this would have been at the gate of the main administrative building. Here the workmen on duty would receive the rations in food, wood, and so forth, brought in from elsewhere by the logistics crew. What other work they had to do is unknown, but somehow it is unlikely that they would be sitting in the shade doing nothing all day. But supposing that they did, then this guard duty may actually have been a very popular job (or a job specially designed for the elderly), because it was decidedly more relaxed than having to hack away at the rock in the Valley of the Kings by the light of flickering oil wicks.

Khaemnun is often attested in the long journals recording the daily events from the reigns of Ramesses III and IV (e.g., O. DeM 32–47, all written by the same scribe). He should not be confused with some of his contemporary namesakes, who acted as scribe and chief of police, respectively. But the latter seldom occur in the Deir al-Medina papers.

The daily records are mostly not as informative as we would like them to be. In the example below (O. Berlin P 12631) we can see that in year 1 of Ramesses IV, fourth month of the *shemu* season, Khaemnun was on duty twice (and it could well be that this was actually one of his grandsons instead of him):

Day 11: Khaemnun. Handing out rations [. . . by] Ptahmose: *pesen* loaves 12; *byt* cakes [. . .]; jars 2. (. . .)

Last day: Khaemnun. From Ptahmose: wood 300. From Amunhotep: wood 310, of which the 110 as the remainder for day 20 (and) the 200 for the last day.

The relationship between O. DeM 32–47 and the Berlin collection is very interesting, because the latter collection houses a number of ostraca found by Georg Möller in the early twentieth century, which in antiquity had broken off from O. DeM 33, 34, 41, and 45. It would be good to know where exactly Möller—one of the greatest hieraticists ever—found these pieces, because the findspot of O. DeM 32–47 is known: the Kom Sûd, a rubbish dump at the southwest corner outside the walls of the village. If Möller's findspot is a different one—why not?—we will have to explain what happened, which we can only do if we know the findspot.

Other pieces that join directly to O. DeM 32–47 are now in Heidelberg, Strasbourg, and Vienna. O. Heidelberg inv. no. 567 was bought by the archaeologist Uvo Hölscher in the season of 1930–31. He was working in Medinet Habu at the time. Since O. DeM 34—to which O. Heidelberg inv. no. 567 belongs—was found by the French excavators in the Kom Sûd (KS) on 17 January 1930, it seems that someone may have decided to sell a piece of the ostracon separately. (The same happened with two of the papyri belonging to the Will of Naunakhte.)

Still, if we look more closely at these records, we can actually learn much about the management of the village, and also about some of the events witnessed by our Khaemnun, things that he would have told Naunakhte about at dinner—for instance, what had happened during his day of guard duty. Sometimes reconstructing parts of someone's past life is not that difficult. If Khaemnun had been on guard duty, Naunakhte would have been told about the ins and outs of it.

In particular, the deliveries of wood and fish could be large—O. Berlin P 12631 mentions 445 deben of fish, which would be about forty kilograms—so that one may ask who was supposed to count or weigh these. O. Turin N. 57038 even refers to 36,000 deben of fish, which is about 3,240 kilograms, but this is probably an annual total. According to O. Turin N. 57080 one man had managed to build up a deficit of 4,200 units of wood, which was duly noted by the scribe. We do not even know what a unit was. A twig, a branch, or a log? But probably a branch, because a shortfall of 4,200 logs would be hard to replace.

Did the men of the logistics crew do the counting (they had quotas to meet, so they must have known about numbers and weights), or did Khaemnun do it when he was on guard duty? Or was it simply his job to fetch the scribe on duty the moment a delivery arrived at the gate? After all, these numbers had to be entered in the daily record and the Egyptian scribes of Deir al-Medina were meticulous. O. Berlin P 12631 once again also refers to the mysterious "passing of the walls," which is believed to refer to a strike. Since in this case it was done to collect rations—and workmen's strikes because of failing rations occurred more often from the end of the reign of Ramesses III onward—it may well be that this entry again refers to unrest of some sort. Unfortunately, however, the daily journal just notes the fact that the walls were passed.

In O. Nicholson Museum R. 97, for instance, which is dated to somewhere between the reigns of Ramesses III and IX, we read how the authorities sent a special commission to Deir al-Medina after the workmen had abandoned their work, because they were hungry and the wages had not been paid. When the committee asked the local court for advice, it stated that the workmen had been right to do so. The crucial passage containing the court's verdict, however, is in lacuna. If Khaemnun and some of his sons had gone on strike too, and they probably did— the peer pressure to show solidarity would be immense in such a small community—this would be the sort of thing he and Naunakhte would have talked about. In fact, Khaemnun may even have taken his family along, as can be inferred from P. Turin Cat. 1880 (the Turin Strike Papyrus), in which the chief of police Montumose—whom we will meet later—told the workmen to take their wives and children to go and protest at a nearby temple. It is not clear whether he was trying to restore order here by getting them out of the way or merely wanted to create more unrest, but one may assume that at least some of Khaemnun's children would have been there, while Naunakhte probably stayed at home. Too old. Even her husband was getting old by now.

The claim was made above that we can actually reconstruct some of the kitchen-table discussions between Naunakhte and Khaemnun. If, for instance, we only look at some of the events described in the journals from the latter part of the reign of Ramesses III and the first years of Ramesses IV in O. DeM 32–47, we can be sure that Khaemnun witnessed these events and discussed them at home. These are the events:

- Coppersmiths arrive at the village to do some work
- A doorkeeper arrives with a message
- The chief of police reports that 'the enemy' has arrived
- The members of the crew stand guard
- Strikes because of arrears of rations
- Amunkha becomes scribe of The Tomb
- Procession of the divine Nefertari
- Death of Ramesses III
- The funerary equipment of Ramesses III arrives at the Valley of the Kings
- Burial
- The crew receives rewards, including silver
- Ramesses IV becomes the new king
- Forty chisels are brought for (?) the divine Amunhotep I
- The crew carries torches (strike)
- Magistrates arrive to listen to the crew's complaints
- The crew receives extra rations for the Opet Festival
- The crew receives nine cows to eat

Then there would be the daily arguments and stories of their neighbors, colleagues, children, and the other people from the village, the court cases, and so on. In O. Turin N. 57380 Khaemnun appears as a member of the court, together with a Neferhotep, maybe his and Naunakhte's son. So we actually know much more about Naunakhte than we think.

Like the other workmen, Khaemnun would have spent much of his spare time working in his own tomb, probably somewhere to the west of the village. The workmen's tombs that have been published so far—increasingly online—are generally of a very high quality. They are beautifully painted, with an incredible attention to detail. These workmen were the best, and they clearly enjoyed the fact that in their own tombs they were allowed to work on a carefree afterlife. One assumes that the workmen assisted each other in the making of these tombs. Draftsmen would prepare the walls for the painters, the workmen with the neatest handwriting would do the inscriptions, and the best stoneworkers would be asked to do whatever needed to be done in stone. In return, Khaemnun would have been working in the tombs of his friends and colleagues.

It is believed by some that, just like the houses in the village, these tombs were state property (apparently not many new tombs were added in Dynasty 20), but it is difficult to see how the authorities would have managed this job asset that was obviously so important to the workmen and their families. Did a tomb revert to the state if a workman was dismissed and had to leave the village with his family? In that case, would the authorities reassign his tomb to someone else (this did occur, for which see below), who would probably not be very keen on other people's mummies in what was now 'his' tomb? What happened to the mummies that were already buried there?

By pure coincidence we do have a well-documented issue about a tomb involving our Khaemnun. O. BM EA 5624 is a limestone ostracon written on both sides. It is a deposition, presumably by the workman Amunemipet. He substantiates his claim to a tomb in the necropolis of Deir al-Medina by describing its history, which includes the inheritance of the same tomb by a long-deceased female relative of his. Most authors who have studied this particular text appear to have mixed up the order of the separate statements by Amunemipet, but it makes most sense to start with what they thought was the last part of the text:

> Year 7 of the King of Upper and Lower Egypt Djeserkheperra, life, prosperity, health, Horemheb, life, prosperity, <health> (1313 BCE). The day on which the <work>man Hay, my (fore)father, entered The Tomb. The majordomo of Thebes Thutmose shared out the places in The Tomb to the crew of Pharaoh, life, prosperity, health. He gave the tomb of Amun<messu> to Hay, my (fore)father, as a commission. He[l], my (fore)-mother, was his daughter who was born to him, whereas he had no male children and his place became abandoned.
>
> Now after (that), in year 21, second month of the *shemu* season, on day 1 (of Ramesses III, so c. 1162 BCE), I stood before (the oracle of) Amunhotep, life, prosperity, health, telling him: "Point at one tomb of the forefathers," and he gave me the tomb of Hay in writing and I have started to work in it.
>
> [Now af]ter (that) I was doing construction work, and the workman Khaemnun was working in his tomb. First month of the *shemu* season, day 6. He was not working and he found {the} the shaft that was in it. He went down in it together with the policeman Neferhotep when I was not there.

Now after (that), in the first month of the *shemu* season, on day 7, I found the chief workman Khonsu, (who was) sitting and drinking. And after that I was standing with Hori son of Huynefer and the workman Bakenwerel and I did not know the (place) where the shaft of my tomb was. The scribe Amunnakhte found the . . . , saying: "Come down and look at the place that opens into the tomb of Khaemnun."

Apart from several reading problems the gist seems clear. Amunemipet had been assigned a tomb by the divine oracle—allotted to his family some 150 years earlier and claimed by him through descent from a female forebear—and had apparently started to work on extending the subterranean vault. Then he accidentally stumbled on the shaft of Khaemnun's tomb. This is strange, because one would expect a skilled workman to somehow notice the risk of breaking through the shaft wall of a neighboring tomb, namely Khaemnun's. The sound alone would have indicated there was a hollow space nearby. Then Khaemnun, assisted by a policeman, descended into the shaft—if that is indeed the correct translation (presumably the same shaft that Amunemipet later said he was unable to locate)—where he found that Amunemipet had taken his construction work a little bit too far, although the latter says he did not know where the shaft was in the first place.

But there is something about the claim of the workman Amunemipet. He states that he has a right to the tomb through some female forebear. So did women own tombs by themselves? They did. There is a graffito on a chapel to the north of TT 321, showing that tombs could be reallocated to a woman. It would have been nice if we knew why this happened in the first place.

> Year 4, first month of the *shemu* season, day 10. Allocating the place [of burial of] the workman (the name is almost gone) [Hori (?)] and the workman Khaemipet, to give it to Taweretherty b[y] the scribe Horshery.

Now the scribe Horshery was the son of the well-known scribe Amunnakhte son of Ipuy. The graffito has been dated to the reign of Ramesses VIII (1126/23–1125/21 BCE) on not-so-certain grounds, but the question is, of course, what happened here? The woman Taweretherty attended the same parties that some of Naunakhte's daughters did, and she is mentioned in connection with a man called Khaemipet in O. Černý 13, although the man's title there is not 'workman.' The context is very unclear, but seems to imply that he "did not know how to drink (properly)." In O. IFAO 1262 she appears in a case before the local court. The complaining party is a woman as well (as usual, the text is broken at the crucial points), but the plea includes the advice that "he should punish her on account of the issue (or statement)." So women could file suit in court by themselves after all—or was this because Taweretherty was the daughter of a chief workman and the complainant belonged to the local elite as well, for whom one would make an exception? The supposition that Taweretherty was well off is not too far-fetched. She even had a so-called *akh iqer (en) Ra* stela made for her (probably when she was dead), published by Demarée (figure 6). Not too many women could do this. It is now in the Szépművészeti Museum under the inventory number 51.232. The idea behind it is that the deceased for whom such a stela was made had become an *akh iqer (en) Ra* 'useful spirit for Ra.' Most of these stelae come from the village, but this may be just due to chance. Acting as mediators between this world and the next, these spirits could come in very handy for their living relatives, which explains their use in the private funerary cult.

Back to the tomb of Khaemnun. There is something interesting about the dates in this text. The entries dated to the first month of the *shemu* season are actually almost a year later than the procedure before the oracle that took place in year 21, second month of the *shemu* season, day 1. This is due to the accession date of Ramesses III, which was day 26 of the first month of the *shemu* season, meaning that each subsequent new year during his reign would start on this day. Through a stroke of luck there is another document recording what happened on this very same day 7 of the first month of *shemu* in year 21 of Ramesses III. P. Berlin P 10496 was bought in Luxor in 1909 by the German Egyptologist Heinrich

Figure 6. Stela Szépművészeti Museum inv. no. 51.232 (courtesy Rob Demarée)

Schäfer, whose *Principles of Egyptian Art*, available in an English edition by the British Egyptologist John Baines, has shaped the way Egyptologists look at Egyptian art (which is mostly not meant to be art, but often just a vehicle to help people cross safely through the afterlife) for generations and generations since.

P. Berlin P 10496 is a dark brown papyrus of 28 × 20.5 cm that is written on both sides. The first text deals with the tomb of Khaemnun; the second is about the illicit entering of other people's tombs (year 24), but this does not concern Khaemnun. The chief workman Khonsu—who was still described as drinking in O. BM EA 5624 (a remark that either seems to imply something unfavorable or simply means that he was off duty on that day)—and the scribe Amunnakhte went down to inspect the situation for themselves, together with a whole team.

> Year 21, first month of the *shemu* season, day 7 under the King of Upper and Lower Egypt Wesermâ'atra Meryamun, life, prosperity, health. On this day: an inspection that was carried out by the chief workman Khonsu, the scribe Wennefer, the scribe Amunnakhte, the deputy [. . .] Inherkha, and the deputy Amunkha, of the shaft that is in the tomb of the workman Khaemnun. They found that the shaft that is in the tomb of the workman Amunemipet was open. The scribe Amunnakhte, the deputy Amunkha, the deputy Inherkha, and the policeman Neferhotep came down to me.
>
> The scribe of the vizier Amunnakhte called to me, saying: "Open (it) at the north end of the column that is in your tomb, so that I can see the opening of your shaft." I was doing construction work together with Hori son of Huynefer and the workman Bakenwerel, whereas the chief workman Khonsu was sitting and drinking on the tomb of Khaemnun. After that the place was inspected.
>
> They found one uninscribed coffin, it was not inscribed with the name of any man in the entire land. There were no dishes or pottery. There was not [. . .] any man on earth placed beside it. And after that [. . . they] wrote to the scribe Akhpet: [. . .] was opened [. . .] the scribe Amunnakhte (. . .).

The text then continues with an official oath, which is damaged, but presumably was about not cutting an opening into other people's tombs again. The authorities were evidently not pleased, because in this specific case the sanctions included mutilation and impalement, which were generally reserved for high treason and similar crimes.

Meanwhile, they may also have wondered why the tomb of Amunemipet only contained a single uninscribed coffin. If he claimed that it had been in the possession of his family for about a hundred and some years, then where were all his relatives who had died? Shipped off by the authorities? Buried elsewhere when the tomb became derelict?

How seriously this case was taken by the authorities is shown by yet another document referring to the same incident, this time involving even more officials. O. Florence 2621 is a limestone ostracon written on both sides. It most likely contains another statement by Amunemipet. The beginning of the text has broken away, but it seems to describe the inspection referred to in P. Berlin P 10496, in which case it may be dated to year 21 of Ramesses III or slightly later. The text also shows that Khaemnun was present on that day, which makes perfect sense, because his tomb had been damaged. We do not know if he brought Naunakhte along with him (she would be rather old by now), but even if he had done so, the scribe would probably not have mentioned her by name. This was official business. And very serious business at that.

> [. . .] the deputy Amunkha, the engraver Iyerniutef, and the workman Khaemnun son of Neferhotep (a cousin of the old Khaemnun?). I went down with the deputy Kha, [. . .] Bakenwer<el>, and Hori son of Huynefer, and I said to them (?): "As for the [. . .] that opens into the place in [. . .]." They said to me: "And as for the place of Khaemnun that [. . .] to the northern column of your tomb. So you will open the entrance of your shaft." I opened it. I took a lamp and I inspected the tomb in the presence of many witnesses. I found one uninscribed coffin lying about there. There was no other equipment.
>
> After that the guardian Penmennefer, he said: "Two tombs are opening into the tomb of Khaemnun." So he said. The scribe Akhpet came up (to the village) to interrogate (me), together with some agents. And the scribe of The Tomb Amunnakhte said to him: "Interrogate (him) and I will look at the places."
>
> I went with the chief of police of The Tomb and I let the chief of police Montumose descend into the shaft. He inspected (it) and said to them: "(There is) only one coffin in the tomb of Amunemipet. And they fetched the guardian Penmennefer and said to him: "Were you in [this] place? Did you [s]ee it?" He said: "I was. [. . .] presence [. . .] all that was there."

One rather hopes that this was the end of it and that the people responsible for the whole affair were ordered to do the necessary repairs, so that Khaemnun's relatives would be able to rest in peace again. Was this Naunakhte's future resting place? And do we know more about Khaemnun's tomb?

Actually, there is one ostracon—a small, round limestone piece of 11 × 11 cm—that records two payments made to a carpenter called Ramery or Meryra (O. Ashmolean Museum 163). Both payments appear to be associated with a coffin, although a coffin is only mentioned on the recto (front), which contains the payment made by a priest called Neferhotep. The text on the other side simply states that Khaemnun paid Ramery four sacks of emmer corn, five bundles of vegetables, and a goat, which equaled three deben of silver. Since coffins in Deir al-Medina were generally much more expensive than that, it may be that this was a down payment, or that Khaemnun had ordered some other item from the carpenter's shop (his account does not mention a coffin).

But it is the date that is perhaps most intriguing. The British Egyptologist Kenneth Kitchen—who published a monumental series called *Ramesside Inscriptions*, which includes almost all of the documentary sources we have from Deir al-Medina—thought the ostracon should be dated to the reign of Ramesses V. If this dating is correct and if Khaemnun really did pay for a coffin, it may be that this coffin is actually the one that Naunakhte was buried in. Then again, one of his sons—most of them moonlighted as carpenters—could have done it for free. Looking at the evidence, it seems everybody in the village had a job on the side, including the women. O. DeM 973 was written in the reign of Ramesses III (one surmises). It is an unclear letter:

So please take these eight (deben) of black yarn to the house of (the woman) Baketsemen, before doctor Kel, so that he can bleach them. And you will then take the fine mat on account of them.

How Mrs. Baketsemen and doctor Kel were related is unknown, but the text shows that she lived in her own house, and did something with textiles. Women did weave at home for others.

Khaemnun was not exactly a nobody. O. Bodleian Library Eg. Inscr. 253 was written in year 23 of Ramesses III. Its interest lies in the fact that this is probably the record of an oath taken before the local court, which this time includes Khaemnun. Telmontu (who was related to Khaemnun through marriage; his daughter Hathor was married to Khaemnun's son Neferhotep) wants his son-in-law Nekhemmut to swear an oath before the court about his wife (Telmontu's daughter). The sanctions facing Nekhemmut if he does revert to his old ways are highly original. Apart from the usual hundred strokes of the stick, he "will be deprived of everything he made with her," meaning that he would lose all communal property the couple had acquired during their marriage. Since the wife was only entitled to one-third of this property in case of a divorce, one has to wonder whether we are dealing with customary law or an ad hoc sanction here, but presumably the latter.

The local court often dealt with property issues, and in year 22 of Ramesses III we see Khaemnun appear in court himself (O. Ashmolean Museum 53).

He did own donkeys, which he occasionally leased out to water carriers, but they could also have been used to work the land, wherever that may have been (somewhere in the fertile plain below). This suggests he must have had a pen or a stable somewhere near the village, and one assumes his daughters had to bring them fodder and water every day as long as they lived in his house; they would also have to do this when he was at work in one of the valleys.

The agricultural activities by the workmen of Deir al-Medina are relatively unknown, due to the few sources that we have, but the mere fact that donkeys were leased out for plowing, in the same way as oxen were leased out to plow in Late Period land leases, suggests that the people from the village could own land, and there is some proof for this. The question should of course be, Why would Khaemnun own a donkey if he was not planning to do anything with it? Although plowing with the use of a donkey is not the best idea ever, by saying 'to plow' the scribe may have meant 'any activity connected with working in the field.'

Apparently the donkeys were not always leased by the water carriers, but simply taken. There is one curious court case involving the workman Parahotep in O. DeM 582 (Ramesses III).

Hearing the statement of the workman Parahotep, to wit: "As for me, my donkey was delivered to my freewoman (a business associate rather than his wife, perhaps), and I went up (into the Valley of the Kings?) for three days. When I returned in the evening, she said to me: 'I have already let the donkey outside.' So I went out to lock her in for the night, but I found that it was loaded with emmer, and with (the water carrier) Kel. I said to him: 'Who gave you the donkey?' And he said to me: 'I found it doing nothing, so I took it to bring the grain assignment to the main administrative building.' I took it, but he said to me: ['Do not ta]ke it. I will give this other [. . . to compen]sate for it.'"

The remainder is fragmentary. Interestingly, the term 'freewoman' was also used by Naunakhte to refer to herself in her statement before the court, indicating that she was in a position to dispose of her property as she pleased. It is a good story, however. A water carrier sees an abandoned vehicle and simply takes it, and then responds almost indignantly to the owner: "Well, the donkey had no license plate, so I thought I could take it, didn't I?"

At least some people in the village did own land, as O. Ashmolean Museum 165 (Ramesses II) shows. In this document, a woman and a police officer are negotiating—or rather, trying to negotiate—the sale of a she-donkey the woman wants to have. It is not known whether this case came to court, but the phrasing seems to suggest it, or else the police officer had it recorded just in case. Why the whole business was conducted through middlemen is unclear.

[I] said: "Give me m[y donkey]," but she sent me the water carrier Tjauherkhet, saying: "The she-donkey, is she all you wa[nt]? Or do you want all of his things that I gave you?" Now I sent the water carrier Tjauherkhet back to her, saying: "No, [I do not] want his things, I [. . .] the *mimi* grain." And she [then sent] this overseer [. . .], saying: "The she-donkey, I want to buy it and I will give you its price in [f]ields in Armant." And I wrote back to her, saying: "I will not take [your] fields. Now give me the donkey itself back right away."

If a woman from Deir al-Medina was in a position to negotiate a deal with someone and promise to pay with some field in nearby Armant— well, a brisk walk away in the fertile plain—one can be sure that some of the workmen owned or at least worked some land there as well, maybe even as contractors of the omnipresent Domain of Amun. The scenes on the walls of their tombs showing the tomb owner and his wife working the land may in some cases actually reflect part of real life, instead of being just another magical pastorale they wanted to take with them in the afterlife. In his letter to his wife Ikhtay, or rather to her coffin (O. Louvre inv. no. 698), the scribe Butehamun refers to their cattle and fields that she had managed when she was still alive. Other people also had fields that were managed by women. In P. BM EA 10412 (LRL 36) from the reign of Ramesses XI, the scribe of The Tomb Nesamunemipet tells his wife (this is what the tone of voice implies), the singer of Amun Mutemipet:

> The deputy of the temple Nesysobek has written to the place where the prophet of Montu is, to wit: "Let them give me an *aroura* of land in Peniufnery adjacent to the household of the priest of Montu Ahautyaâ, so that I can cultivate it with fruit." He then said: "I will give it. Send someone to receive it." When my letter reaches you, you must send Sobeksankh to where the prophet of Montu is to receive from him this *aroura* of land north of the household of Ahautyaâ (. . .).

The mention of the verb 'to receive' is actually much more exciting than would appear at first sight. We must assume that land lease contracts were made throughout the whole history of ancient Egypt, but the tangible evidence to support this—written contracts—only appears from Dynasty 25 onward. Ninety-nine percent of the leases would have been arranged orally anyway. In the Late Period there were two scribal and legal traditions in Egypt, due to the fact that the land had been split up into two separate, smaller empires. Demotic from the north would win in the end in Dynasty 26, becoming the writing vehicle for the next thousand years or so. But the southern tradition—abnormal hieratic— was still very much alive and kicking in Dynasty 25, and it seems that some of the legal terminology used in these southern texts comes straight from the tradition that also shaped the Deir al-Medina legal terminology. P. Louvre E 7851 recto and verso were written by the same scribe in year 26 of King Taharqa, so probably around 665 BCE. Both texts are land leases by the same mortuary priest, in one case accompanied by a business partner. Before we look at the translation, however, the reader should be warned that at present there are only very few Egyptologists worldwide publishing abnormal hieratic texts, because they are too difficult to read.

That is why the translation includes several question marks. The texts were published for the first time more than a hundred years after they were bought by the Louvre.

> Year 26, fourth month of the *peret* season, day 14. Have said the choachyte Hetepamun son of Dyamunpankh and the choachyte Amunpayfit son of Ituru to Mrs. Heryamunese: "We have received from you these two shares of endowment field of Osiris (a field dedicated to someone's mortuary cult) which are in Pakhjenen. To the north, the field of . . . (?) which is the field of Amun . . . (?) for what we will produce as remainder for it, for a quarter (the share for the landlord), whereas the one-tenth is for the . . . (?) scribe, seed corn included, for what we will produce from the grain for it, whereas I will have nothing to discuss with you (afterward)."

But the verso of the text holds the real cliffhanger, because there the same scribe writes that the lessee 'received a field to plow.' Since the sources from Deir al-Medina sometimes mention that a donkey is leased to cultivate some field ('give to plow'), and there is one abnormal hieratic source from the same archive as P. Louvre E 7851 stating that a field was 'given to plow,' it seems that the legal terminology of Deir al-Medina may have been not just from Deir al-Medina, but Theban, or even more broadly southern. It was previously thought that the fact that the mortuary priest Hetepamun from P. Louvre E 7851 recto referred to the fields he was to plow as fields that he had 'received' was a mistake for 'received to plow' (as written by the same scribe on the verso of the papyrus), but in the light of P. BM EA 10412 (LRL 36) we may now actually have to rethink this text, and surmise that in New Kingdom Deir al-Medina one referred to the leasing of a field as 'receiving' it, which is of course a highly ambiguous term.

What is also very interesting about P. Louvre E 7851 recto and verso is that in both cases the lessees are choachytes—funerary priests who brought offerings to the dead in return for payment—but that the landlords in both texts are women. The fields they are leasing out are called "these two shares of the offering field of Osiris" and "this share of the offering (foundation) of Osiris," respectively. This strongly suggests that these fields had been given to them as a mortuary foundation, as often happened in ancient Egypt. People would die, and their relatives would establish a mortuary cult that was meant to last forever (although they must have realized this was not a very realistic prospect). Since the deceased would become an Osiris after death, the fields these landlords—landladies—leased out were probably donated to them to establish a cult for some deceased person in return for the proceeds of this field, just as the kings donated land to the temples to make sure that the priests would maintain a specific cult. It would be interesting to know why P. Louvre E 7851 mentions two landladies leasing out land to the same person, but there could be any reason for that. They could even be related to the lessees. These texts also tell us that these landladies were not planning to work the land themselves. This makes sense, because they were probably choachytes themselves working in the necropolis. However, there are other possibilities. It could, for instance, also be that these landladies had inherited the lands from their parents and that they had nothing to do with the funerary cult. We simply do not know.

But where were we? We went from Khaemnun's donkey to agriculture in Deir al-Medina to land leases from the Kushite period (Dynasty 25), with an anonymous woman offering a field for a donkey in between, in O. Ashmolean Museum 165. On the other side of this ostracon there is a dispute over donkeys between a workman, a water carrier, and the chief of police Sobekhotep. As we will see below, the policemen and their chiefs were always striking deals with the workmen. Scholars used to think this was because the policemen could move about freely while the workmen could not, but there actually seems to have been little restriction on the mobility enjoyed by the workmen and their families. For one thing, they could go to the market on the riverbank, where ships would moor with produce from everywhere. Naunakhte's son Maaninakhtef traveled to downstream Hu for business, and the woman owning fields in Armant whom we met above would have to go there from time to time to see how her crops were doing. Women were also doing business by themselves in Thebes, as P. Turin Cat. 2087 verso shows:

> Year 13, third month of the *peret* season, day 9. On this day, going to Thebes by (the woman) Takhjenemheb. Trading took place for 10 deben copper . . . gold.

So if there were checkpoints around Deir al-Medina (and one assumes there were), they were there to keep other people out, not to keep the villagers in.

But we were talking about policemen and business. And owning fields and donkeys. There is one small text, a question really, that was most probably laid before the divine oracle of Amunhotep, and one surmises this was done by a man who did not feel very comfortable with an upcoming business deal. So perhaps he put two questions on either side of the road where the oracle would pass, watching closely which way it swerved when passing his personal question. But suppose there were twenty people with a question for the oracle on this day; would they all do the same? The oracle would probably have a hard time satisfying all its customers, unless it had sent some literate person ahead to prepare the route, which sounds altogether too efficient. Alternatively, the supplicant could—as in later times—have brought two ostraca, one positive, one negative, asking the oracle to return the right answer. The more we know about Deir al-Medina the less we seem to know. How did they do it? Approach the oracle and simply ask?

Should one plow the fields of the chief of police Nebsemen?

We do know more about the chief of police Nebsemen and donkeys. The same man may be mentioned in O. DeM 918 from the end of Dynasty 19, but this is very uncertain, because there may have been three chiefs of police called Nebsemen all living at the same time. Like all police officers, Nebsemen (whichever one) did business with the villagers, but O. Turin N. 57456 (either Ramesses III or IV) shows that, unlike his colleague Montumose (see chapter 10, "Was Neferhotep a Wimp?"), he did keep up his end of a bargain. This is a typical sale from Deir al-Medina:

Regnal year 5, third month of the *shemu* season, day 20. Given to Hay by the chief of police Nebsemen: ox 1, which makes 120 deben. What he (Hay) has given: fresh fat 2 jars, which makes 60 deben. Smooth tunics 5, which makes 25 deben. Fine loincloth 1, which makes 20 deben. Hide 1, which makes 25 deben.

It is not known why someone would have to ask the oracle whether or not to plow Nebsemen's fields, although people resorted to it for all kinds of issues, including crime. If, for instance, something had been stolen, the oracle could provide the solution by telling the supplicant what the entire village probably already knew. The oracle could also be consulted if the other party was too powerful to sue in court. One such case may be found in O. Ashmolean Museum 4 (see chapter 5, "Criminal Women"), in which the oracle seems to confirm that the daughter of the scribe Amunnakhte was a thief.

Deborah Sweeney, who has done much for the study of women in the village, looked at this oracle from a gender perspective, with some surprising results. We know the statue of the god would be carried on the shoulders of six or eight men (not women), but this procession probably also involved other priests and female singers of a god. In theory, therefore, we can imagine that Naunakhte—when she was younger—would have been an active player in such an event, since she was the wife of the senior scribe and a singer of Amun. In her statement before the court she did not refer to her profession, most probably because she was no longer active as a singer. The only reason we know she had been a singer of Amun is that her son Qenhirkhopshef mentions it on Stela BM EA 278. Sweeney does point out a picture of the oracle in the tomb of Amunmose, where the god is hailed by women playing the sistrum, castanets, flutes, and tambourines. Just like the smells of the past, the sounds have faded for good, which is a shame because they form an integral part of the picture we are trying to build of life in this village in the New Kingdom. Deir al-Medina was probably noisy and smelly too. In short, carrying around the statue of the deified Amunhotep I was not a solemn and silent affair, but perhaps a rather loud event, with emotions running high. As we saw earlier, the questions to the oracle could often be brief, such as "Did Ramesses steal my bike?" which always reminds me of a Roman Catholic church in Leiden where people still write notes to God, Jesus, and Mary and pin them to the signboard on the wall for them to read.

Sweeney investigated how many female suppliants she could identify among the oracle questions from Deir al-Medina. If we look only at the named men (38) and women (2) and the anonymous men (34) and women (5) found by her, we immediately get interesting statistics. Also, some issues are clearly reserved for the men, such as appointments and wages. In between the few cases laid before the oracle by women, O. Berlin P 10629 (dated to both Dynasties 19 and 20) takes a special place, because it is a cry for help in a conflict between a mother and her daughter. This is the text:

Come to me, My Lord. My mother has created a conflict with my siblings, saying: "I have given you two shares of copper that my (or: your) father had given to me (or: you): a *dydy* vessel, a razor, a *nu* vessel, and a [. . .]. It was the scribe Pentaweret who gave them to me." But she took them and bought a mirror. May My <Lord> establish its value (?). My father gave me emmer: 5 sacks (and) barley as barley: 2 sacks. They belong to my husband in his seven-year term. He only received barley: 4 sacks.

The text on the verso appears to be related:

"There are a man and a woman. Receive two shares." So she said, that is, my mother.

Translating and interpreting texts such as these are notoriously difficult, so it is perhaps best to simply reproduce Sweeney's translation in full (from her article "Gender and Oracular Practice in Deir el-Medîna," 2008):

Come to me, My Lord. My mother is causing me to argue with my siblings, saying, "I gave you two shares of copper, which your father gave to you: a metal dish, a razor, a nw-vessel and a ? when it was the scribe Pentaweret who gave them to me." And she took it away and she traded it for a mirror. My <lord> will make for them a price in deben.

What my father gave me: five sacks of corn and two sacks of barley which belong to my husband for the period of seven years, and he received (only) four sacks. "It belongs to one man and one woman who receive two shares," she said to me, did my mother.

This much is clear: this woman felt swindled out of her rightful share of the inheritance by her mother, who—and the image is too good not to highlight—used part of it instead to buy a *mirror*, which did not come cheap. It seems the mother had been responsible for the division of the inheritance of her late husband among her children, who inherited directly and separately from their father and mother, although here clearly the mother had a say in things. Part of the marriage agreement with the daughter's husband seems to have included grain deliveries by her father for seven years, and the amounts mentioned are probably annual amounts. But these fell short almost by half, year after year. Now the daughter could have gone to court, but instead she resorted to the oracle, although it is difficult to say in what way. Did she put this cry for help before the oracle during a procession, or leave it at his temple (where one does not suppose that any woman was allowed to enter just like that)?

It seems the recto and verso of this text are indeed connected, and one ingenious solution was proposed by the Finnish Egyptologist Jaana Toivari—the author of *Women at Deir el-Medina* (2001)—who thought that the mother may have wanted to compensate her daughter for the shortfalls in the grain deliveries, but on second thought decided against it. Sweeney suggests that the conflict between the daughter and her siblings was actually about the inheritance of the mother and that the daughter wanted a bigger share of it because part of her father's inheritance had been appropriated by her mother, and her father had not held up his end of the deal either. In her view the conflict was therefore between the children and about money, as always, but the sequence of her explanation managed to lose me, which is not surprising because O. Berlin P 10629 permits many interpretations, all of which are equally valid until someone comes up with the right answer.

But it is high time to get back to our Khaemnun and his donkey (O. Ashmolean Museum 53). The official record dryly notes that he had already complained to the court four times, but without success. Once again one likes to think that this court was in the main administrative building and that many villagers went there to see the show, maybe even Naunakhte and some of the couple's children.

> Year 22, second month of the *peret* season, day 5. The court on this day: the four agents of the interior (and) the four agents of the riverbank. The workman Khaemnun complained to them, saying: "As for me, the water carrier Penniut took my donkey and her foal. They both died with him. I have now complained about it (already) four times in court. And the(se) four (times) he was ordered to reimburse me for the donkey and the foal, but he has not given me anything."
>
> His (Penniut's) deposition was heard. He said: "This workman is right. I have really been ordered (to reimburse him)."
>
> He was given a punishment and he repeated the Oath of the Lord, life, prosperity, health, again, saying: "I will [. . .] Penniut [. . .]."

On the back of this ostracon there are two lines of another text recording the payment that the water carrier brought to Khaemnun. It was pathetically little (twenty liters of barley), and it had apparently cost Penniut twenty days to collect these, so that this case would surely have ended up in court again if the parties had not come to some agreement in the meantime.

> He did bring me in year 22, second month of the *peret* season, day 25, barley as barley, one oipe.

And that was not the only court case the water carrier Penniut had to worry about. Several other texts mention him in conflicts about a donkey or money (e.g., O. Ashmolean Museum 196 and O. DeM 569), so that one would have expected that everybody in the village knew that he had something of a reputation when it came to paying. Everybody except Khaemnun.

There is one more ostracon which sheds more light on the daily life of Khaemnun. O. Vienna H. 1 was republished together with its then missing part O. IFAO 628—now O. DeM 828—by the Dutch Egyptologist Louis Zonhoven. Since the text mentions the scribe Amunnakhte son of Ipuy right at the end (and at the beginning, by the way), the editor assumed that he was also the person who wrote this ostracon, but the handwriting is clearly that of the scribe who wrote O. DeM 32–47, which are daily accounts of the events taking place at the gate of the main administrative building, including guard duties and deliveries. This suggests that our anonymous scribe, who is not mentioned on the ostracon, was also present on the scene that day. From the composition of the team involved, it appears that this was official business. But the case may have been brought to the attention of the authorities by the scribe Amunnakhte son of Ipuy himself, because his tomb was directly facing the tomb that was inspected.

> Regnal year 25, first month of the *shemu* season, day 9. Account of the investigation of all the things found in the ruined tomb opposite the place of burial of the scribe Amunnakhte son of Ipuy.

After this brief introduction the text goes straight into what was found in the tomb: various coffins, an ebony footstool with duck heads (repaired), headrests, and a sizable number of baskets and vessels of all kinds of materials. Some of these contained assorted items, including a knife, a pin, a bowl, a jar for libations, a razor case, and various razors.

Strangely enough, the text then continues with the people who were present at the investigation. Nothing is said about why this inspection was held.

> The chief workman Khonsu, the chief workman Kha, the officer Neferhotep, the officer Khaemipet, the guardian Penmennefer, Khaemnun, Weserhat, Aânakhte, Irsu, Huynefer, Neferher, the scribe Amunnakhte.

Since the dating to year 25 of Ramesses III is secure, we may be sure that this is our Khaemnun. Aânakhte may be his son (who did not live to see Naunakhte's epic statement, although Weserhat's father was also called Aânakhte), and Weserhat could be his son-in-law (the husband of Menatnakhte). But is it significant that his name comes first after the mention of the officials involved, and what was he doing there in the first place? Perhaps we should not read too much into this list and simply assume that Khaemnun and his fellow workmen had been summoned to come along in case there was some heavy lifting or clearing to do (which would be strange, because he was already too old for that). At the top of the ostracon there is one additional line stating that the tomb was sealed (again), which suggests that the entrance had to be blocked in some way, which may have been why the workmen were there. In any case this tomb must have been close to the village, meaning that Khaemnun returned home later that day, with another good story to tell his wife.

7

A Day in the Life
of Menatnakhte

The women of Deir al-Medina (or some of them, at least) could divide their own property the way they saw fit, but, as often happens with property divisions, these can lead to both happy and sour faces. For this we only have to look at the Deir al-Medina court cases dealing with inherited family property. They invariably show that property—a direct reflection of the owner's relative status in the village—was an important asset, as it still is today.

The most famous case of a Deir al-Medina woman dividing her inheritance is the so-called Will of Naunakhte. An extensive account of this rather complicated arrangement has already been given in *Mrs. Tsenhor* (2014), but here we want to look at it from the perspective of one of Naunakhte's daughters, namely Menatnakhte, or Menat for short.

The Will of Naunakhte consists of four papyri. Two of these were acquired by Alan Gardiner sometime after 1928. In 1945 he presented them to the Ashmolean Museum in Oxford, where they are now kept under the inventory numbers 1945.95 and 1945.97. The two other papyri were found in situ during the excavations in Deir al-Medina by the IFAO in 1928 (P. DeM 23 and 25), so it is possible that all four papyri had been found together, and then two were stolen and sold on the market. Or they had been found by illicit diggers after the French excavators had left the site at the end of the season. The French team also found a large number of fragments, which turned out to be letters and a literary text. The largest Naunakhte papyrus—43 × 192 cm in the handwriting of two different scribes—is P. Ashmolean Museum 1945.97. It was written in year 3 of Ramesses V. This may have been around 1142 BCE, but it could also have been slightly earlier. The professional discussions about dating issues in Egyptology are often so boring that it is difficult not to lose interest at some point, mostly after a minute or so.

P. Ashmolean Museum 1945.97 records the oral statement by Naunakhte before the local court. She was very old by this time and did not have much longer to live. And what she had to say in court does shed some light on the position of the ancient Egyptian *materfamilias* and her right to divide the family estate. As a young girl Naunakhte had been married off to the prominent Deir al-Medina scribe Qenhirkhopshef, who was probably forty years older. We do not know whether the couple had any children. From Stela BM EA 278—which was commissioned by the family of her son Qenhirkhopshef—we know that she was a singer of Amun. After her husband Qenhirkhopshef's death, and having inherited from him some movables and real estate, Naunakhte married the workman Khaemnun, to whom she bore eight surviving children. That is, only eight were there to see the division of her inheritance. For the reader's convenience a family tree is reproduced here once more, with the names of the women in italics (for the extended family tree from *Who's Who*, see figure 1):

Qenhirkhopshef × *Naunakhte* × Khaemnun

Maaninakhtef
Qenhirkhopshef
Amunnakhte
Wasetnakhte
Menatnakhte
Neferhotep
Henutshenu
Khatanub

In P. Ashmolean Museum 1945.97 Naunakhte states that some of her children will not inherit from her, because they had not looked after her when she was old. They will not share in the division of the estate of her first husband, Qenhirkhopshef, although they will still inherit from the property she had acquired with their own father, Khaemnun. It is probably the property that she had (presumably) inherited from Qenhirkhopshef and from her father that would have been the most valuable (apart from

Qenhirkhopshef's library). Unfortunately there are no sources telling us what happened to the property, although we do know what happened to the library. It was given to her son Amunnakhte and after that it came into the possession of his brother Maaninakhtef. Both could read and write. This suggests that there must have been more documents in which Naunakhte allocated the real estate to specific children, but these have never been found. Or it could be that her husband had been instructed to manage and divide it at will, which sounds improbable.

Behind the statement by Naunakhte we sense disappointment with some of her children, who had apparently been too busy or careless to look after their mother. This raises the intriguing question of what would have happened if Naunakhte had died before she had gone to court. At least two of her daughters—Henutshenu and Khatanub (aka Khanub)—may rather have hoped for this to happen, because in the end they received nothing from their mother. Or would they? Henutshenu named one of her daughters after her mother, as we can see from O. Cairo CG 25705 + O. IFAO 1322 + O. Varille 38 (see chapter 11, "Women Can Party Too"), but most probably this was done long before she chose not to support her mother in her old age. She was not the only one of Naunakhte's children to name her daughter Naunakhte (her disinherited son Neferhotep did as well), but most of these girls are mere names.

According to the official record, Naunakhte—described as a female citizen and a freewoman, a person free to dispose of her belongings—made her statement in year 3, fourth month of the *akhet* season, day 5 of Ramesses V, about 1142 BCE. The court where she did this was composed of no fewer than fourteen men (no women). Apparently this statement was a big event, so the court included the two chief workmen of Deir al-Medina, two scribes, two draftsmen, two district officers, and several workmen. Although it is nowhere explicitly stated, one assumes that her children and her second husband were present on this day as well, and probably even many of the village people. Nothing like a family scandal to brighten up the day.

After these preliminaries there follows the statement of Naunakhte:

As far as I am concerned, I am a freewoman of the land of Pharaoh, life, prosperity, health. I have raised these eight servants of yours. I gave them a household outfit of all things that is usually done for the likes of them.

Now see, I have grown old, and see, they are not taking care of me in turn. As for anyone among them who laid his hand on my hand (cared for me), I will give him my things. As to the one who has not given me, I will not give him from my things.

Note how Naunakhte states that *she* was the one who enabled her children to start their own households, not her husband Khaemnun. One has to assume here that part of what she had inherited from Qenhirkhopshef was used to give her daughters a dowry and fit out her sons with the wealth that would enable them to find the wife of their choice. Perhaps she even provided some of them with a house.

Then there is a list of the children who will inherit from her and those who will not. What is striking is that her son Qenhirkhopshef—named after her first husband and believed by some to be Naunakhte's eldest son—receives an extra portion. This may have been because, as we will see below, he would take care of his father after Naunakhte had died. Our Menatnakhte, standing there and expecting at least something, now heard that she would receive her part of the inheritance from Naunakhte's own property, but slightly less, because she had not contributed to her mother's pension, unlike some of her brothers and her sister Wasetnakhte:

List of the workmen and women to whom she has given: the workman Maaninakhtef, the workman Qenhirkhopshef. She said: "I have given him a bronze washbowl as a reward and, as an additional share above the others, also ten sacks of emmer corn." (And) the workman Amunnakhte, the female citizen Wasetnakhte, and the female citizen Menatnakhte.

As for the female citizen Menatnakhte. She said about her: "She will have a share in the division of all my things, except the oipe of emmer corn that my three male children and also the female citizen Wasetnakhte have given me, and my hin of fat that they gave me in the same manner."

The inheritance divided by Naunakhte consisted of various lots: a storeroom that she had inherited from her father, plus the property of her first husband, Qenhirkhopshef, that she had inherited from him, almost suggesting that he may have adopted her to guarantee her rights to his inheritance. Sources such as P. Ashmolean Museum 1945.96 (the Adoption Papyrus) and possibly also P. Geneva D 409 + P. Turin Cat.

2021 recto tell us this could be done. They were the right age for a father–daughter relationship.

Then there was the property acquired by her and Qenhirkhopshef, and the property acquired by her and her second husband, Khaemnun, of which one-third was hers to dispose of. Some of this would also go to the children who had been negligent toward her, but her own property and the property inherited from Qenhirkhopshef was hers to divide, and hers alone. That was where the real money was and from this they would get nothing.

This explains the next division listed by the scribe, who makes a crucial mistake, once forgetting to write 'not' where he should have:

> List of her children of whom she had said: "They will not enter into the division of my one-third, but they will enter into the division of the two-thirds of their father."
>
> The workman Neferhotep, the female citizen Menatnakhte, the female citizen Henutshenu, and the female citizen Khatanub.
>
> As far as these four children of mine are concerned, they will <not> enter into the division of all my things. And as for all the things of the scribe Qenhirkhopshef, my husband, and also his places and this storehouse of my father and likewise this oipe of emmer corn that I and my husband collected, they will not share in them.

The mention of the movables (which may have included slaves) and immovables of Qenhirkhopshef is intriguing. Naunakhte is referring to his real estate here, and Qenhirkhopshef may have been quite wealthy if he had really inherited from his tutor, the scribe Ramose. We know he had a large house in the village (did she still live there?), the most luxurious hut on the col between the village and the Valley of the Kings, and probably lots more. Somehow one gets the impression that Qenhirkhopshef had married Naunakhte as his 'staff of old age,' in return for which she would become his heir, in exactly the same way in which Qenhirkhopshef may have been the person caring for Ramose and Mutemwia and, after one of them died, for the person left behind. Still, at this point one would have expected Naunakhte to list what went to whom, but the protocol does not say.

Four children were excluded from the division of the property from Naunakhte's first marriage with Qenhirkhopshef, although she could not prevent them from sharing in the inheritance of their own father

Khaemnun. So far the statement is not entirely clear about the share that Menatnakhte would or would not receive, and we have to assume that the latter would be very confused at this point, to say the least. What exactly would she get out of it?

The scribe's mistake in not writing 'not' at a crucial spot in the statement above—indicated by the angled brackets—could of course have led to fierce legal battles afterward.

> As far as these four children of mine are concerned, they will <not> enter into the division of all my things.

The atmosphere was probably tense when this document was written, after Naunakhte had made her statement before the court, unless it was recorded more or less verbatim. We have to assume that all the people involved in the division of her inheritance were present. It would have been nice to know whether the family all went there at once, or whether Khaemnun and Naunakhte went on their own, and their children (and their husbands and wives) followed later.

We do not know if the children knew what was coming (apart from her son Qenhirkhopshef, who had already received his extra share), although it seems likely, because a daughter not caring for her mother in her old age, as she was expected to do, would be bound to expect a repercussion of some sort. Nor do we know whether Naunakhte had discussed her plans with her husband and (some of) her children. One would assume so, because she also makes a public statement about the division of her second husband's property, saying that each of their children will receive an equal share. This suggests that Khaemnun and Naunakhte had prepared her statement together (including his pension plan). In any case, it was up to Naunakhte to make a coherent oral statement in front of all these people, including the children who would be disinherited— now glaring at her—so one would very much like to know how she felt when she made it. Was she sad because she knew she was dying? Was she happy because this was payback time? Perhaps both?

One certain outcome of Naunakhte's statement was that family relations would remain uncomfortable for many years to come, because most of the people involved would still be living in the same small community afterward. Also, her son-in-law Weserhat and the workman

Telmontu (who was related to the family through marriage) had been members of the court that heard (and probably endorsed) her statement, and Weserhat in particular may have had some explaining to do to his wife Menatnakhte.

But Naunakhte was far from finished. One of her sons received some extra punishment, although he is not mentioned by name. He was the black sheep who needed support time and again. The obvious candidate would be her son Neferhotep, as is suggested by the addendum to the protocol made a year after Naunakhte's statement (see further below). From Naunakhte's words we may take it that Neferhotep was not very good at taking care of himself, and more than once called on his mother for support. Only three of her sons and a daughter made sure that she received a monthly oipe of grain and some fat. We probably do not have to guess which son did not contribute.

> As for the kettle that I gave him to buy bread for himself, and likewise the chisel of seven deben and likewise the vase of seven deben, and likewise the adze of six deben, which makes forty deben, they will form his share. He will not enter into the division of any copper. It will be for his brothers and sisters.

If these forty deben were all that Neferhotep were to receive, this suggests that Naunakhte had plenty to give away, apart from having set up her children in life, and that instead of supporting his old mother, Neferhotep had to be supported by her. But as we will see below, he was not satisfied with his share and presumably contested the will in court at some later time.

When the protocol was done, the record was signed by the scribe Amunnakhte son of Ipuy, the same person who wrote the Turin Strike Papyrus (P. Turin Cat. 1880)—about the strikes in year 29 of Ramesses III—and many other documents from Deir al-Medina.

There is a little addendum to the official record that is dated one year later, in year 4, third month of the *akhet* season, day 17. It says that on this day the workman Khaemnun and his children went to court again. This time the court consisted of the two managers of the crew, the scribe Horshery (the son of Amunnakhte son of Ipuy), and two district officers, one of whom had also witnessed the official statement by Naunakhte the year before. Khaemnun—who was not a very rich man—and his children had come to make a statement of their own:

> As far as the writings are concerned which the female citizen Naunakhte has made about her things, they are thus exactly, exactly. The workman Neferhotep will not share in them. He will take an Oath of the Lord, life, prosperity, health, saying: "If I turn back on my word again, he (I) shall receive a hundred blows and be deprived of his (my) things."

From this we may surmise that—as was to be expected—Naunakhte's will had created some dissent in the family. Her son Neferhotep clearly did not agree with the way things had gone, and the fact that the addendum states that Khaemnun and his children had gone to court again probably does not refer to the time they were there to hear Naunakhte's statement the year before, but to subsequent hearings about the validity of the division.

We do have two more papyri showing that some of the property owned by Naunakhte was physically divided among her children. These were found by the French excavation team in Deir al-Medina in 1928, and they are now known as P. DeM 23 and 25. Both are small, 21 × 12 and 23.5 × 9 cm respectively, and they were written in different hands on recycled papyrus (reusing a papyrus from Qenhirkhopshef's library?). They record the division of some of the things belonging to 'your mother,' Naunakhte (the 'your' suggests that the texts were written by some of the husbands of Naunakhte's daughters, unless it is a mistake for 'our,' in which case they may have been written by some of Naunakhte's sons), and their content is nearly identical, mentioning the items received by Amunnakhte, Wasetnakhte, Maaninakhtef, Menatnakhte, Nebnakhte (the husband of Wasetnakhte), and Qenhirkhopshef. Although these lists are tedious reading, they are included to show how meticulous property divisions in Deir al-Medina could be. They only concern household objects of lesser value. The names of the women are in italics, as are the Egyptian words that defy translation.

P. DeM 23

Recto

List of the division of the things of your (mistake for 'our'?) mother.
Given to Amunnakhte: millstone 1.
Given to *Wasetnakhte*: millstone 1.
Given to *Menatnakhte*: wooden *iqer* 1.
Given to Qenhirkhopshef: wooden *iqer* 1.
Given to Maaninakhtef: wooden box 1.

Given to *Menatnakhte*: mortar 1.
Given to Amunnakhte: mortar 1.
Given to Qenhirkhopshef: mortar 1.
Given to Nebnakhte: mortar 1.
Given to Maaninakhtef: wooden box (?) 1.

Given to Amunnakhte: wooden box 1.
Given to Menatnakhte: wooden *tepu* 1.

Verso

Given to Qenhirkhopshef: legs of a wooden *maset* 1.
Given to Maaninakhtef: wooden *kerty* 1.

P. DeM 25

Recto

List of the division of the things of your (mistake for 'our'?) mother.
Given to Amunnakhte: millstone 1.
Given to *Wasetnakhte*: millstone 1.
Given to *Menatnakhte*: wooden *iqer* 1.
Given to Qenhirkhopshef: wooden *iqer* 1.
Given to Maaninakhtef: wooden box 1.

Again, another division.
Given to *Menatnakhte*: mortar 1.
Given to Amunnakhte: mortar 1.
Given to Qenhirkhopshef: mortar 1.
Given to Maaninakhtef: wooden box (?) 1.
Given to *Wasetnakhte*: mortar 1.

Again, another division.
Given to Amunnakhte: wooden box 1.
Given to *Wasetnakhte*: wooden cage (?) 1.

Given to Qenhirkhopshef: legs of a wooden *maset* 1.
Given to Maaninakhtef: wooden *kerty* 1.

Given to *Wasetnakhte*: wooden cage (?)1.

Given to *Wasetnakhte*: wooden cage (?) 1.

Again, another division.

Given to *Menatnakhte*: oipe 1.
Given to Amunnakhte: oipe 1.
Given to *Wasetnakhte*:
oipe 1.
Given to Qenhirkhopshef:
sledge 1.
Given to Maaninakhtef:
sledge 1.

Given to *Menatnakhte*: oipe 1.
Given to Amunnakhte: oipe 1.
Given to *Wasetnakhte*:
oipe 1.
Given to Qenhirkhopshef:
sledge 1.
Given to Maaninakhtef:
sledge 1.

Again, another division.

Given to Qenhirkhopshef:
wooden ... 1.
Given to Amunnakhte:
wooden *hetep* 1.
Given to Nebnakhte:
hetep 1 and mortar 1.
Given to *Menatnakhte*:
stone *khed* 1.
Given to Maaninakhtef:
stone *gat* measure 1.

Given to Qenhirkhopshef: wooden
... 1.
Given to Amunnakhte: leg of a
wooden *hetep* 1.
Given to *Wasetnakhte*: *hetep* 1 and
mortar 1.
Given to *Menatnakhte*:
stone *khed* 1.
Given to Maaninakhtef:
stone *gat* measure 1.

Again, another division.
Given to Amunnakhte:
wooden *sheqer* 1.
Given to Qenhirkhopshef:
stone footrest 1.
Given to Maaninakhtef:
stone footrest 1.
Given to *Menatnakhte*:
stone footrest 1.
Given to *Wasetnakhte*:
stone footrest 1.

So we have two papyri that obviously deal with the same division of some of Naunakhte's inheritance. As Černý, who published the Naunakhte documents, noted, however, the items divided were not the most precious ones, the division leaving out all the metal commodities (which were the equivalent of cash money).

Also, exactly who in the end received the most valuable possessions of Naunakhte—such as the real estate—is unclear, but it is no coincidence that the five children involved in the division recorded in P. DeM 23 and 25 are the same as the ones mentioned in Naunakhte's opening statement of P. Ashmolean Museum 1945.97 seen earlier.

> List of the workmen and women to whom she has given: the workman Maaninakhtef, the workman Qenhirkhopshef. She said: "I have given to him a bronze washbowl as a reward and as an additional share above the others, also ten sacks of emmer corn." (And) the workman Amunnakhte, the female citizen Wasetnakhte, and the female citizen Menatnakhte.

One assumes that P. DeM 23 and 25 were written after Naunakhte had died and the children were clearing out the house (in which their father Khaemnun would still be living). Both texts record the same division, listing (almost) the same people in the same order, receiving the same items from the inheritance. The scribe of P. DeM 23 chose to separate the various steps involved in the procedure using a horizontal stroke, whereas the scribe of P. DeM 25 introduced each session with a separate header "Again, another division." There may even have been several more of these lists that went into the separate archives of the heirs, and the fact that these two lists were written suggests that the people involved wanted to be very sure about who had taken what.

P. DeM 25 lists one extra division that is not recorded in P. DeM 23. So if these texts were not written at the same time (either one being used to make a copy), it is difficult to tell which was written first. If it was P. DeM 23, then why does P. DeM 25 include an additional (sixth) division that is not in P. DeM 23? If P. DeM 25 was written first, then why was this sixth division excluded from P. DeM 23? The same question applies if both texts were written at the time of the physical division, or if they are both copied from another text.

According to Černý, P. DeM 23 and 25 are the records of a division that involved multiple visits to empty Naunakhte's house:

> We may, therefore, picture the five heirs paying six visits to their mother's house, and on each occasion dividing up a set of objects of approximately equal value. (*Journal of Egyptian Archaeology* 31)

This procedure could, and probably would, have unfolded in a much simpler way. Perhaps the five siblings were all in the house and simply took turns choosing items from the inheritance. Later demotic sources, such as the Ptolemaic legal manual P. Mattha (c. 250 BCE), suggest that the children took turns according to their order of birth if their father had died intestate, first the boys and then the girls. But they could also decide to cast lots to determine the order in which they would pick the items of their choice. This would help to explain why this division took place the way it did.

For instance, in the second division in P. DeM 23 and 25 we see four siblings each receiving a millstone, leaving the fifth with some wooden object. This somehow looks like what people would do today: "So you're taking a millstone? Right, then so will I." Also note that in the last division Naunakhte's son Amunnakhte—the first to pick this time—chose a wooden *sheqer*, whereas the other four siblings each received a stone footrest, clearly the least popular item of the lot (which may explain why this is not even listed in P. DeM 23). For one thing, they would have to schlep it home. So even tedious documents such as accounts from ancient Egypt often conceal deep emotions that researchers tend to overlook. That is, of course, because emotion is not very scientific. We cannot measure it, and certainly not with a few millennia in between.

Looking at the order in which the five siblings took their pick from their mother's household items, a strange picture emerges. This is the picking—or rather pecking—order of this particular division (the names of the women are in italics):

NAME	Div. 1	Div. 2	Div. 3	Div. 4	Div. 5	Div. 6
Amunnakhte	1	2	1	2	2	1
Wasetnakhte	2	5	5	3	3	5
Menatnakhte	3	1	2	1	4	4
Qenhirkhopshef	4	3	3	4	1	2
Maaninakhtef	5	4	4	5	5	3

Note that in the second division in P. DeM 23 Wasetnakhte('s husband) is mentioned fourth and Maaninakhtef fifth, whereas in the same division in P. DeM 25 it is Maaninakhtef who comes before Wasetnakhte.

We see that Amunnakhte was clearly a favorite of some sort—at least in this division of Naunakhte's household goods—always picking first or second. As has been convincingly shown by the Dutch demotist and legal historian Pieter Willem Pestman, Amunnakhte also inherited his mother's extensive library (collected by her first husband, Qenhirkhopshef), something that may have raised his status in the village considerably. Poor Maaninakhtef in most cases came last, doing even worse than his sister Wasetnakhte. But as we will see below, he started a rather successful business in carpentry, most likely with some of his brothers.

Menatnakhte gets to choose first twice, and second once, which is better than all the other siblings except her brother Amunnakhte. Why this was so we do not know, and in the light of Naunakhte's own statement in P. Ashmolean Museum 1945.97 one would rather have expected some of the other four being allowed to take their pick before her, but this is clearly not what happened. Then again, we do not know who received the lion's share of Naunakhte's inheritance, and until new evidence comes up we probably never will.

Nebnakhte is the odd one out. He is not listed among Naunakhte's children who are mentioned in her own statement, and the simplest solution is that he and Wasetnakhte were husband and wife and that he assisted in the division. Nebnakhte also appears in the last papyrus of the series as a witness to a statement made by Naunakhte's second husband, Khaemnun, presumably representing the interests of his wife in what had become a highly volatile family affair. It makes one wonder whether women were actually allowed to participate in procedures such as this. Looking at the demotic evidence—thousands of papyri, in which the witnesses to a contract are invariably male—it almost seems as if women did not count as credible witnesses in the ancient Egyptian legal system, which is not true, because there are court records showing that they did.

The fourth papyrus from the series is not as straightforward as the rest. It actually predates the Will of Naunakhte by a few weeks. The papyrus, which measures 21 × 43 cm, is now known as P. Ashmolean Museum 1945.95.

It is in two hands, one neat and professional and the other rather sloppy. It is not certain whether we are dealing with another court session here, since the following transaction between Khaemnun and his son Qenhirkhopshef only involves ordinary workmen, asked to witness the transaction (or maybe some of them represented the interests of the sisters who were not there on this day). Qenhirkhopshef's brothers would be there.

> Has said the workman Khaemnun before the workman Anynakhte, the workman Qedakhetef, the workman Hornefer, the workman Neferhotep, the workman Amunnakhtef, the workman Maaninakhtef, and the workman Khonsu: "Look, I give this washbowl which is thirteen deben of copper. It is for Qenhirkhopshef. No son or daughter will discuss it. His statement shall not be heard. It is not in any (other) division."

Since the economy of Deir al-Medina revolved around bronze and copper, this represented a serious amount of cash. It seems reasonable to assume that this washbowl is the same as the one mentioned by Naunakhte in her court appearance a few weeks later. Khaemnun explicitly states that the washbowl will not be part of any division, presumably of Naunakhte's inheritance. His statement was then formally put into writing again, meaning that it is recorded twice. Or could it be that Khaemnun first stated his plan to donate the washbowl to Qenhirkhopshef in front of witnesses and that after this—and not necessarily on the same day—they went to court or to an individual scribe to have it recorded in writing? It is in any case strange to see his statement being recorded twice on the same papyrus. According to Černý the first part of the text refers to Khaemnun's promise before the court to give the bowl, whereas the second records the actual transfer.

Only then are we told why the washbowl was given. We know that Naunakhte was old and intended to make the statement in court about her inheritance a few weeks later. We also know that Khaemnun was not a rich man and that in ancient Egypt children were a man's (and woman's) pension.

> Delivering on this day in front of the workman Anynakhte, the workman Qedakhetef, the workman Nebnakhte, the workman Khonsu, the workman Neferhotep, the workman Amunnakhte, and the workman Khaemnun himself, whereas the workman Qenhirkhopshef has said: "I will give to him 2¾ sacks (of grain)." And he took an Oath of the Lord, life, prosperity, health, saying: "As Amun endures, as the Ruler endures, life, prosperity, health. If I take away the ration of my father my reward shall be taken away. I will give a pair of sandals to the workman Amunnakhte and he (I?)

will give to him a chest, namely Maaninakhtef, on account of the writings that were made concerning the statement of their father."

One is really tempted to speculate here. Nebnakhte was the husband of one of Naunakhte's daughters. Pestman thought that Khonsu was married to another of her daughters (which is not believed by others), but that is where it stops. The other men must have been friends or relatives, because otherwise Khaemnun would never have asked them to witness this statement, but one would so much like to know more.

Although the last part of this text is particularly obscure, Qenhirk-hopshef promises to take care of his father after the death of Naunakhte. In return for this he receives the washbowl, as a bonus on top of his share of the inheritance. Since 2¾ sacks were slightly more than two hundred liters of grain, one does wonder what was the precise arrangement between father and son. These 2¾ sacks would be more than half of the normal monthly income of a workman and Qenhirkhopshef could probably not afford to give this to his father each month (although he added to his income by working as a carpenter)—unless perhaps there would be some future compensation, such as a larger part of the inheritance of his father (who was not rich). As a yearly amount, 2¾ sacks sounds even more unlikely, unless all eight children of Khaemnun and Naunakhte were to chip in, so that Khaemnun actually received 8 × 2¾ sacks = 22 sacks per year, which would be an extremely good pension. But that would never happen, of course. We know that three sons of Naunakhte and one of their sisters contributed to her monthly oipe of grain, and what Qenhirk-hopshef is saying here is that he alone will make sure that his father will be provided for with an oipe per month. Since the 2¾ sacks promised by him would only be 11 oipe, one assumes the rest would have to come from the other brothers or Khaemnun himself. This ration would presumably be supplemented by other food and drink, and ointments, but the statement does not say. The reader is reminded that Naunakhte also willed him ten sacks of grain. Was this actually the pension plan for her husband, paid some years in advance?

Since Khaemnun's daughters Henutshenu and Khatanub had never cared for his wife when she was old—and where was he, by the way?—the chance that they would care for him may have been slim as well, although we do not know. Which brings us to Naunakhte's daughter Menatnakhte, one of the children for whom a special provision had been made by Naunakhte that robbed her of part of her inheritance.

From some of the official sources we may take that Menatnakhte—just a workman's wife, and thus not very prominent in the records of Deir al-Medina—was more than once involved in household trouble—her own household, that is (see chapter 9, "So Who Gets the Kids?"). She is one of the better documented of Naunakhte's daughters, although one should not be too optimistic here. For instance, the still unpublished O. IFAO 1253 is an account titled "List of the th[ings . . .] that are with Menatnakhte," which are many mostly wooden—and thus valuable—items, varying from carrying poles to a large bed, along with several types of ointments. If this were a list of items (or at least their value) owed by one person to another, the combined value would be astronomical and it is unlikely that anyone in the village would be prepared to lend her commodities to this value. It seems more likely that we should connect O. IFAO 1253 with a marriage (what Menatnakhte brought into the marriage), a divorce (what she got out of it) or—and why not?—an inheritance. But this would also be problematic. Menatnakhte was only one of several heirs, five in the case of Naunakhte's inheritance, and presumably eight in the case of the inheritance of their father Khaemnun. Would either of the parents have owned so much movable property that Menatnakhte could have inherited all this? If Naunakhte had owned eightfold of what is listed here, where would the couple have kept all these wooden items in the house? One never stops wondering.

8

A Boy with a Golden
Pair of Hands

We do not know where Maaninakhtef ('I have seen his power'), whose name is generally shortened to Maanakhtef and sometimes written Pamaanakhtef, came in the line of succession, although when Naunakhte's children went to clear out their mother's house—which is described in detail in P. DeM 23 and 25 (see chapter 7, "A Day in the Life of Menatnakhte")—and took turns picking the items of their choice, he was quite often last in line. Then again, these were not the most valuable items of the lot, just the household goods.

Maaninakhtef was part of the regular workforce and is securely attested in the daily records O. DeM 41 and 44–47 from years 1 and 2 of Ramesses IV, where he occurs side by side with his father Khaemnun. In O. Cairo CG 25533 (year 3 of Ramesses IV) he is mentioned with his father and his brother Qenhirkhopshef. This daily journal once again records that the workmen passed the guard posts in search of their grain rations that were late (as usual by this time). One assumes these three men joined this protest too.

So do we know more about this man? Yes, in fact we do know a lot. If we look for a specific person in Deir al-Medina, the first thing to do is to check the village 'telephone directory': Benedict Davies, *Who's Who* (1999), to see where else he occurs. The incredible amount of work that Davies went through to compile this directory is not something every Egyptologist would have been prepared to do. He does mention some of the above sources, but not all (new evidence has turned up in the meantime), so that the obvious thing to do in the near future is to convert his invaluable book into an extendable database. That is the trouble with printed encyclopedic works: the moment they are published they are obsolete. Archaeologists find new things.

The story of Maaninakhtef also becomes quite complicated even before it starts. According to Andreas Dorn, O. Cairo CG 25533 actually contains the names of two contemporary workmen both called Maaninakhtef, using the designations (iii) and (iv) from *Who's Who* to distinguish between them. Number (iii) would then be Naunakhte's son Maaninakhtef. The original sources also make a fine distinction between the two in hieratic, because no. (iv) is always written with two additional alephs in the verb *maa* 'to see' at the beginning of his name, which are always absent in no. (iii). Dorn's suggestion is tempting, but it has its flaws. For one thing, it is built on the hypothesis that both no. (iii) and no. (iv) worked in the Valley of the Kings, but that only no. (iii)—our man—did guard duties at the gate of the main administrative building and that no. (iv) only worked in the royal tomb. In the Valley of the Kings the Swiss team found a number of exercises in letter-writing which Dorn then attributed to both no. (iii) and no. (iv). Two workmen called Maaninakhtef living at the same time, and both practicing writing letters to the vizier? This is perhaps too much to take in all at once. The final proof can only come from a study of the handwriting in all the ostraca and papyri written by (whichever) Maaninakhtef. And that is something for the future.

In any case, the workman Maaninakhtef (iii) son of Naunakhte is actually the same person as the carpenter Maaninakhtef mentioned in some of the papyri of that time, such as P. DeM 8–11. This suggestion was made earlier by Pestman in his brilliant essay on the library of the scribe Qenhirkhopshef, showing how it ended up with his widow Naunakhte, then possibly her second husband Khaemnun, then their son Amunnakhte, and finally Maaninakhtef. But much has happened since in Deir al-Medina studies.

While in Leiden scholars were working on the *Deir el-Medina Database* from 1998 onward, Egyptologists from Munich—Günter Burkard, Stefan Wimmer, and Maren Goecke-Bauer—were compiling their own database of the sources found during the German excavations, such as by Georg Möller in the early twentieth century. This database is also online for all to use *(Deir el-Medine Online)*. It was seen earlier that Möller's finds sometimes show a striking overlap with some of the finds made by the French archaeologists at Kom Sûd near Deir al-Medina. In the case of

Maaninakhtef the Munich team actually almost doubled the then known material mentioning him. The excavations by Andreas Dorn in the Valley of the Kings have added yet more new material.

This allows us to paint a rather complete—albeit rather one-sided—picture of this man, the son of Naunakhte and Khaemnun. He clearly worked on the side as a carpenter and apparently a very good one at that. The only bad news is that, as so often in Deir al-Medina, women play no role in his dossier. We know that he had at least four sons, but the name of his wife is still unknown.

O. Berlin P 14262 is undated but extremely important, because it firmly connects the *workman* Maaninakhtef with carpentry. It is tempting to identify the workman Weserhat mentioned in this text with his brother-in-law, the husband of his sister Menatnakhte.

> Account of the silver [that the workman] Weserhat [gave] to the workman Maaninakht[ef . . .] the bed: barley as barley [. . .] sacks [. . .], basket 1, filled with emmer, makes [. . .], basket [. . .], filled with barley as barley, makes [. . .].

This deal between Weserhat and Maaninakhtef is also described in two other ostraca from Berlin. This is O. Berlin P 14357. It is a limestone piece that was scrubbed clean to remove an earlier literary text.

> Account of the silver that the workman Weserhat gave to the workman Maaninakhtef in return for the bed: barley as barley 2 sacks 2 oipe, which makes 6 deben. Emmer corn 2 oipe, which makes 1 deben. Goat 1, which makes 2 deben. Again: goat 1 (?), which makes 2. Baskets 2, which makes 2 deben. Total of what came from him: 10 deben copper. His remainder: 4 deben.

O. Berlin P 14365 is surely about the very same deal:

> [. . .] that Weserhat gave me in return for the bed: [. . .], which makes 5 deben. *Kebes* basket, which makes 1 deben. Goat 1, which makes 2 deben. I gave him 1 hin of *merehet* oil.

The 'me' and 'I' in this last text suggest that Maaninakhtef wrote some of these accounts himself. The fact that he was the last known owner of the library of Qenhirkhopshef suggests that he could read and write (he did). In fact, one should seriously consider the possibility that he had been taught by his mother, who in turn had been taught to write by her first husband, Qenhirkhopshef. She was probably well aware of the status the ability to read and write would bring. Surely this library would have provided the impetus to learn to read. But why three accounts for one bed? They could be installments (simple solutions are often the best).

Maaninakhtef and his brother Amunnakhte called themselves 'scribe' on numerous occasions, such as in O. Glasgow D.1925.68 (O. Colin Campbell 3), which is a list of workmen excused from work because the vizier had some carpentry for them to do, including the door of a tomb, a chest, and a bed. There are indeed some similarities in the handwriting of the accounts O. Berlin P 14357 and 14365 between Weserhat and Maaninakhtef, but O. Berlin P 14262 is clearly in a much hastier script. Then again, we only have to look at our own handwriting for notes, official letters, and drafts of book chapters to be aware that people can write in many different ways and still be the same people. It seems Maaninakhtef even had a literary handwriting, which is quite distinct from his business hand. Although the first editor could not read the scribe's name in the colophon of the teaching of Kemyt on O. Munich 1638, his French colleague Georges Posener was able to identify it as 'Maaninakhtef.' If this is indeed our man, we now know he was very well educated indeed.

The identification of the anonymous handwritings of the Deir al-Medina scribes—allowing us to assign a corpus of texts to an individual scribe—is still in its infancy. This new line of research actually started in Leiden several years ago and is now carried on in Munich by Maren Goecke-Bauer, but there are several other studies, including a dissertation on scribal hands in the so-called necropolis journals by the British Egyptologist Stephanie Hudson (Oxford), *The Twentieth Dynasty Journal of the Necropolis of Deir el-Medina* (2013). The book is eagerly awaited.

On the recto of the literary P. Chester Beatty III—Qenhirkhopshef's Dream Book—Amunnakhte added his own colophon (trying to pass himself off as the real author of the Dream Book?), which tells us that some other brothers also worked as carpenters and could read and write. Note that he does not mention any of his sisters.

Made by the scribe Amunnakhte son of Khaemnun, brother of the carpenter Neferhotep, brother of the carpenter Qenhirkhopshef, brother of the scribe Pama[anakhtef]. Made by the scribe Amunnakhte.

One of the texts that does not seem to fit the picture is O. Berlin P 14260 recto (one or two lines have broken off at the bottom), believed to be from the reign of Ramesses IV. Here we see Maaninakhtef himself paying the carpenter Aâpatjau. The obvious thing would be to assume that he paid for some wooden product, but the text does not mention this, so it could also be the payment for any other item, even carpentry lessons by Aâpatjau.

Account of all the things of the workman Maaninakhtef, which he gave to the carpenter Aâpatjau: *meses* tunic 1, which makes 5 deben. Goat 1, which makes 1½ deben. Vegetables 3 bundles, which makes [. . .] deben. Straw for sleeping [. . .]. Mats 2, which makes [. . .] deben for his companion, barley (?) [. . .]. Sleeping mat [. . .].

These men knew each other well, occurring side by side in a number of sources. O. Cairo CG 25532 is a journal listing various workmen who are absent because they were attending some feast (*ll.* 3–4 of the verso). The interesting thing is that in this text Aâpatjau is also referred to as a *sesh* 'scribe,' although from the looks of it he was a simple workman (e.g., O. Cairo CG 25599). In fact, Maaninakhtef also referred to himself as a scribe, and in the end would own Qenhirkhopshef's library. But so did his brothers Amunnakhte and Qenhirkhopshef the Younger, and there is even one other son of Khaemnun and Naunakhte who also called himself 'scribe,' a certain Pagafy, who did not live to see the division of his mother's inheritance (O. Berlin P 15295). But the evidence, including O. Cairo CG 25716, O. Petrie 6 (which is not in the *Deir el-Medina Database* because it is a prayer to Amun and not a documentary text), and Graffito no. 774a, is not entirely conclusive.

More puzzling is O. Černý 20 (still unpublished), an account listing painted coffins, garments, and various other objects, but also payments made by both Maaninakhtef (for a painted coffin and assorted items) and Aâpatjau. It would appear that both men, whose payments are listed together, had placed an order for the painting of a coffin and these other items, but not for the coffin itself. Does this mean they owned a business together in which Maaninakhtef's brothers Neferhotep and Qenhirkhopshef were also partners?

Let us return to the problem of the two contemporary workmen both called Maaninakhtef, no. (iii) in *Who's Who* being our man. Dorn suggested that the person of that name who paid the workman Pentaweret for a piece of woodwork in O. Ashmolean Museum 66 (possibly from the reign of Ramesses V) *would have to be* the other Maaninakhtef (iv), because of the double aleph in his name and the fact that *surely* (my italics) our Maaninakhtef (iii) son of Naunakhte would have been able to make this piece of woodwork himself. Of course he would. But one of the first lessons you learn in real-life business is that sometimes demand quickly outgrows your own capacity to meet it. The obvious solution is to have other people do the work for you, pay them for their work, and add a percentage when you deliver. This may have been precisely what our Maaninakhtef did every now and then.

Maaninakhtef was, from the looks of it, an avid letter-writer. O. DeM 418 (reign of Ramesses V) is a letter to the carpenter Qenhirkhopshef the Younger (his brother):

> The carpenter Maaninakhtef greets the carpenter Qenhirkhopshef. In life, prosperity, health. In the praise of Amunrasonter. To wit: I have arrived in Hu. Amunmose and Pahemnetjer have made all (kinds of) splendid provisions for me in bread, beer, oil, and clothing. When this letter reaches you, you (must) let one door be brought to me and also a (wooden) cubit measure. May Amun give that your health is good.

So Maaninakhtef had sailed downstream to Hu (present-day Hiw) on some business. One can easily see that taking a door to Hu would not be the first thing a person would think of when traveling north, so this makes Maaninakhtef's message all the more mysterious. Did they not have carpenters and doors in Hu (or cubit measures, for that matter)? And who are Amunmose and Pahemnetjer? It is obvious that Qenhirkhopshef knew these people too, although the letter suggests that they were the reception committee in Hu itself. There is one papyrus kept in Geneva and Turin that is believed to have once been part of the scribe Qenhirkhopshef's library that ultimately ended up with Maaninakhtef: P. Geneva MAH

15274 + P. Turin CGT 54063 (reign of Ramesses III or IV). On the verso of this text—firmly embedded in a Deir al-Medina context—we meet a policeman Amunmose and a scribe Pahemnetjer (if we had just this one text he could also very well be a carpenter, by the way). This is probably too much of a coincidence, so it seems safe to assume that it may actually have been these two men who had traveled from Thebes to Hu ahead of Maaninakhtef to welcome him there when he got off the ship.

There is, however, one other Amunmose in the Maaninakhtef dossier. And he may actually have lived in Hu, at least some of the time, because in year 4 of Ramesses IV we see a scribe Amunmose, Maaninakhtef, and a man called Nakhtamun sitting in "a court to know what they (the declaring parties) say" (O. DeM 10084). This was a private case between the water carriers Paân and Iuferikh ('What use is he?', which is not your average name, although I knew a Parisienne once who had a terrier called 'Pourquoi,' which conveys more or less the same idea), who wanted some official setting to make a statement about a debt. This would be the sort of thing Maaninakhtef would have talked about at his parental home, assuming that he visited his mother every now and then. So would be the visit of the king himself. O. DeM 956 informs us that Ramesses IV or V had arrived in Thebes, and perhaps he did cross the Nile to pour water for his forefathers, as the vizier did on more than one occasion. Maaninakhtef is seen taking five loaves from the (official) granary to celebrate this event.

The Naunakhte papers also include a number of personal letters, possibly dating to the reign of Ramesses IX. They show that there was a firm connection between Maaninakhtef and the city of Hu. There is a letter (P. DeM 18) that is addressed to a woman whose name is lost, but was apparently to be sent on to the now chief carpenter of the Lord of the Two Lands Maaninakhtef by the scribe of the temple of Hathor of Hu, Amunmose. It would of course happen more often that a letter would be addressed to person A, but was intended to be read aloud to person B. In the letter Amunmose tells her that he is impatiently waiting for some furniture, so it seems the woman addressed in the letter was asked to go over to Maaninakhtef's workshop and demand that he finish this order right away. But if the presumably sealed letter was indeed sent to Maaninakhtef as the address would suggest, surely he would have been the first to read it. The problem would solve itself if the woman was

Maaninakhtef's wife, and she was also on intimate terms with Amunmose, suggesting that he may have been a relative.

> What is this, your not writing to me about your health? What have I done to you? As soon as my letter [arrives at the place] where you are, you (must) let this (wooden) *maset* and this small bed be finished. When Nakhtmin comes, you (must) let them bring <them to me>.

From the looks of it, this same order from the scribe Amunmose is also referred to in P. DeM 8 recto, so someone was desperately waiting for Maaninakhtef to finish his work and send it to Hu (presumably). Since the verso of the papyrus contains a letter from Amunmose to Maaninakhtef himself, who is called "brother," but which was apparently left unfinished, and the "you" on the recto is referred to using the masculine pronoun (and no introduction at all), it seems only close examination of the handwritings in these papyri will tell us who wrote what to whom, or copied these letters. If P. DeM 8 is not damaged at the top, we once again have a letter on our hands without the obligatory flowery introduction. This is the recto, which is in a decidedly sloppier hand than the text on the verso:

> And as to the writing that you did about the (wooden) *maset*, [I] will not tell you [. . .] equip your house with carpentry products. As to the [thing I wrot]e about, it is not finished and your companions are not here at all . . . and you (must) let someone bring it so that I know that you are without, like [the] little [bed] of which I already told you to busy yourself with. When my letter [arrives at the place] you are, you are to finish the little bed and the (wooden) *maset* and [have] Nakhtmin (?) [come] as quickly as possible and bring them, the two (pieces). Do not go [. . .] the (wooden) *maset* or lag with the bed, so that he may bring you what is in store (?) for you. [. . .] I have written to you already twenty days ago, and you will write [. . .].

The longer one stares at this letter, the more difficult it becomes to understand who wrote this and who was supposed to read it. Was it really Amunmose writing to Maaninakhtef? But his letter to Maaninakhtef is on the verso of the papyrus. It looks unfinished:

The scribe Amunmose of the temple of Hathor, Mistress of Hu, greets his brother, the [chief] carpenter of the Lord of the Two Lands Maaninakhtef. In life, prosperity, health. In the praise of your august god Amunra[sonter. May he give you life, prosperity, health, a long life and a good old age], health, life, and sweetness in your heart. May [I see] that you are young and thriving in happiness unto eternity, every day. To wit: the [policeman] Basa arrived here with me and found me. We then went . . .

This letter on the verso was apparently unfinished, but both sides of the papyrus were clearly meant for Maaninakhtef to read. The verso actually contains the expected beginning of a letter, whereas the recto, which has always been treated as a separate letter, jumps straight into the message without further ado. So could it be that the text on the verso of the papyrus—which was always less smooth than the other side, so that scribes usually started on the recto, where the fibers run parallel to the writing—was actually the beginning of the letter and the text on the recto its continuation? But then why was the verso left unfinished (this happens more often in the dossier, in P. DeM 9)?

From P. Harris I ("The Great Harris Papyrus" or P. BM EA 9999), which is a gigantic list of donations made by Ramesses III compiled in the reign of his successor, we know that the king allotted twelve people to the temple of Hathor, Mistress of Hutsekhem (Hu), the same temple that employed Amunmose. Not exactly the biggest royal donation ever, and it would have been wonderful if we could somehow have connected Maaninakhtef's exploits in Hu with this historical (?) fact, were it not that the correspondence between him and the scribe Amunmose is much later in date.

It is a shame that letters never seem to contain a date, so they are sometimes arbitrarily assigned to a specific reign. O. Ashmolean Museum 273 is also said to come from the reign of Ramesses V. It is a letter by Maaninakhtef to a Mr. Paneferemdjedu, who is mentioned as a scribe of The Tomb in P. Geneva MAH 15274 + P. Turin CGT 54063. After the flowery introduction Maaninakhtef cuts to the chase right away:

Do not let your hand off the commission that I told you (to do). I am not at all without a heart. I will make for you a (wooden) *sheqer* at your cost (?) and I will supply you with the writing that I told (you) about as well. May your health be good before Amun.

This is not just a workman speaking. Maaninakhtef's tone toward the scribe of the village is frank, to say the least, even if Paneferemdjedu was the son of the scribe Amunnakhte son of Ipuy. But why on earth would he have to do some writing *(sesh)* for a scribe *(sesh)*? Probably because Maaninakhtef was referring to a paint job *(sesh)*, but we do not know whether he would have done this himself or commissioned someone to do it for him. As we saw above, O. Černý 20 seems to suggest he did employ draftsmen to do work for him.

The short letter O. Michaelides 79 may corroborate this. It has been dated to Dynasty 19 by some, in which case this would not be 'our' Maaninakhtef, but alternatively to the reign of Ramesses V. The latter date would fit perfectly, and since Maaninakhtef is here referred to as a scribe, we may be fairly sure that this is our man, but only fairly, because Andreas Dorn believes that this Maaninakhtef is actually no. (iv), not the no. (iii) that we are interested in. But if he is, this letter tells us something new. He was apparently also an expert sandalmaker, and was requested by a draftsman to send him some leather items. It is still a mystery why people in the village sent each other letters to get things done, when it would have been so easy to send a boy or girl to relay a message by mouth. Or were the sender or recipient always somewhere else? Then again, people receiving and reading letters were probably looked up to by the illiterate villagers (of which there were no doubt many), so a public display of the ability to read and write, by a member of the work crew like Maaninakhtef, would be a big thing.

We can only wonder what lay behind the very short note by the scribe of The Tomb Hori to Maaninakhtef (O. Vienna H. 3):

The scribe Hori to the scribe Maaninakhtef. Look. The gum that is here. You have not said anything (about it). Look. [. . .] bring [. . .] you . . .

Yes, ostraca can be very boring little pieces, but they are also a gold mine. If the assumption that the workman Maaninakhtef was actually also the carpenter Maaninakhtef, who liked to refer to himself as the scribe Maaninakhtef, is correct (and it probably is), one of the senior scribes at the time—Hori, who may have written O. DeM 32–47 and many more texts (66 have been identified so far by Goecke-Bauer)—in this letter did acknowledge Maaninakhtef's status in the village by addressing him as a fellow scribe. Although this is not a real letter, but a memo that might be construed as an order by a superior to a subordinate, we could also view it as an exchange of views between two equals. Hori addresses Maaninakhtef as the scribe Maaninakhtef. And it does not stop there.

There is even what seems to be a model letter (O. BM EA 50723) that Maaninakhtef wrote to the vizier, and this perhaps should really make us wonder whether it is possible that the workman, the carpenter, and the scribe were indeed one and the same person. This ostracon did in fact make the editor, Rob Demarée, wonder whether there were two contemporary Maaninakhtefs (as did Dorn), although Demarée's suggestion is couched in a most cautious note.

Are the workman, the carpenter, and the scribe all one and the same person? Are there actually two workmen called Maaninakhtef? The workman and the carpenter yes, and the carpenter did write (and often about carpentry) and own a library. Did he call himself a scribe because he could write just a little? No way.

This is a model letter that was never sent. The angled brackets indicate that Maaninakhtef forgot to write something. The suggestion that the scribe Qenhirkhopshef taught Naunakhte to read and write, and that she taught some of her children (or had someone else do this for her), becomes more appealing by the minute. This would also do much to explain the strange preponderance of the male members of the Naunakhte family to add their names to the graffiti left by Qenhirkhopshef in the Theban hills. Was it he who had elevated this family from mere workmen to the upper middle class? Still, Maaninakhtef did not get it quite right this time.

[To the royal fa]n [bearer] on the right side (of the King), overseer of Thebes and vizier Neferrenpet. The scribe Maaninakhtef inform<s His Lord (*oops, mistake*)>. This is a letter so that My Lord knows. Another m<essage (*oops, another mistake*)> to My Lord. To wit: I say to Amunrasonter [. . .], Mut, Khonsu, and all the gods and goddesses of Thebes (and) to Parahor[akhty] . . . healthy [. . .]. Let him be in the [favor] of Pharaoh, life, prosperity, health, His Lord. [. . .] of Pharaoh . . .

This little text tells us that Maaninakhtef was *au courant* with the way official letters were written, so he either had a model letter before him from Qenhirkhopshef's archive or from his own correspondence, or he knew it by heart.

But the story gets better still. The recent excavations in the workmen's settlement in the Valley of the Kings by the Swiss team led by Andreas Dorn have yielded multiple new practice letters on ostraca that Maaninakhtef wrote to the vizier Neferrenpet but never actually sent. According to Dorn's record he found six or seven of these, of which four can be attributed to our Maaninakhtef with absolute certainty, namely O. KV 18/2.415, 18/3.576 verso (Raum 43), 18/5.757, and 18/6.951. They were all excavated in the settlement of the workmen east of the tomb of Ramesses X (KV 18; 1107/1103–1103/1099 BCE) or in the rubbish heaps left by earlier excavators. They can be dated to the reign of Ramesses IV without doubt, due to the stratification of some of the finds. Dorn did not stop there. He checked the record and found some other pieces that may belong to the same corpus. O. Cairo CG 25747 is another practice letter by Maaninakhtef to the vizier Neferrenpet. It was found in the 1907–1908 excavations between KV 17 (Sethy I) and KV 21 (perhaps an Amarna princess) by Edward Ayrton and Theodore Davis in House *omega*. The text has been dated to the reign of either Ramesses II or Ramesses IV, but the mention of the vizier Neferrenpet makes the latter dating very appealing. O. Cairo CG 25750 is a similar text written by our Maaninakhtef to a scribe Nebnefer. The dating to Dynasty 19 by Černý is surely incorrect. So more unknown texts written by Maaninakhtef surface every day, and in the end only handwriting identification will allow us to draw reliable conclusions.

Why the library of the scribe Qenhirkhopshef was passed on to Maaninakhtef when his brother Amunnakhte died is unknown. One would have expected it to go to, for instance, Amunnakhte's son Khaemnun (iii). But it did go to Maaninakhtef, with devastating consequences. As we saw above, Maaninakhtef loved to write letters, and some of these were found with his archive (e.g., P. DeM 12–13). If Pestman's theory about the subsequent owners of the library is correct, it was actually Maaninakhtef who sometimes cannibalized the literary papyri if he needed a piece of papyrus to write on.

P. DeM 10 is another of his business letters to the scribe Amunmose from the temple of Hathor in Hu, but it still shows traces of a literary text that was erased, probably by none other than Maaninakhtef himself.

The letter (c. 21.5 × 14.5 cm) is damaged and the content not exactly clear, apart from the mention of a delivery of some sort, the castration of Amunmose's calf, and the request by a (female) singer of Amunrasonter for a calf (another?). Also, Amunmose is being asked to have grapes sent, and this seems rather awkward if they were to travel all the way from Hu to Deir al-Medina.

Some strips in the middle and at the end of P. Chester Beatty VIII were simply cut out of the papyrus for reuse, probably also to write letters. In summary, we can say that several important literary works from ancient Egypt may have been lost forever because a carpenter from Deir al-Medina—and one of Naunakhte's sons, at that—wanted to write a letter.

9

So Who
Gets the Kids?

We know that Naunakhte's daughter Menatnakhte was married to—or officially cohabited with—the workman Qenna, but in the otherwise very turbulent year 29 of Ramesses III she had apparently also found time to have sex with the workman Weserhat. The verso of the Turin Strike Papyrus (P. Turin Cat. 1880) contains a number of memos mentioning this man.

The first (verso col. V *ll. 2ff.*) is an account listing what Weserhat paid to a doctor, and then from col. V *l.* 13 onward there is another entry about what appears to be a property division between Weserhat and our Menatnakhte, although some authors have chosen to interpret her name—written as the abbreviated 'Menat'—as the word for 'wet nurse.' In so doing, they read the element that Ramesside scribes commonly used to write *nakhte* ('(is) strong') in personal names as the determinative of the striking man, without any phonetic value, which would be a very disconcerting determinative for a wet nurse. The date mentioned in col. V is year 29 of Ramesses III, fourth month of the *akhet* season, last day, and this date probably refers to all three entries dealing with Weserhat. The second entry runs as follows:

What is for Menatnakhte and is with Weserhat, which one will divide:
Necklace of red jasper 3, makes 15 deben.
Log of wood 1, makes 10 deben.
Chest (?) 1, makes 2 deben.
Ivory comb 1, makes 2 deben.
Sandal strap 1 (pair) and fat 1 hin, makes 1½ deben.
Total copper: 30½ deben.

What is for him: copper 20 deben. What is for her: copper [10] deben. Total: 30 deben.

Apparently these two entries are to be connected with a court case involving Weserhat (verso col. VI *ll. 2ff.*):

Said by Weserhat in front of the court of listening, (namely) the chief workman Kha, the scribe Amunnakhte, and the entire crew:

"As Amun endures, as the Ruler, life, prosperity, health, endures, one will not take away my three daughters from me, and one will not take me away from them."

The presence side by side of a doctor's bill, the allocation of ten deben to a woman—the name Menatnakhte being read by some as 'wet nurse'—and the mention of three daughters whom Weserhat apparently refuses to give up have led some authors to believe that Weserhat's wife had died and that he now needed a wet nurse to bring up his children, although there may be something wrong with the translation. This raises an interesting (and very easy to answer) question: If this entry is really a payment to a wet nurse, why would the scribe mention the amount that would go to Weserhat himself, namely twenty deben? All the scribe would have to do is list the items that were paid to the wet nurse. This is what the scribes normally did: they just listed the payment made.

The problem solves itself immediately if we choose to read 'Menatnakhte' (her name is clearly there on the papyrus), of whom we know she had a sexual relationship with Weserhat. In that case the 20 + 10 = 30 deben correspond exactly with the division of the conjugal property of a married couple. When Naunakhte divided her inheritance, she could only give away her own property and one-third of the property that she had acquired together with her second husband, Khaemnun.

This passage in the Turin Strike Papyrus has also been interpreted as a property division between a husband and his wife as the result of a divorce. In that case the oath taken by Weserhat that he refuses to be separated from his three daughters would make perfect sense, since a divorce generally includes a bitter fight over the children. In Weserhat's case these were three girls, but it is somehow very difficult to believe that these girls could have stated their own preferences as to where they wanted to live after the separation. Still, in the present state of our knowledge we must assume that they did and that in that case Menatnakhte went to live somewhere else, perhaps even with her mother Naunakhte.

As we will see below, however, there may be something wrong with this interpretation. The literal translation of the crucial statement made by Weserhat in this oath is "One will not bring my three daughters on me," and this sounds like a strange way to describe his refusal to let his three daughters go. It actually suggests the exact opposite, namely that he wants them off his back. Ancient Egyptian legal language contains many references to physical acts, such as 'stand in front of someone' (to claim something), 'be far from someone' (having no more claim on that person) or 'be far from something' (having relinquished the property right), and 'be at the back of someone' (having a claim on this person). As we will see below, the property division between Weserhat and Menatnakhte could actually also be interpreted as a financial agreement on account of their marriage. (In fact, this possibility has already been proposed by B.G. Davies, *Who's Who* (1999), p. 255.)

But there is more, because col. IV *ll. 1ff.* on the recto of the Turin Strike Papyrus decribes some serious charges against the same Weserhat. These were brought forward in year 29 of Ramesses III, first month of the *shemu* season, day 16, by the workman Penanuqet. He made them before the scribe Amunnakhte son of Ipuy and the chief workman Khonsu. After stating that the official oath he has taken—which made him an employee of the state—obliges him to report any illicit activity taking place in the necropolis, Penanuqet accuses the workmen Weserhat and Pentaweret of stripping a royal tomb. Also, one of these men—referred to only as "he"—had stolen an ox with the brand of one of the nearby royal mortuary temples and had apparently been stupid enough to park it in his own stable. To top it all off, this anonymous man—none other than our Weserhat, as becomes clear from other sources—"had sex with three wives with a husband, (including) the female citizen Menat (short for Menatnakhte, no doubt) who was with Qenna (. . .)."

Of course we only have the date on which these accusations were made, meaning that the offenses mentioned in Penanuqet's accusation were obviously committed by Weserhat earlier. So how, then, do these data connect?

The property division between Weserhat and Menatnakhte took place in year 29 of Ramesses III, fourth month of the *akhet* season, last day, and if this was done as the result of a divorce, the accusation by Penanuqet in the first month of the *shemu* season (only four and a half months later) that Weserhat had had illicit sex with the same Menat(nakhte)—the vulgar expression used is *nek* 'to have sex (implying a four-letter word)'—would make little sense, unless this illicit sex had been between Weserhat and his then ex-wife, who was now with Qenna.

That is, if this property division was really about a divorce. What if, for instance, Weserhat had had sex with Qenna's wife Menatnakhte some time before the property division, and that this sex—and the ensuing love, or vice versa—had led to the decision to live together? In that case the property division should perhaps be connected with their marriage, clearly defining the one-third that would from now on be Menatnakhte's share of the conjugal property. From later abnormal hieratic sources we know that, if a woman committed adultery, she would receive nothing of the conjugal property—abnormal hieratic contracts being the direct descendants of the legal contracts made in southern Egypt in the New Kingdom—so maybe Menatnakhte had been kicked out of the house by Qenna, and now needed compensation for the one-third of the conjugal property she had left behind with her former husband. Far-fetched this may be, but there is much we do not know about customary law in connection with marriage in Deir al-Medina.

This still leaves us with the statement that Weserhat made about his three daughters. As far as our knowledge goes, nowhere does it say that these were the daughters of Weserhat and Menatnakhte and, as we saw above, the interpretation of Weserhat's oath allegedly refusing to be separated from them is based on the ambiguous expression "One will not bring my three daughters on me."

And there is more, namely the still unpublished P. Turin Cat. 1966, which is generally assigned to year 6 of Ramesses IV. In col. III *ll.* 1–4 on the verso of this papyrus there is another oath by Weserhat about Menatnakhte (the transcription of which Rob Demarée kindly made available to me):

Year 6, second (?) month of the [. . .] season, day 12. On this day [the workman (?)] Weserhat son of Aânakhte took an Oath of the Lord, life, prosperity, health, saying: "As Amun endures, as the Ruler, life, prosperity, health, endures, whose might is greater than death. One will not bring the female citizen Menatnakhte daughter of Naunakhte on me. One will not bring [. . .] to (?) her, (or) he will be under blows of the stick. I have been justified as to the thing that one has given her . . . [. . .]. ."

This phrasing is exactly as in the oath he took years earlier about his three daughters, which has always been understood in the sense that he refused to let them be taken away from him. As a result, we have to assume that the statement "One will not bring my three daughters on me" from his oath on the verso of P. Turin Cat. 1880 has exactly the same (legal) meaning as his statement here in P. Turin Cat. 1966: "One will not bring the citizen Menatnakhte daughter of Naunakhte on me." Now this is very strange. In the standard reference work by J. Toivari-Viitala, *Women at Deir el-Medina* (2001), p. 238, both P. Turin Cat. 1880 and 1966 are said to be connected with the divorce of Weserhat and Menatnakhte, the second (from year 6 of Ramesses IV) being a statement made during a court case, when the couple had still not settled their grievances after the property division in P. Turin Cat. 1880, which occurred in year 29 of Ramesses III. In her view the couple's daughters also stayed with Weserhat.

But if we accept the translation "One will not take away my three daughters from me" for the literal "One will not bring my three daughters on me," it follows that the statement by Weserhat in P. Turin Cat. 1966, "One will not bring the citizen Menatnakhte daughter of Naunakhte on me," should mean "One will not take away the citizen Menatnakhte daughter of Naunakhte from me." And this would then be a statement made at a time when—if we accept the property division from P. Turin Cat. 1880 to be the result of a divorce—the couple had already been living apart for years? This really makes very little sense.

So perhaps it is time to rethink. Perhaps the intentional use of 'one' as the acting party in both oaths taken by Weserhat may have some significance, indicating a third party besides him and his daughters, and him and Menatnakhte, respectively. Who else could this be but the authorities? In the oath from P. Turin Cat. 1966 Weserhat states that he has been justified concerning the things—the phrasing is again frustratingly imprecise—that have been handed over to Menatnakhte. And exactly for this reason this anonymous 'one'—namely the authorities—should not bring Menatnakhte on him. This sounds more like a request to the court to declare any of Menatnakhte's future claims unfounded, which suggests that there may have been a divorce after all.

If that is correct, the oath he took in P. Turin Cat. 1880 would refer to a similar request to the court to ignore any claim by his daughters (or by him), and this can only have happened if these daughters were not his and Menatnakhte's, but his daughters by another (previous) wife at the time he decided to leave her and go to live with Menatnakhte. It would fit very well in the hypothesis that the property division in P. Turin Cat. 1880 was not the result of a divorce, but in fact the exact opposite, namely an agreement about the division of the conjugal property prior to his marriage to Menatnakhte. This all sounds extremely complicated, but as far as we can see it still seems more plausible than the existing theory. In short, it is a mess.

In any case, when Menatnakhte came to listen to her mother Naunakhte's statement about the division of her inheritance, she was not a mere name, as is suggested by P. Ashmolean Museum 1945.97, P. DeM 23, and P. DeM 25, but a woman hardened by life.

Menatnakhte is one of the few daughters of Naunakhte who does sometimes, although only rarely, pop up in the official records. In the so-called Stato Civile, which is an official record of the households in the village, listing the occupants for each house (the large and small fragments that are left can be dated between the reigns of Ramesses IV and IX), she is mentioned as the wife of the workman Weserhat and the mother of a daughter called Tanitpaipu (who is also mentioned in another fragment), which does not mean she had only one daughter, but rather that this daughter was still living in her household. So they did get married after all. The fact that this girl is not mentioned in Davies, *Who's Who* (as are many other people) is the best reason to start thinking about putting all the known inhabitants of Deir al-Medina in an online database.

O. Louvre N 696 verso (years 23 and 25 of Ramesses III) is another mystery in this respect, because it may actually mention three of Naunakhte's daughters in *ll.* 5–7 of what the editor of this text dubbed Document A, and the mystery is of course why they are in this text in the first place. Did they receive some extra rations because their husbands had done some extra work? This is the text (the names of the women are in italics):

Amount of the fresh vegetables that will be [received] from the doorkeeper Ankhjerter:

[*N.N.*]: 10. Entered.

Henutkha: 5 (and something). Entered.

Weser: 10. Entered: 8 [. . .] 2.

Menat[. . .]: 5. Entered.

Henut[. . .]: 5.

Huynefer: 5.

Hay son of Huy.

Entered: 28. Remainder: 22 [. . .].

To try and understand the signficance of the consecutive mention of the people called Weser, Menat[. . .], and Henut[. . .], we will have to go back to P. DeM 23 and 25. There the name of Naunakhte's daughter Wasetnakhte was actually written Wesernakhte, which was probably nothing more than the scribe mishearing the name. The 'r' at the end of many written words had disappeared in daily speech by this time, meaning that even if scribes wrote an 'r' at the end of a word (resorting to the spelling they had learned), as in classic Middle Egyptian *sewer* 'drink,' this had become *sewe* or something similar in speech. So *weser* '(be) strong' and *waset* ('Thebes') would have sounded more or less the same, namely *wese*. We can picture the scribes of P. DeM 23 and 25 (presumably relatives) entering the house of Naunakhte with her children to clear it out, and each time asking the siblings who were about to choose: "Right, who's next?" and people would say their name. In the case of Wasetnakhte her name would be written down the wrong way. This assumes that one papyrus was a copy of the other, or both were a copy of an original. Otherwise one would have to assume that P. DeM 23 and 25 were written simultaneously by two scribes who made the same mistake, whereas one would prefer to think that this division of Naunakhte's household goods was recorded by someone who knew her children. This is strange, by the way, because both *weser* and *nakhte* are words denoting strength, so someone was not paying attention.

We saw above that the name Menatnakhte was probably abbreviated to Menat in the official record and then most probably also at home. So why not assume we can also abbreviate Wasetnakhte (or Wesernakhte) to Waset (Weser)? Seeing that Amunhotep could become Huy, and Amunemipet could be shortened to Ipy, this is not that far-fetched after all, although it does lean heavily on the reconstruction of the next two lines as 'Menatnakhte' and 'Henutshenu,' two other known daughters of Naunakhte. It all seems to fit the outline but, even if it is correct, we will never know why this ostracon was written.

10

Was Neferhotep
a Wimp?

B ernard Bruyère found two fragments of a limestone seat in the
village containing the names of both Neferhotep and his brother
Maaninakhtef. Does this mean they shared a house, or could this
actually be their carpenter's shop? The latter seems unlikely. It is difficult
to see how the cramped environment of the walled enclosure could have
accommodated a carpenter's workshop, with all the bustle that would
ensue. Apart from being a workman, a colophon made by Neferhotep's
brother Amunnakhte in one of the Chester Beatty papyri also refers to
him as a carpenter, so that O. Turin N. 57040 from year 22 of Ramesses III
probably refers to our man. In this text the policeman Paiuemiteru ("The
island in the river") brings two pieces of wood to Neferhotep in return
for a coffin. The verso of the text mentions a carpenter and a "year 28."

When his mother Naunakhte made her statement in court she was
very clear about Neferhotep's share, but strangely enough the official
record does not include his name, so that it is only the later statement by
his father Khaemnun (see below) that suggests it was really Neferhotep
who was excluded from the main part of the inheritance. He had knocked
on Naunakhte's door for support (and received it) so often that he was not
going to share in the division of the copper objects from her inheritance.
One wonders whether the word 'copper' used by Naunakhte actually
referred to anything of value, including Naunakhte's real estate, but the
record is unclear. Her statement was humiliating to Neferhotep, especially
if we imagine the entire village population standing around to watch the
show, and one almost has the impression that the official scribe deliberately
chose to keep his name out of the record, because everybody in the village

knew who would be meant anyway. It is either that, or a mistake, or Naunakhte did not mention him by name this time, only earlier in her statement about the children who would not inherit from her.

> As for the kettle that I gave him to buy bread for himself, and likewise the chisel of seven deben and likewise the *irer* vase of seven deben, and likewise the adze of six deben, which makes forty deben, they will form his share. He will not enter into the division of any copper. It will be for his brothers and sisters.

Forty deben of copper to buy food? What his mother did here was actually tell the villagers what everybody knew already. Neferhotep was a wimp who was unable to make ends meet, and instead of supporting his mother in her old age she had to support him.

Neferhotep contested her will after she died. The Naunakhte papers contain a short note stating that he will no longer be able to contest the division or risk punishment, meaning that the court found nothing wrong with Naunakhte's statement. In the year after that, Khaemnun, who was responsible for dividing her inheritance, appeared in court again to make a statement that Neferhotep no longer had a claim, suggesting some heated discussions had taken place in the family.

> As far as the writings are concerned which the female citizen Naunakhte has made about her things, they are thus exactly, exactly. The workman Neferhotep will not share in them. He will take an Oath of the Lord, life, prosperity, health, saying: "If I turn back on my word again, he (I) shall receive a hundred blows and be deprived of his (my) things."

One gets the impression that Neferhotep may have been the slow one in the family. This would not be entirely unexpected (the family does show evidence for cousin marriages, which was one way to keep the family estate intact), but on the other hand, he was competent enough to be part of the regular workforce (e.g., O. Ashmolean Museum 14).

In O. BM EA 65938 (O. Nash 5) we see Neferhotep on the receiving end. He is mentioned in connection with the delivery of a bed, so we may be fairly sure that this is our man. The ostracon lists two cases of assault: the first involves a woman who was beaten by her husband, and the second case concerns our man.

[Regnal year 20, third] month of the *shemu* season, day 13. Day of complaining which the [work]man Neferhotep son of Khaemnun did before [the court. The chief] workman Khonsu, the scribe Wennefer, the scribe Amunnakhte, [the deputy Amun]kha, the deputy Inherkha, the [work]man [. . .], the work[man] Parahotep, and the officer Kha, saying: "[As for] me, I was sitting in the house of Amunhotep, life, prosperity, health, [. . . t]he bed to the riverbank, after [. . .] the tent. You said to me [. . .]: 'I will beat (you?) up in front of [. . .] the magistrates (. . .).'"

This rather confused statement would be in line with the assumption that Neferhotep may have been a bit of a wimp in real life. But he could read and write and did marry a Mrs. Hathor. He fathered a daughter called Naunakhte, as we can see from the Stato Civile 7, I *ll.* 8 and 10. But the Stato Civile actually tells us more, specifically that he also named one of his sons after his father:

The house of Neferhotep son of Khaemnun, his mother being [Nau]-nakhte:
    His wife Hathor daughter of Telmontu, her mother being [Raya];
    Her daughter Naunakhte daughter of Neferhotep, her mother being Hathor;
    His son Khaemnun son of Neferhotep, his mother being Taweretsankh;
    (in red ink) His daughter Naunakhte, idem, idem, Hathor.

So he was married twice. The name Taweretsankh is very rare in Deir al-Medina. It is only known from one list of names (O. DeM 10004). Lists such as these occur more often (e.g., O. DeM 110 and O. VM 3000) but, if they contain only names, it is unclear why they were written. O. DeM 10004 is just a list of women, where she is called Tawerethersankh.

Whether Neferhotep named his daughter after his mother because it was the thing to do or out of recognition for her financial support—as was not very subtly stated by Naunakhte when she divided her inheritance in court—the story does not say. O. DeM 121 is a letter to his wife:

The scribe Neferhotep to the singer of Amun Hathor. When my letter reaches you, you must have some beans brought to me. You know that I am on watch duty (?), but I do not like my bread at all the way it is, even if there was a basketful. Look, I am already counting (?) beans.

This is not the most romantic note ever, although it does show that the sender and receiver knew each other intimately. Perhaps Neferhotep was even trying to make a joke here. If he did, it is not the best joke ever. People wrote little notes about beans fairly often, such as the person who wrote O. DeM 10253, but in that case it was to check on a delivery that never arrived. Note that this message is not addressed to the woman, but to a man called Paherypedjet (perhaps he had to read it to her?):

> To Paherypedjet. To wit: please ask Iy, the mother of Tjaunedjem: what did you give Tjaunedjem?

The verso of this ostracon seems to hold the answer:

> Well, I gave him neither beans nor salt.

Even these few lines contain problems that appear unsolvable. The editor thought that Tjaunedjem ('Sweet breath') was a girl, and that the text on the verso still belonged to the text on the recto, in which case the sender apparently wants to inform her mother that he gave her (the scribe used the masculine pronoun here) nothing. But then why ask the mother if she had given something? The use of the masculine pronoun only makes sense if Tjaunedjem was a boy and the text on the verso was the answer by the mother. The writing on the verso looks slightly sloppier than the writing on the recto.

In the other example we have of this name (P. Milan E 0.9.40127 + P. Turin Cat. 2074), it is used for a man. The text is included here because it touches on the subject of female literacy. We do have letters from women to women, and there are also various graffiti ascribed to women, but somehow we seem unable to prove that these were actually *written* by these women. In O. DeM 10253, as so often, the memo is to a man who can read and then transmit the message to the intended addressee, a woman.

Speaking of jokes, the French Egyptologist Pierre Grandet once published a charming article about the names that some of the villagers gave to their donkeys, showing how they looked at these animals. Of course the fact that they named their donkeys does tell us that they recognized their personalities, something that we can still understand today. These are the names that a Mr. Sennefer from the village gave to his pet animals: Excellent Cat (perfectly able to ignore the boss), Another Companion (somehow I miss my old donkey), Wolf (probably best not to lease this one out to everyone), Pig (my God, the way you gobble your fodder), Jackal (not my best purchase after all), Goat (get off the shed now!), Rower (a little less movement might be nice, thank you), one illegible name, and Dog (will you stop barking at everyone?). Apparently he also had a donkey that in some way reminded him of someone he knew, so this one was called Ramesses. After more than 3,000 years we can still sense that Mr. Sennefer had a great sense of humor, and we can be sure that parents in the village would have warned their kids not to go near the donkey called Jackal, or pay the price. We do not know where the villagers—including Khaemnun and his son Neferhotep—kept their donkeys, but it would have been within walking distance, because these animals required daily care.

So who was this Sennefer? That is something of a riddle, but Grandet proposed that he was probably the owner of TT 1159 A to the west of the village, which is actually a double tomb, in which between 1905 and 1909 the Italian excavators led by Ernesto Schiaparelli found several remains of the burial of a Mr. Hormes, the chief workman of the left side of the crew from year 8 of Ramesses VII to year 17 of Ramesses IX. But in 1928 Bernard Bruyère looked a bit closer, and on 7 February opened another (undisturbed but also undecorated) level containing the burial of 'our' Sennefer, who lived in Dynasty 18. So Sennefer did not name his donkey after the (reigning) king, as some readers may have hoped, because the Ramesside kings were still a thing to come when he was alive. The tomb contained two adult burials and one child's coffin. After almost ninety years one can still marvel at Bruyère's detailed excavation diaries. Egyptologists working on Deir al-Medina really do owe him.

There were other jokers besides Sennefer. One such was a man (or a woman) who wrote these words on a piece of silex no bigger than 4.5 × 2 cm:

Another small stone.

Remarks such as these suggest that the parties these people had (see chapter 11, "Women Can Party Too") were probably just as much fun as they are today. O. Cairo CG 25234 from year 7 of Ramesses IV tells us that parties could be very large indeed. One may well wonder whether in this case it is significant that the children are mentioned first, so one feels almost forced to translate 'even' instead of 'also.'

> Year 7, third month of the *peret* season, day 29. One was at the Great Festival of Ki[ng] Amunhotep, life, prosperity, health, the Lord of the Village. The crew was rejoicing before him for four entire days, drinking with their children and also their wives, sixty from the inside and sixty from the outside.

But we have to get back to Neferhotep, because even if his wife had a job, O. Glasgow D.1925.78 (O. Colin Campbell 13) seems to corroborate the suggestion that he somehow needed more support than others.

> [. . . Neferhote]p son of Khaemnun. [. . .] sandals 1 (pair), staff of *awenet* wood, [. . .] torn loincloth, *heqeq* fruit 1 basket, [. . .] large [*she*]*qer*. Given to him through the retainer [. . .] desert Pa[. . .]. Given to him again through him: [. . .] jar of cut meat, [. . .] razor, [. . .] jar. Given to him [through the poli]ceman Amunkha [. . .]: jug of beer.

The text is battered but, if these were actual payments to Neferhotep for carpentry, one would have expected the value of each item to be listed, so one is left to assume that the items were given to Neferhotep. One can only wonder why. We do know that he did business with policemen fairly often (including Amunkha), as O. Turin N. 57151 (years 13 and 15 of Ramesses III) shows. Just like his father Khaemnun, Neferhotep may have leased out his donkey(s) for payment. This text is a little memo stating that in year 13 of Ramesses III the policeman Amunkha took his donkey, and two years later the water carrier Kel did the same. No payments are mentioned. Since people would not have given a donkey to someone else without any compensation, we must assume that they were leased.

Not all Neferhotep's encounters with the police appear to have been successful. O. DeM 10082 (O. Černý 1) from the reign of Ramesses III or IV is a memo (or a complaint) about items totaling forty-seven deben of copper that were given to the chief of police Montumose, although we do not know what really happened here. The text simply states that items were given, although one suspects that these were the installments of a payment. The reader is invited to try and figure out who the "I," "you," and "he" in this text really are, which is the perfect way to illustrate the problems we have with texts from Deir al-Medina. They are often imprecise.

> Memo/complaint about all the things of the workman Neferhotep. Given [to] the chief of police Montumose: [. . .] that you collected. I gave a folding chair with footrest. [. . . sea]l set in silver and [a wooden *sheq*]*er* (?) which makes 15 deben. [Given to him]: smooth piece of textile, which makes 10 deben. [Give]n to him: emmer 3 sacks and barley 1 sack 2 oipe, 1. One (other?) time: 2 oipe and 1 sack. [Give]n to him: fresh fat 5 hin, which makes 2½ deben. [Again] given to him: *neheh* oil 3 hin, which makes 3 deben. Given to him: smooth garment 1, which makes 5 deben. Again given to him: emmer 1 sack. [I] gave a mirror, and you gave it to the soldier of the interior who was with (?) you [. . .] temple of Wesermâ'atra, life, prosperity, health [. . .]. Total: 47 deben of copper.

According to the editor of the text, Grandet, who is continuing the brilliant publication of the IFAO series of administrative ostraca from Deir al-Medina that was started by Černý, the temple mentioned here is actually the small temple in the Mut complex in Karnak, not Medinet Habu. The policemen were among the most mobile people of the lot, often doing business with the villagers, and not always with the best results. In one specific case, the chief of police Montumose managed to not repay a loan—or pay for a delivery—for eighteen years, despite repeated appeals in court by his creditor, the workman Menna (O. Oriental Institute Museum 12073).

> Year 15, first month of the *shemu* season under the Majesty of the King of Upper and Lower Egypt, Lord of the Two Lands Wesermâ'atra [. . .], life, prosperity, health, Son of Ra, Ramesses, Ruler of Iunu.
>
> On this day: giving the jug of fresh fat by the workman Menna to the chief of police Montumose, saying to him: "I will return it to you in barley as barley through this brother of mine on whom one has a claim to fulfill my obligation. May Ra cause you to be healthy." So he said to me.
>
> But I have spent three times accusing him in court before the scribe Amunnakhte of The Tomb. He has not given me a single thing to this day. Now look, I accused him (Montumose) before him (the scribe Amunnakhte) again in regnal year 3, second month of the *shemu* season, day 5 of the Majesty of the King of Upper and Lower Egypt, Lord of the Two Lands Heqamâ'atra Setepenamun, life, prosperity, health, Son of Ra,

Lord of Appearances Ramesses Mâ'aty Meryamun, life, prosperity, health, which amounts to eighteen years.

He (Montumose) took an Oath of the Lord, life, prosperity, health, saying: "If I fail to repay him for his jug by regnal year 3, third month of the *shemu* season, day 30, he (I) will be subject to a hundred strokes, it (the payment due) being against me being doubled." So he said before the three supervisors of the interior, the agents from outside, and the entire crew.

Regnal year 4, second month of the *peret* season, day 14. The chief of police brought Menna a fresh ox, amounting to 130 (?) deben. What had come to him from the property of Rety: a coffin of 35 deben. What was given to him by Menna: 40 hin of fat, which makes 30 deben. Total: 65 deben. His remainder: 65 deben to be given to the chief of police Montumose by the scribe Amunnakhte of The Tomb, the deputy Amunkha, the guardian Khay [. . .], Penpaiu, and the draftsman Horshery.

The chief of police Montumose took an Oath of the Lord, life, prosperity, health, saying: "These 65 deben of copper is what I will demand from Menna."

What is interesting about this text is that people could actually sue each other over twenty liters of fat that had not been paid for eighteen years. By this we mean not paid by the chief of police. It is easy to see why the scribe Amunnakhte was not very eager to sentence someone who was responsible for law and order in the village and its surroundings. Montumose was apparently keenly aware of this, and thus managed to prolong the case forever. When he finally did pay Menna, he did so later than promised in his oath taken in court, but there is no record of him receiving the dreaded hundred strokes of the stick.

Then there is something amiss with the amounts paid. Menna was to receive double the amount of the thirty-deben value of the fat (because Montumose had exceeded his term of payment). The editors of the text— Joe Manning, Gary Greig, and Sugihiku Ichida, at the University of Chicago at the time—transcribed the value of the ox as '130,' and indeed there is a small sign that with some imagination could well be read as '100.' If we choose not to read '100' we are left with an intrusive and inexplicable sign, which is equally unsatisfactory. Prices for a healthy ox could indeed rise to over a hundred deben, whereas people paid thirty deben for a calf. Apart from this, Menna also received a coffin worth thirty-five deben. But does it make sense to pay 165 deben if you only have to pay 2 × 30 = 60?

It becomes more complicated still, because Montumose now demanded half of this payment back. The record states that it is to be paid by the scribe Amunnakhte and others, but the meaning is probably that they would be responsible for the repayment by Menna. So it seems this conflict over a jug of fat boomeranged in the face of Menna, eighteen years later, and it could well be that Montumose's intention was in fact to pay more than required, so that he could sue Menna in turn.

We may have one court case involving Neferhotep at hand in O. UC 39622 (O. Petrie 21), which was published by Rob Demarée in one of the first books from Leiden that was entirely devoted to the village: *Gleanings from Deir el-Medina* (1982). Since the text is dated to year 27 of Ramesses III, the Neferhotep mentioned in it could well be one of Naunakhte's sons, although this is not an absolute certainty. The text is very difficult. It appears to be about two cases laid before the divine oracle, and here we see the supplicants simply asking the oracle aloud what they wanted to know. It is interesting to note that these cases were apparently not taken to court without any recourse to the oracle, unless of course the court had ordered them to consult the oracle because it felt unable to decide. Either this, or the supplicants did not feel confident that they could win their case in court. This raises the question of whether the oracle could be bribed (probably).

> Year 27, first month of the *shemu* season, day 19. On this day, the workman Khaemwaset complained to King Amunhotep, life, prosperity, health, s[aying: "Come] to me, My Lord. Judge between me and the workman Neferhotep. Will [one] seize the hut of my forefather Baky that is in the Valley of the Kings because of the (hereditary) share of (the woman) Sakhmetneferet, My Great Light?" The god moved backward decidedly. It was then said to him: "Should one give it to Khaemwaset?" And the god moved forward decidedly. Before the chief workman Khonsu, the chief workman [In]herkha, and all the bearers.
>
> He (the oracle) [said to I]yerniutef: "Do not go into the hut."
>
> Plea to Amunhotep, life, prosperity, health, to wit: "My [Great] Light [...] Hori [...] a stela. He set it up in the hut on [...] exactly." The god then said to him: "Do not enter [this hut and] remove your stela [from it]."

The presence of the two chief workmen is surprising. Did they form the local court of the day? Or were they the main or only witnesses to the verdict, apart from the bearers? That would be strange, because an oracle consultation would be most effective if there were as many witnesses as possible, preferably the entire crew, as happened more often. And one has little doubt that the villagers would not have missed any occasion to see some live action. Besides, this would not be the only case put before the oracle on this day.

The way the translation stands we seem to be dealing with two separate cases, which would be expected, because if the oracle was being carried around there would be more people wanting to present their case. However, as Demarée points out, one would rather have seen the oracle tell Neferhotep to vacate the hut and remove his stela (which probably indicated ownership). The presence of Hori is likewise a mystery, unless these are, after all, two separate cases.

Now there were other Neferhoteps at the time (including the husband of Neferhotep's own sister Khatanub), who could have been in dispute with Khaemwaset about this hut in the Valley of the Kings, but in the duty roster, the calendar listing the workman on duty at the gate of the main administrative building north of Deir al-Medina (the "turnus lists"), there is always a workman Neferhotep on duty two days prior to a Khaemwaset (e.g., O. Ashmolean Museum 113 and O. Berlin P 12631), and the accepted view appears to be that this Neferhotep was the son of Khaemnun and Naunakhte. So with whom else could Khaemwaset have picked this fight than with another workman active in the crew? The Neferhotep from O. UC 39622 could therefore be our man. A bit of a wimp after all?

11

Women Can
Party Too

I t often happens that an ostracon does not survive antiquity in one
piece, so that parts of it end up in various collections worldwide. Such
is the case with O. Cairo CG 25705 + O. IFAO 1322 + O. Varille 38 (or
O. Cairo CG 25705⁺ for short), which is dated to the reign of Ramesses III
or IV. It is made of pottery and consists of no fewer than thirteen separate
fragments that have been rejoined in modern times.

At first glance the text appears to deal with a women's drinking party
in honor of Hathor. These did occur in the village, as we see from O.
Ashmolean Museum 61, which combines a memo about the death of a wife
and the food and drink this involved, and the items brought for a festival of
Hathor, which in this case is without doubt the goddess Hathor. The text
also mentions Telmontu, who was related to Naunakhte through marriage:
her son Neferhotep was married to his daughter.

Now Hathor was not only the goddess of sexuality and dance, but also
the only divinity who knew the exact length of children's lives at the time
they were born, so she was pretty important in the village women's lives.
But these were only a few of her many aspects. As Sakhmet-Hathor she
had been responsible for the (mythical) destruction of mankind, until some
clever god—yes, it happens—finally came up with the solution of getting her
drunk. Fortunately, after she had sobered up she became her old gracious
self again. It may not be too far-fetched to connect O. Cairo CG 25705⁺ with
a similar, but much more private and modest ceremony in Deir al-Medina—
probably women only, although the text also mentions several men.

Since the name Hathor has the seated woman determinative instead
of the divine determinative, however, one has to assume that this was not

the goddess Hathor after all, but the birthday girl herself (or perhaps a girl who had just had her first menstruation or child). The personal name Hathor is actually not all that uncommon in Deir al-Medina. O. DeM 121 is a letter from Naunakhte's son Neferhotep to a singer of Amun by that name (his wife), which is dated to the reign of Ramesses III. As a personal name Hathor occurs twice in P. Milan E 0.9.40127 + P. Turin Cat. 2074 verso (Ramesses IX). The presence of some of the guests in O. Cairo CG 25705⁺ actually suggests that this party was thrown for Neferhotep's wife Hathor. Incidentally, she was the daughter of Telmontu.

In theory this drinking party could even refer to a memorial service for a deceased Hathor, a custom known from the demotic evidence, although the latter is much later in date. O. DeM 570 does, however, suggest that the tradition of last drinks with a departed loved one by the relatives was already established in New Kingdom Deir al-Medina (see chapter 2, "Where Was the Management Located?").

One of the women mentioned in O. Cairo CG 25705⁺ was a Mrs. Henutshenu, the mother of a Naunakhte. These names are too rare for this to be a coincidence, especially in such a small village, so she was definitely family. We can also assume that, like Henutshenu, all of Naunakhte's other daughters attended similar events. It is just that we lack the written evidence. Then again, parties such as the one described in O. Cairo CG 25705⁺ were probably by invitation only.

In Chart 25 of *Who's Who* (figure 1), Benedict Davies suggests that the Naunakhte mentioned in this ostracon was actually the *materfamilias* who made the famous will. This is not entirely impossible, because some women in the village lived to become very old (as Naunakhte did), but somehow still not plausible. By the time people reached the age of forty they would start to have physical problems. So once again, this supposition requires some calculation.

It is agreed that Naunakhte's first husband, Qenhirkhopshef, had become the senior scribe by year 40 of Ramesses II, which would be around 1240 BCE (O. BM EA 5634). Let us assume he was twenty at the time. He married Naunakhte when he was about fifty years of age, in about 1210 BCE. Naunakhte is believed to have been forty years younger, so she must have been born around 1220 BCE. She died shortly after she had made her will, which would have been in about 1140 BCE. The dating of O. Cairo CG 25705⁺ is not very specific, namely Ramesses III or IV, or Dynasty 20 if we include the dating given by Černý, but this dating is too imprecise to be of any help here.

If O. Cairo CG 25705⁺ was written in year 1 of Ramesses III, 'our' Naunakhte would have been thirty-seven, so the Henutshenu mentioned in the text could indeed have been her mother. Most texts we have from the reign of Ramesses III, however, date to the end of his reign. If we assume that the text was written in that period or—for the sake of argument—in year 1 of Ramesses IV, Naunakhte would have been about sixty-eight, so that the Henutshenu mentioned in the Cairo text was more probably her daughter (and the mother of a daughter named after Naunakhte), rather than her own mother. The fact that the text also mentions a woman called Menat—who could very well be Henutshenu's sister Menatnakhte— would seem to support this alternative. Menatnakhte had also brought her daughter Tapaipu, who was still living at home when the authorities recorded all the households in the Stato Civile. Naunakhte herself was by now probably much too old to attend parties. It is believed that in Deir al-Medina women were considered old once they had grandchildren.

We know that Henutshenu was excluded from Naunakhte's (rich) inheritance, because she had not looked after her mother in her period of need. But that period was actually only about to start at the time O. Cairo CG 25705⁺ was written, which explains why Henutshenu's daughter was named Naunakhte. Mother and daughter had not yet fallen out with each other when Henutshenu's own daughter was born and duly named Naunakhte. This is the document (the names of the women and the untranslated Egyptian words are in italics):

Given (by) *Ese*, [the wife (?) of] Nebnefer: 10 *sesh* loaves, 1 ash-baked loaf, 1 *menet* jar for the drinking of Hathor. *Meresger* . . . : . . . *sesh* loaves . . . *Merut*: . . . *Taweretemheb*: 5 *sesh* loaves. *Tamerut*: 10 *sesh* loaves. *Ese*, the mother of . . . *Tahenuttaiwa*: *akek* loaves. *Hemestiherawyes*: 10 *sesh* loaves. *Tahenut*, the mother of Nebnefer: 5 *sesh* loaves. *Tanedjemetkhabet*: 5 *sesh* loaves. *Henutshenu*, the mother of *Naunakhte*: 30 *sesh* loaves: 1 *seshqed* loaf, 2 *menet* jars, (and) 2 *gen* vessels for a wreath. *Wabet*, the mother of Kha: 5 *sesh* loaves. Anynakhte: 10 *sesh* loaves, 1 *menet* jar, 1 ointment jar with sesame oil, . . . Bes: 1 white triangular loaf. *Hely*, the mother of *Raya*: 5 *sesh* loaves. *Merutmut*, the mother of *Taseket*: 1 white triangular loaf. *Mutemipet*: 1 white triangular loaf. *Taâtmerut*: 1 white triangular loaf. *Taweretherty*: 1 *akek* loaf. Hori: 10 *sesh* loaves, 2 *menet* jars. *Henutwaty*, the mother of Mes:

5 *sesh* loaves. *Tapaipu*: 1 *sesh* loaf. *Dewaitneferet*, the mother of *Sheritra*: 5 *sesh* loaves. *Dewait*, the mother of Khonsu: 10 [*sesh* loaves], 1 *seshqed* loaf. *Ta* . . . : 1 white triangular loaf, . . . *Takamenet*: 5 *sesh* loaves. *Tui*: 1 *sesh* loaf. Seba: 1 *akek* loaf. *Tameket*: . . . triangular [loaves]. N.N.: 10 *sesh* loaves. *Takhy*: 1 *sesh* loaf. *Menat*: 1 *sesh* loaf. *Henutdjuu*, the mother of *Kenya* (?): 1 *sesh* loaf. *Henutmeter*: 1 *sesh* loaf.

There is another inscription in bolder hieratic mentioning the king, but this may be entirely unconnected. Note how the women are often identified as "the mother of," which would help the person who kept this ostracon remember exactly which Ese had brought goodies to the party and which one had not. In other ostraca people are referred to as "the wife of," "the son of," "the daughter of," or, if they had a prominent position, by their title.

The publication history of this ostracon is also something that is not uncommon in Deir al-Medina studies. The Cairo fragments were published by Černý in his magistral edition of the ostraca from the village in the Egyptian Museum in Cairo, whereas the texts from the IFAO and Varille's collection are only known from Černý's *Notebooks* that are now kept in the Griffith Institute in Oxford. His transcription there already includes the Cairo fragment. Somehow Černý had all the written sources from Deir al-Medina in his head.

In a groundbreaking article in the *Journal of Egyptian Archaeology* 68, Jack Janssen showed that reciprocal gift-giving was a big thing in ancient Egypt, as it would have been in Deir al-Medina. People did not simply give each other gifts; it was actually a social obligation and in a way an essential part of village economics, as in other premodern cultures. According to Rob Demarée, who has visited the area for the last fifty years, this system of gift-giving is still in place in Qurna today, and called *wajib*. These party accounts—of which there are more—always carefully list who brought what to the party, and the only reason for this seems to be that it served as an aide-mémoire for future reference.

The idea has been proposed that the people who brought the most (valuable) items were mentioned first, reflecting their status in the process, but in the surviving lists this does not always appear to be so (as in O. Cairo CG 25705[+]). Does this mean that the names reflect the actual order in which people arrived? This we do not know; nor do we know who wrote these lists. There are in any case far too many items and names to remember afterward, so notes must have been made on the spot. (The people in Deir al-Medina did use a separate notation system that was somewhere in between writing and pictorial jottings that was very effective, so maybe even a semiliterate doorman could have taken notes that would later be turned into a formal record by a more literate person). This brings up the interesting problem that in O. Cairo CG 25705+ there are only a few men present. Did one of them write this memo? Was it the birthday girl herself (not very likely, because she would have been too busy entertaining the guests), or was there someone else to do this for her?

The problem of these party accounts kept occupying Janssen, as we can see from his chapter IV ("Women and Gifts") in one of his last—and probably intentionally desk-cleaning—publications on daily life in Deir al-Medina: *Village Varia* (1997), which also included the text translated above, using the transcription by Černý. The present account is based on Černý's and Janssen's work, as are some of the findings below. But not all, because the entire framework of reciprocity seems to be blown out of the water right from the start by Henutshenu's own contribution to the party for her sister-in-law Hathor. Bringing five *sesh* loaves appears to have been the socially accepted minimum. Note, for instance, how the four women who brought only one loaf—among whom was Henutshenu's own sister Menatnakhte—were neatly relegated to the bottom of the text by the scribe. This also disqualifies the theory about people being listed in their order of arrival.

Henutshenu crashed the party carrying thirty *sesh* loaves, one *seshqed* loaf, two *menet* jars, (and) two *gen* vessels for a wreath. The *gen* vessels and the connection with the wreath totally puzzled Janssen—who probably knew more about ancient Egyptian commodities than anyone else ever living on this planet—and all Egyptologists after him. Even in translation it makes no sense, so it may be best to not pursue this question any further. What we can say is that the *menet* jars mentioned in this text most probably contained beer, even if Janssen felt slightly uncertain here. He did point out, however, that it would have been very bad form to show up at a party with an empty jar. This was, after all, a party. If the amount brought by Henutshenu reflects anything besides the fact that she could afford to bring such gifts, it must be the relationship she had with her sister-in-law Hathor. But how do we explain the fact that some women—including

Henutshenu's sister Menatnakhte—brought only one loaf? Does this also reflect their relationship with Hathor (or their own financial situation)? Or something else we are no longer aware of?

There is one very interesting party account (O. DeM 222) from the reign of Ramesses III. It counts no less than six columns containing 110 short lines of text. Most of the people who attended the party brought a good number of snacks. The workman Neferher (col. II *ll.* 17*ff.*), for instance, brought a number of water-bread loaves, three *meh* dishes of cooked (meat), one *meh* dish of fish, five mixed loaves, one *qedjedj* loaf, one *remenet* jar, and five bundles of vegetables. This is more or less the typical entry per person. So this was a major party. By contrast, the scribe Amunnakhte son of Ipuy—one of the top dogs in the village—brought only two mixed loaves (col. VI *ll.* 15–16). Does this explain why he was only recorded in this list almost at the bottom? After him there is only one line of text, telling us that the workman Kasa did even worse. He brought one single loaf. If these gifts were indeed formal expressions of friendship or kinship, Amunnakhte and Kasa clearly had their own explicit opinion on the host of the day.

O. DeM 134 is a similar list, mentioning only women, including Menatnakhte and Naunakhte, who is either our Naunakhte—which is not very likely—or again Henutshenu's or her sister-in-law Hathor's daughter. Their brother Qenhirkhopshef the Younger also had a daughter called Naunakhte. Together the women account for cakes, loaves, fish, and possibly also fruit (no beer). The text was dated to Dynasty 19 by Černý, but Dynasty 20 (Janssen) seems to be the better alternative, although Janssen preferred to leave open the question whether Menat was simply an abbreviation of her full name Menatnakhte, whereas we have little doubt that this was so (see chapter 7, "A Day in the Life of Menatnakhte").

The woman Taweretemheb, present in O. Cairo CG 25705⁺ and O. DeM 134, is also known from the account O. DeM 145, which is dated to year 30 of Ramesses III. She was actually the wife of the scribe Amunnakhte son of Ipuy, so the Dynasty 20 date seems certain.

P. Turin Cat. 1885—showing the plan and dimensions of the tomb of Ramesses IV—was published as early as 1917 by Howard Carter and Alan Gardiner, who had the following to say about the work on this papyrus by its previous editors:

The texts on the verso of the Turin plan have been published, or, to speak more precisely, very inadequate facsimiles of them have been given, in Pleyte-Rossi, *Papyrus de Turin*, pls. LXXI–II; comments on them, equally inadequate, will be found on pp. 100–2 of the volume of letterpress accompanying the plates. (*Journal of Egyptian Archaeology* 4)

Perhaps it was just as well that both Pleyte and Rossi were already dead by this time. For us, the interest of P. Turin Cat. 1885 lies in the fact that on the verso there is a small note about the division of part of Amunnakhte's inheritance, apparently carried out by the scribe Hori and Amunnakhte's widow Taweretemheb, who was also the first to take her pick. But as in the case of Naunakhte's inheritance, it seems that the items that were divided formed only a small part of Amunnakhte's inheritance. In both cases, we do not know who inherited the real estate (women's names and untranslated Egyptian terms are again in italics).

(Verso col. II) Year 7, second month of the *shemu* season, day 5. On this day: division [of the] property of the scribe Amunnakhte for his children by the scribe of The Tomb Hori and the female citizen *Taweretemheb*. Given to the female citizen *Taweretemheb* as a share of his clothing: fine *daiu* dress (used) 1, fine *rudju* dress (used) 5, fine *djay* dress 1, fine *rudju* dress 2. Clothing: total 2. Heavy wooden chest 1, mats 3. Given [. . .] *Taweretemheb*: honey 2 hin. [. . .] of The Tomb: honey 1 hin. *Taa[mun]-nakhte*: 1 hin. Paidenu: 1 hin. *Ta[. . .]. Tagerpet*: 1. Pentaweret: 1 hin. Given [to . . .]: resin 4 hin. *Hel*: 1¼ hin. Paidenu: [. . .] hin. Given to Ta to compensate for his chest: tamarisk, making 10 deben.

(Verso col. III) Given [to the female ci]tizen *Hel*. Given to her from the clothes (. . .).

Since the children would inherit directly from their father, the fact that Amunnakhte's wife seems to be allowed to take the first pick makes one wonder whether this is not simply the division of the couple's communal property, of which Taweretemheb owned one-third. But surely this was not all of it.

One may be fairly confident that Pentaweret and Ta were two of Amunnakhte's many sons, but some of the women mentioned in this text seem unrelated, such as Mrs. Hel, who received 1¼ hin of resin (a monthly ration?) and also some of the clothes. Still, in this division Amunnakhte's widow received the most. These women did know each other. Both had attended the party described in O. Cairo CG 25705+ and we cannot exclude the possibility that they were family. Otherwise, why would Hel have inherited from Amunnakhte in the first place?

Taweretemheb appears in a few other texts from Deir al-Medina, including an official journal (O. DeM 145). It is perhaps a coincidence that her husband once attended a party, bringing just the smallest gift he could think of, and that Taweretemheb took the largest part of his clothes after his death. And if something looks like stinginess and smells like stinginess, it is probably stinginess. There is one letter that may be addressed to her, urging her to intervene on the sender's behalf (O. Berlin P 12630), and this definitely looks like a case of someone (her husband) not willing to pay:

> (Recto) Memo from the workman [Mose (?)] to the ci[tizen . . .]. To wit: the scribe Amunnakhte, your husband, has taken one coffin from me, saying: "I will give you the ox to pay for it." To this day he has not given it. I told it to Paâkhet and he said to me: "Give me a bed for it and I will bring the ox for you when it has grown up." I gave him the bed. No coffin, no bed to this day. (Verso) If you (want to) give the ox, then let it be brought. If no ox (?), then let one bring the bed and the coffin (back).

The language is terse, the sentences short. One is very tempted to ascribe this to the irritation felt by the sender of this short letter, clearly a man who could afford to address the wife of the senior scribe this way. Again, no flowery and polite introduction. The handwriting is, however, neat and clearly from a professional scribe. But as we will see below, this could equally well have been a letter addressed to the wife of Amunnakhte son of Naunakhte.

As we saw above, parties were not always only women. O. Cairo CG 25660 + O. Cairo JdE 37649 from the reign of Ramesses III or IV lists thirty-six guests, of whom only five are women. There are twenty lines of text, and there is another text that includes workmen's marks, which was a parallel notation system in which the names of workmen were replaced with single, often crudely drawn, signs representing their names and simple notes. Anyone, including the women, would know which sign represented which household, which may explain why they are listed here.

Just this once the text will be rendered as it appears on the ostracon. The translation again leans heavily on Janssen's edition in *Village Varia* (1997), checking this against the edition and Černý's *Notebook*. This was a serious party in view of the amounts brought. The names of the women and the untranslated Egyptian words have been italicized.

Qedherikhetef: 5 large loaves, 20 mixed loaves,
1 *gay* jar of meat and fish, 1 *gay* jar of grapes and *heqeq* fruit,
1 oipe of cakes.
Pentaweret son of Amunnakhte: 3 big loaves, 17 mixed loaves, 1 *gay* jar of fish.
Ramose: 5 big loaves, 15 mixed loaves, 1 *gay* jar of meat, 1 oipe of cakes.
Pahemnetjer: 13 mixed loaves, 1 *meh* dish with 3 cuts of meat, 1 oipe of cakes.
Nebnakhte: 20 mixed loaves, 1 *meh* dish of meat. Amunemheb: 10 mixed loaves, 1 *gay* jar of fish.
Pentaweret: 4 mixed loaves. Amunnakhte son of Kes: 5 mixed loaves. Wesekhnemtet: 5 mixed loaves.
Penniut [son of] Mes: 7 mixed loaves. Amunpahapy son of Aânakhte: 10 mixed loaves,
1 *gay* jar of cuts of meat. The scorpion wizard Amunmose: 4 mixed loaves. Minkha: 3 mixed loaves.
Nehesy: 5 mixed loaves. Hornefer: . . . mixed loaves, fish. Nebnefer son of Pentaweret: 5 mixed loaves.
Sethy: 10 mixed loaves. Amunnakhte son of Reshpeteref: 6 mixed loaves. Penamun: 3 big loaves, 17 mixed loaves,
1 *meh* dish of fish, 3 oipe of cakes. Montupahapy: 5 big loaves, 11 mixed loaves,
1 *gay* jar of meat. Amunkha: 5 big loaves, 20 mixed loaves, 1 *meh* dish of meat.
Qenna son of Kha: 6 mixed loaves. Nesamun: 5 mixed loaves. Qenhirkhopshef son of Khaemnun:
5 mixed loaves. Hormin: 5 mixed loaves. Nebnefer: 5 mixed loaves. *Hathoremheb*: 5 mixed loaves.
Rek: 5 mixed loaves. *Henutan*: 5 mixed loaves. Nakhtamun: 4 mixed loaves. *Takamen*: 4 mixed loaves. Anynakhte: 5 mixed loaves. Buqentuef: 7 mixed loaves.
Sheritra: 3 big loaves, 17 mixed loaves, 1 *meh* dish of fish.
Qenhirkhopshef: 5 mixed loaves. Neferhotep: 7 mixed loaves.

Assuming that this was a hot day or evening, one thing immediately springs to mind. There is no mention of any beer, but it is very hard to imagine these people sitting there eating bread, cake, and (partly salted or sun-dried) fish without anything to wash it down. In this case one has to suppose that the host or hostess provided the drinks, which immediately sheds another light on the previous texts, where there is hardly any mention of *menet* jars. So maybe in most cases such a party meant drinks only, with the guests expected to bring the food themselves? It is either that, or the guests would have gone home with very dry mouths.

Apart from the fact that this particular party was attended by a few of Naunakhte's sons—namely Qenhirkhopshef and Neferhotep (although this Neferhotep could also have been the husband of his sister Khatanub)—and perhaps his sister's husband Nebnakhte, the other remarkable thing about it is that some of the guests apparently brought an entire oipe of cakes. In grain measures the oipe represents approximately twenty liters, but in this case three people together brought five oipe, and surely a hundred liters of cakes would be almost enough to feed the village, not just the people at the party. The scribe presumably meant to say that these people brought a sack full of cakes the size of an oipe.

In Deir al-Medina studies new texts surface almost every day, and one of these actually seems to mention Naunakhte's husband Khaemnun attending a similar party. O. DeM 10166 mentions him and several others in connection with loaves. This could of course be a coincidence, and in that case the editor of the text is right in assuming that this is merely an account of the distribution of loaves, although it is very tempting to treat it as another party account.

The other side of the coin seems to be represented by O. Berlin P 12635 from Dynasty 20. In this text an anonymous workman noted down the food that he had given to other people during several (religious) feasts. The recto is mostly taken up by the things he gave to his daughter, but on the verso we see him celebrating with other people, including Naunakhte's son Maaninakhtef:

> Again: the Coming of the Gods from the East, him drinking a *menet* jar and eating a large loaf and five sweet melons with Amunpahapy son of Neferhotep. Again: at my Feast of Taweret together with Maaninakhtef, him drinking two *tjer* jars and one *menet* jar. (. . .)

Again: first month of the *peret* season, day 2 at the Khoiak Festival, him eating one large loaf and two (pieces of) pickled meat together with his sister, and he said to me: "I love my sister more than meat." So I gave him one (more piece of) pickled meat. (. . .)

The pregnant hippopotamus goddess Taweret protected young children right after they were born and during the first period of weaning and, if our interpretation is correct, Maaninakhtef may have been boozing to celebrate someone's birth by drinking other people's beer (which was in turn noted down by the donor with care). The second event was the Khoiak Festival, celebrating the finding and reconstruction of the deceased Osiris from his various body parts by Isis. People would pay special attention to their dead relatives during this festival, and here we see Naunakhte's son eating with his wife—who is often referred to as "sister" by her husband—and a friend (or a brother?), and telling one of these ancient Egyptian jokes that are not very often understood, unless he meant to say "I love to eat, but sex is better." In that case it is not likely that this anonymous sister was one of his siblings. Or that she would be amused. We do not know if the ancient Egyptians paid any attention to foreplay (although the demotic story of Setne and Tabubu shows that women knew very well how to arouse a man). We do not even know whether Maaninakhtef's wife was circumcised, in which case the fun would not be hers to begin with. Still, it would have been nice if we knew that they were having this picnic near Naunakhte's tomb, but the story does not say.

Maaninakhtef also attended a party mentioned in our last account, O. Berlin P 14328. The header is problematic:

Account (lit. 'So that one knows') of the thing(s) that the workman Minkha took on account of (?) the drinking in his house.

What follows is the usual list of people bringing all kinds of goods, and we know that three sons of Naunakhte were there. Amunnakhte and Neferhotep are mentioned in the same line, so they had either arrived together or were now sitting together, whereas Maaninakhtef is mentioned later on in the text. Amunnakhte brought only five loaves, but Neferhotep—the son who had received so much support from Naunakhte that he was excluded from the copper items of her inheritance—had, just like his sister Henutshenu on another occasion, decided to bring more than anyone else. We do not know why (perhaps he loved the person who threw the party), but we also do not know why this party was held. It could be anything from a birthday, a religious feast, or the birth of a child to the celebration of a marriage with the closest friends. The foremen Nekhemmut and Inherkha were there too, carrying the minimum of five assorted loaves. One sometimes has the impression that the first menstruation of a daughter—or worse, the possible removal of her clitoris—would be a reason to throw a party. In O. Berlin P 10631 (Dynasty 20) gifts are given to a woman called Henutwaty on account of the advent of her *hesmen*, which authors believe is the word for menstruation (among other possibilities). Did this occur around the twelfth year—the age often ascribed to Naunakhte when she married Qenhirkhopshef—or actually slightly later due to malnutrition or other factors? In that case Naunakhte may have been slightly older than twelve when she married.

12

Qenhirkhopshef
the Younger

As was seen earlier, Qenhirkhopshef the Younger received a larger share of the inheritance of his mother in the form of a copper vessel and ten additional sacks of grain, presumably because he would take care of his father. He was a regular workman, but from some of the correspondence with his brother Maaninakhtef we know that he also worked as a carpenter (e.g., O. DeM 418), perhaps as part of a family business. He attended parties, just like his sisters and brothers, and is altogether much better documented than some of his siblings, some of whom are hardly known beyond the Naunakhte papers.

But there may actually be one ostracon (O. BM EA 50737) from Dynasty 20 that mentions both him and his sister Khatanub. She is there called Khanub, which could be a simple mistake by the scribe (in his publication of the Naunakhte papers Černý transcribed her name into hieroglyphs as 'Khatanub,' but in his translation reverted to 'Kha'nub'). This is of course the very last resort if one wants the evidence to fit the story, which we desperately do, but the name is also written Khanub in the Stato Civile and other sources. The fact that she is a singer of Amun does not come as a surprise, because a stela made for Qenhirkhopshef the Younger and some of his deceased children (see below) informs us that his mother Naunakhte had been one too.

Naunakhte's daughters do sometimes appear in the records buying carpentry, as in O. DeM 195, where one of the carpenter's clients is called "the female citizen [. . .]nakhte," which can be Wasetnakhte, Wesernakhte (which is another way to write Wasetnakhte), or Menatnakhte. It could even be Naunakhte herself or one of her granddaughters. What is more surprising is that in O. BM EA 50737 Qenhirkhopshef charges his sister for the making of a bed (although Maaninakhtef did the same with his brother-in-law Weserhat):

> Account of the silver for the bed that the singer of Amun Khanub gave to the work<man> Qenhirkhopshef.

There follows a list of the commodities that Khatanub paid, including grain, up to a total of nineteen copper deben. But this was at least a bed for sleeping. O. Varille 4 (Dynasty 20) is an account of coffins and other funerary items made or decorated on behalf of a number of men and women by the draftsman Hormin (the name is not read with confidence), and one of the women mentioned is a Mrs. Khanub, although the fact that someone ordered a coffin for her (she may have done so herself) does not mean that she was dead by that time. Could our Khatanub not have simply been called Khanub in daily life, in a village in which many people would be known by their household nicknames? Or could 'Khatanub' be a simple writing mistake in the statement by Naunakhte?

It is a shame that the ostracon is not dated, but we can be certain that it was made after Naunakhte's death, as was O. BM EA 50737, because Khatanub was there to hear her mother's will, only to be told that she, her sister Henutshenu, and their brother Neferhotep would receive nothing, and their sister Menatnakhte not a full share. Since her brother Qenhirkhopshef had supported his parents and she had not, he may have seen no reason to give her a free ride in O. BM EA 50737 as well. So he charged his sister for the bed. Of course Khatanub could also have decided to look for a carpenter who was not family. O. Varille 4 was bought in Luxor in 1933. It is broken on all sides, but her name (in italics, as is the name of the other woman) is there:

> Given (delivered) by the draftsman Hormin [...] Buqentuef. The *wet* coffin for Anynakhte, painted, makes 20 (deben). The *wet* coffin [for ...] *Ese*: the inner coffin 1, makes 11 (deben). The inner coffin for *Khanub* [...]. Two *wet* coffins of wood, makes 10 (deben) ... wood 1½, makes [...] *wet* coffin for a woman, makes 8 (deben).

The text on the verso seems to be related to the recto in some way because it again mentions the workman Buqentuef. Somehow this sort of thing always happens. One starts out on a chapter dealing with Qenhirkhopshef the Younger, only to be distracted by the fact that the women Khatanub and Khanub are of course one and the same (even if the editors of the Stato Civile still doubted this), so all of a sudden some new pieces of the puzzle can be added to Naunakhte's family.

Some texts were already mentioned in *Who's Who*, but O. Varille 27, which is only known from Černý's *Notebooks* and the online *Deir el-Medina Database*, seems to be new. Parts of the text are incomprehensible, but it mentions not only her but also a Khaemnun, who could be 'our' Khaemnun (and her father). The text further refers to "this evil deed," but that is on the verso in connection with a Mr. Kel, whereas the other names are on the recto.

Apart from one other unclear source (O. BIFAO 76 no. 4) mentioning her (the text was not transcribed into hieroglyphs in the edition), that seems to be all we know about her, so we cannot really say that we have come to know Naunakhte's daughter Khatanub ('The Golden One (Hathor) has appeared') any better, even if she has now gained a little more personality than she was given in Černý's brilliant edition of the Naunakhte papers, where she was still just a name.

Deir al-Medina will always keep surprising us, however, because she is also mentioned in the Stato Civile, albeit as a mother's name only, but the information is interesting enough. It turns out that Ramery (or Meryra), the son of Khatanub and a Mr. Neferhotep, had actually married Tanitpaipu, who was the daughter of Khatanub's sister Menatnakhte and the workman Weserhat. One could speculate forever about the desirability of these kinds of marriages (and the reasons behind them), but this was probably not the first such marriage in Naunakhte's family, and not the last either. Clearly the ancient Egyptians had fewer problems with such marriages than we do today.

Finally, there is one unpublished ostracon from the collection of Černý that is reputedly kept in Prague (O. Černý unnumbered), mentioning both Khanub and her sister Wasetnakhte, albeit in a tantalizingly unclear context. After the header, "What he brought to compensate [...]," there are several short lines mentioning copper and grain, and then it becomes interesting.

Khanub: *daiu* dress 1, deben copper 1 (and) 6½ kite.

Given to the female citizen Wasetnakhte: jars of strong (?) *mersu* wine 5, jars of *agenen* 2 . . .

Year 3, first month of the *peret* season, day 14. Settling the account for Nebnakhte and Wasetnakhte. What he compensated her for: 25 copper deben.

At first sight this text is about three or four payments or deliveries (or possibly gifts) to two of Naunakhte's daughters, but the last entry is the most interesting, provided that the "he" mentioned there is Nebnakhte and the "her" is Wasetnakhte. In that case we are dealing with a sizable payment by Nebnakhte to his wife. Or should we rather say ex-wife? It may well be that we are looking at the financial arrangement of the couple's divorce here. O. Černý unnumbered was written in year 3, first month of the *peret* season, day 14. Naunakhte's statement was made in year 3, fourth month of the *akhet* season, day 5 of Ramesses V, and we know that Nebnakhte and Wasetnakhte both participated in the division of her household items, which took place after Wasetnakhte's mother had died. One has to assume they were still married at the time, meaning that the "year 3" from O. Černý unnumbered has to be Ramesses VI or later. But this ostracon could equally well *not* be about a divorce, in which case one could even theorize that money was already changing hands shortly after Naunakhte had made her statement. The problem with this, however, is that Khatanub received nothing of Naunakhte's inheritance, so that we are back at square one.

Anyway, let us return to Qenhirkhopshef the Younger, a man who seems to have been more versatile than other workmen, although one has the impression that Naunakhte's sons were all a bit special in the first place, because they could read and write. And once in a while this Qenhirkhopshef would set out into the hills of the Theban necropolis and write a graffito here and there, in some cases very near a graffito left by his namesake, his mother's first husband. Did he know where to look, or did he just stumble by accident on one of the old Qenhirkhopshef's many graffiti? In some of his own graffiti Qenhirkhopshef the Younger suddenly refers to himself as "the priest of Amun-Ra of the Good Encounter." The word for priest is *wab* 'pure one,' which does not necessarily mean that he was employed at the temple permanently, but eligible, for example, to carry the divine oracle statue as it made a tour of the village and beyond.

There is also something about him and stelae. He seems to have been the only one of Naunakhte's children to have left stelae to posterity (although this may be just a question of finder's luck). Bernard Bruyère thought that he had found a stela belonging to him in Hut R (E) on the col between the village and the Valley of the Kings, and another one that was actually made by him for an elite client (and these were wont to look only for the best craftsmen). Although this observation by Bruyère has not received much support, it would be rather sensational if it were true, because it would mean that Qenhirkhopshef was also a sculptor, meaning that he could seemingly try his hand at any craft and succeed. But then, we also saw how his brother Maaninakhtef rose to become chief carpenter of the Lord of the Two Lands, which suggests that the latter at that time had better things to do than work in the royal tomb (which raises the question of whether he would still be allowed to live in the village). In some cases, therefore, the fact that someone is no longer mentioned as a member of the crew could also mean that he had found a better job. Conversely, the fact that Khaemnun was still mentioned as part of the crew at the end of the reign of Ramesses III does not necessarily mean that he was still obliged to do the hard work in the tomb. And it could, of course, be that this late Khaemnun was in fact Khaemnun's grandson Khaemnun by his son Neferhotep.

We do know that one of Qenhirkhopshef's relatives (perhaps even his wife) did commission at least one stela, which was published by Černý alongside the Naunakhte papers. It is known as Stela BM EA 278. The text refers to him as *mâa kheru* 'true of voice,' which generally (although not necessarily) means that a person is dead. Černý was the first to note that the man who dedicated this stela to Hathor and Amun of the Good Encounter was actually the same as the son of Naunakhte who agreed to take care of his father after his mother had died, and therefore received an extra bonus. This stela was found in a Theban tomb and was then acquired by the Earl of Belmore, whose biography tells us he was quite a character. He financed Belzoni's excavations in Thebes and one can assume that this is also where this stela comes from.

Tomb KV 30, which was excavated by Belzoni, is called Lord Belmore's Tomb to this day. Apart from collecting Egyptian antiquities—he sailed up the Nile to Luxor with his wife, two sons, and Rosa the dog—just like the old scribe Qenhirkhopshef he loved to leave his mark, so that his carved inscriptions may be found from the Ramesseum to the pyramid of Khufu (near the top).

The fact that Qenhirkhopshef the Younger (or, more probably, a relative of his) commissioned this stela tells us that the family had done well. Still, some of the execution of the stela as it is reproduced here (it has not been checked against the original or a photograph, because that would ruin the story) does make one wonder about the skill of the man who made it. The stela tells us that Qenhirkhopshef had several sons, who also appear in Graffito no. 803 in the Theban hills. The graffito does not mention any daughters, and one wonders why, because the stela seems to do so, but in the weirdest possible way. This is Stela BM EA 278:

Figure 7.
Stela BM EA 278, commissioned by the family of Qenhirkhopshef the Younger (courtesy of the British Museum and the *Journal of Egyptian Archaeology*)

This is a very old drawing. One supposes the artist did not get all the signs right, and some weird readings were therefore tacitly corrected by Černý in his publication of the Naunakhte papers. Whoever commissioned this stela, he or she may have been slightly disappointed at the result. The message is all there, but when the sculptor had to add the names of the beloved relatives, he found that he had used up all of his space in the bottom part (did he not make a draft beforehand?). So what he did was cram in the names of two of Qenhirkhopshef's sons—Nebseta (written with the female element *nebet* instead of the masculine *neb*) and Amunemheb—in the empty line that originally separated the so-called lunette text (the part shaped like the half moon) at the top, like this:

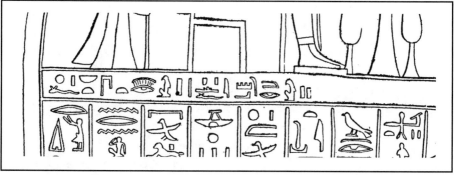

Figure 8. Stela BM EA 278. Not a very elegant solution

He also had to get the name and title of the *materfamilias* Naunakhte in somewhere, and he obviously did not want to put her in this same line (or maybe he actually chiseled the names of the two sons only after thinking about where to put Naunakhte). So she went up into the first line on the right in the lunette text, which almost suggests he did this section last. Otherwise he would have started his *hetep di nesu* ('an offering that the king gives') formula—the formal prayer for the dead—in the right vertical column, which was now used to chisel in the name of Naunakhte.

An accomplished artist would have gotten this right, but this one certainly did not. Instead of writing *mutef* 'his mother,' the plate suggests he wrote *mutek* 'your mother,' so either the drawing is wrong, or the artist knew Qenhirkhopshef, or something else was amiss, because the sign for *mut* 'mother' also looks like anything but the proper sign for

Figure 9. Stela BM EA 278. A mess

'mother.' The signs in the title of Naunakhte face left (althought the lower arm sign across the reed plant actually faces right), meaning that we are supposed to read it from left to right and then from top to bottom, but when he carved her name he suddenly switched to the opposite reading direction, from right to left and top to bottom. It is a mess. Had Qenhirkhopshef been there, he would have noticed, and suddenly it becomes easy to see why these people sued each other so often. Why pay for a stela that is not right?

It does not stop there. The artist still wanted to slip in the name of Qenhirkhopshef's daughter, but for some reason he chose not to include it in the line between the lunette and the main text, where there was some space left. Instead his eyes fell on the space beneath Qenhirkhopshef's arms, raised in adoration to Hathor, whose horns go all the way up to the edge of the stela (see figure 7), and Amun of the Good Encounter. And even there he managed to slip up.

The artist did get the name Naunakhte right this time, carving from

Figure 10. Stela BM EA 278. Qenhirkhopshef son of Naunakhte

left to right and top to bottom, although the striking arm sign (the name does after all mean 'Thebes is strong') is followed by another inexplicable sign, unless it is again the first sign of *mâa kheru* 'true of voice.' But the filiation *satef* 'his daughter' is written *saes* 'her son' and is written in the wrong order (from right to left and top to bottom), with the ideogram stroke denoting an entity seemingly preceding the sign of the egg, a nice way to denote offspring. So in the end the artist wrote *saes Niutnekhet* 'her son Naunakhte,' so that one would love to have seen the response by the sculptor's client when he (or she) saw the stela. Note, by the way, Qenhirkhopshef's belly. This is a man who could take care of himself. He (or his family) could afford to have a stela made. Then again, also note the ridiculously long legs and feet (figure 7). Someone slipped up here.

13

Thrown Out

Divorce in Deir al-Medina was easy. A man could 'throw his wife out' of the house—that is almost the literal translation—and a woman could just as easily decide to 'go away,' although this would of course have emotional and financial consequences. If she had been a faithful wife, she could expect to get her own possessions back, as well as one-third of the conjugal property. But where would she live? In Deir al-Medina we more than once see women receiving real estate, sometimes by the riverbank (the villagers used the same word for 'market,' which was located there), and it may be that in some cases this was the result of a divorce. Would the wife be taking all the children with her or just the small children? There are indications that from about seven years onward the boys' education and further upbringing became the task of the husband. And why was it always the woman who should leave the house? That one is easy. A house in the village was state property and directly connected with the husband's job (see, for example, the case described in O. UC 39656 below).

There are, however, also instances where we see the man leaving the house to live with another woman. One such case is P. Geneva D 409 + P. Turin Cat. 2021 recto. In the original publication by Černý and and the British Egyptologist Thomas Eric Peet in 1927, the Geneva fragment was still missing. Together with two other pieces, this was acquired by Gardiner in 1937 in exchange for what is now P. Geneva MAH 15274, and presented by him to the Museo Egizio in Turin. The text has been assigned to Dynasty 20 or 21 and the reign of Ramesses IX or XI, respectively, and it presumably comes from nearby Medinet Habu.

What makes this text special—apart from informing us how complicated the mutual property relations could become after a divorce—is that it directly involved the vizier himself.

The right part of the text has broken away, except for a number of fragments at the bottom. This is a shame, because this column would have told us about the date of the court session, the composition of the court, and perhaps also more about the previous history of the declaring party, a Mr. Amunkha, who was a god's father, presumably in one of the mortuary temples on the western bank of the Nile. He starts by telling the court why he, two of his eldest sons, and his second wife, Ineksunedjem—"this woman standing in front of the vizier"—have come to the court today.

> [. . . the citi]zen Inek[sunedjem . . .]. I entered [the house of (the father of the woman) Tatjarya with the consent of (?)] the great god. She became [the mistress] of my house and I built [a house for my] children. I (also) [provided for (?)] their children. But the god turned me away and I [swo]re about her in the court of the temple (divorced her) and I made two-thirds to one-third out of everything that I had acquired with her and [I entered] the house of (the father of?) the female citizen Ineksunedjem, this woman standing in front of the vizier.

In short, Amunkha tells the vizier that he was married once, which is shown by the expression "I entered the house of N.N.," in which N.N. is either his first wife, as some authors believe, or the house of his future father-in-law to collect his bride. (The latter is more likely, because we see this happen in Deir al-Medina and later abnormal hieratic sources such as P. Louvre E 7846 and 7849.) But the marriage did not work out and he took an oath, supposedly in Medinet Habu, to annul the marriage. Just as Naunakhte told the court of Deir al-Medina that she had been a good parent, establishing households for her children, he states the same. Not only that, he even provided for his grandchildren, meaning that he was rather old. Still, he had now moved in with his second wife, Ineksunedjem, and together they had built up an estate.

> I bought four slaves [wi]th her. She has been good to me and she agrees with my character. And she has done for me what a son or [daugh]ter would do. I gave her the female servant Numutery, the female servant Bupuymutkhaen, and their child[ren as he]r one-third. I further presented (?) her with the

servant Sapeterdjehuty, the servant Gemamunpash, these two [sla]ves of mine, as a share out of my part of all that I have made (acquired) with her, as a child [just li]ke the children of my former wife, exactly exactly, who are in my house, whereas I did not put a single loved one above (?) the other.

Amunkha is rather eager to underline his role as a good father, and this of course always goes down well in front of a court. In the case of his second wife he also appears to hint at regarding her not just as his wife, but also as a faithful daughter, and as a daughter she will receive two additional slaves from his own two-thirds of the conjugal property. Right then he hastens to add that he has never favored one particular child. He loves them all.

But now it was time for business. Amunkha specifically states that he wants each of his children to know what his or her share will be, and one assumes that this includes his wife, Ineksunedjem. It reminds one of the famous New Kingdom Adoption Papyrus in which a man adopts his own barren wife as his daughter, so that she will be able to inherit his property (P. Ashmolean Museum 1945.96) instead of his own brothers and sisters. As part of the deal the couple bought a female slave who bore him three children, and these were raised by his own wife. After his death she freed the slave children and adopted them, as well as her younger brother, who had married the oldest slave girl (one hell of a wedding present).

In the case of P. Geneva D 409 + P. Turin Cat. 2021 recto we have no way of knowing what exactly Amunkha had discussed beforehand with Ineksunedjem and perhaps even his first wife, or at least his two eldest sons, but we do know that during the entire procedure his second wife, Ineksunedjem, remains silent, which may be explained by the fact that this was a family issue that first and foremost required a settlement between him and his sons who were present, because only then could he be sure that they would not sue Ineksunedjem after his death.

Amunkha then reveals the real reason for his appearance in court: it is a pension plan for his second wife, including a generous compensation for the children of his first marriage. And just to make sure that this plan will not fall through, he cites a decree by the king stating that a man can do with his property as he likes, and when he states that his two-thirds will be on top of her one-third—suggesting it will become Ineksunedjem's after his death—one starts to wonder whether he did not in fact adopt

Ineksunedjem to make sure that she would also inherit the rest of the conjugal property after his death. Otherwise, Amunkha's siblings would have a legitimate claim to it. And if they did not come forward to stake a claim, his sons might.

> Now see, I have come before the vizier [and the] magistrates of the court so that every one of my children knows his share. This plan that I will make for the female citizen Ineksunedjem, this woman who is in my house today. Pharaoh, life, prosperity, health, has said: "Cause that every man shall do according to his wish concerning his things (property)." I give everything I have acquired with the female citizen Ineksunedjem to her, the woman who is in my house today, namely the two male slaves and the two female servants, total 4, and <their> children, whereas the (my) two-thirds is on her one-third.

The only way to make sure Ineksunedjem's future would remain secure was to compensate his first wife and children. And generously so. It is easy to imagine that his children were probably not very pleased when he left their mother for another woman, and since Amunkha already had grandchildren he would have been rather old, and—who knows?—Ineksunedjem very young.

So the children get a large share of the property. (Amunkha only mentions servants, slaves, and the house of his father and mother, but there must have been more to divide of which nothing is said.) Note that in his statement Amunkha first says that he himself entered the house of Ineksunedjem (or was it the house of her father after all?), but all of a sudden she has become "this woman who is in my house today."

He ends his statement with a lame excuse. He would have given his children more, even from the property he had acquired with his second wife, but hey, the Law of Pharaoh, what can you do? A woman—including his second wife—must have her dowry.

> I will give the nine slaves that have fallen to me as my two-thirds with the female citizen Tatjarya to my children, as well as the house of father and mother that is with them. They will not be robbed of anything that I have acquired with their mother. I would have given to them from what I have acquired with the female citizen Ineksunedjem, but Pharaoh, life, prosperity, health, has said: "Give the dowry of any woman to her."

From what we know of ancient Egyptian legal practice we may assume that Amunkha, Ineksunedjem, and Amunkha's sons—who are mentioned by name—were standing in front of the court. In the famous tomb of the vizier Rekhmira of Dynasty 18 (TT 100) we see the tomb owner dispensing justice, comfortably seated in a chair, with forty-two objects in front of him on a mat, which have been interpreted as either papyrus rolls constituting a law book or whips or rods representing the nomes (provinces) of Egypt.

Remaining seated while listening to people forced to stand when making a statement was a very subtle way to show who was in charge here. But there would also be a practical reason. During Amunkha's statement the vizier and the magistrates probably also sat, because this would not be the only case they would hear today.

Then the vizier speaks, and it is clear that he wants to hear from Amunkha's sons themselves what they think of the pension plan devised for their stepmother.

Said by the vizier to the priest (and) overseer of work Ahautynefer and the priest Nebnefer, the children of the god's father Amunkha, who stood before him, the eldest brothers of his children: "What do you say about the statement that the god's father Amunkha has made, your father? Is there truth in (the statement about) these nine slaves of which he has said: 'I gave them to you as my two-thirds to divide with your mother, as well as the house of father and mother?'"

They said with one mouth: "Our father is in the right. They are with us, really."

Said by the vizier: "[And what do you say about] this plan that your father has made for the female citizen Ineksu[nedjem], this (second) wife of his?"

They said: "[. . .] what our father has done. As for what he has done, who could discuss (dispute) it? His things (property) are his. Let him give them [. . .]."

Said by the vizier: "And (what) if she is not his wife at all, but a Syrian [or a Nubi]an, whom he loves, and he gave his things to her, who would (try to) annul what he had done? Give her [the four] slaves [that he acquired] with the female citizen Ineksunedjem and all he acquired with her, saying: 'I give her my two-thirds on top of [h]er one-third, and no son or daughter will discuss (dispute) this plan I made for her today.'"

It is evident that the vizier was trying to get to the bottom of this situation, probably because in his office he had seen family tragedies like these far too often. Strangely enough there is no record of any answer by Amunkha's sons. Apparently living with a Syrian or Nubian woman was frowned upon, although it was probably allowed, and perhaps troublesome when it came to the division of the family property.

So it is time for another aside. This intricate arrangement made by Amunkha may have been standard practice in the elite circles he was moving in, but was it the same for the average citizen, such as those from the village? There is evidence that the village also harbored Canaanites, Libyans, and Hurrians. For instance, the Hurrian Tjer or Tjel (which was the Egyptian way to write Zilli) was married to the woman Aty (not a very Egyptian name either), but they named their daughter Iyneferty (a very Egyptian name), and she married the workman Sennedjem who built TT 1, which housed three generations of dead relatives. But which law would apply if someone in this mixed family were to divorce, for instance?

Back to the case at hand. One gets the impression that Amunkha had discussed the matter with his eldest sons, saying, "Look, this is my pension plan for the woman I love and this is in it for you and your mother. It is a generous plan, so I advise you to accept it." And so they did. All the vizier now had to do was to wrap up the business at hand.

> The vizier said: "Make a copy of what the god's father Amunkha, this god's father who stands before me, has said."
>
> The vizier instructed the priest (and) scribe of the mat Ptahemheb of the court of the temple of Wesermâ'atra Meryamun, life, prosperity, health (Medinet Habu), saying: "Record this decision that I have made on a roll of papyrus in the temple of Wesermâ'atra Meryamun, life, prosperity, health."
>
> And a copy was made for the Great Court of Thebes before many witnesses.

The list of witnesses is impressive indeed, but it is very difficult to decide whether the eighteen lines of subscriptions are not actually just sixteen witnesses in all, as would later become more or less the fixed number of witnesses in demotic contracts ('more or less' because practically anything was possible), or many more, because the subscriptions include two lines, one of which reads "the chiefs of the Medjay (policemen) of

The Tomb," and one cannot be sure whether this means that all chiefs were present but were not mentioned by name (meaning that there were more than sixteen witnesses), or that the names that directly follow this and the other line are actually the chiefs in question. Since the purpose of such a witness list was also to be able to trace a witness if there were to be another court case, these two lines are probably the header.

The people from Deir al-Medina must have faced the same problems, namely the future of the family property and their children, apart from their personal grief. If we look at some of the sources, such as O. Gardiner AG 19, one almost gains the impression that divorce happened rather frequently in the village. It is a small limestone ostracon from the reign of Siptah, containing six lines of very damaged writing. Why this curious little text was written we do not know, although it is probably safe to say that nobody would write this down just for fun. In particular, the mention of Nekhemmut throwing Ese out of the house is spicy in view of the date (reign of Siptah), because in year 25 of Ramesses III both would be imprisoned for questioning (if they were indeed the same people), and by that time Ese was married to the workman Anynakhte (O. Turin N. 57556), who could have been Nekhemmut's son and would not have been pleased with the news (the names of the women are in italics).

[. . .] with [. . .] of Paser. With Amunhotep. He threw out *[N.N.]*. [. . .
] threw out *Wabet* and (?) *Nedjemmut*. Telmontu [thr]ew out *Henutnefer*.
Nekhemmut [threw] out *Ese*. Sawadjy, the drafts[man . . .].

If this Telmontu was the father of Naunakhte's daughter-in-law Hathor, his divorce may have occupied her mind for some time. Then again, the text is dated to the reign of Siptah, so this may be rather too early for her son Neferhotep to already have been married to Hathor.

Sources from Deir al-Medina do hint at a property reshuffle after a divorce, as one would expect. In O. Ashmolean Museum 157 (O. Gardiner 157), for instance, which is dated to the reign of Ramesses VII (1134/32–1126/23 BCE), a Mr. Nakhtmin is seen dividing his property between his sons Nebnakhte and Pentaweret, and for a reason:

Inventory of the things of the workman Nakhtmin, which are in his house after he threw out Wabty, his former wife.

As the text states, this inventory was prompted by Nakhtmin's divorce from his wife, who presumably took her own property and one-third of the conjugal property with her, although this is nowhere stated.

A property division between a man and a woman is also described in O. DeM 239 (Dynasty 19), a limestone ostracon that was found in the Kom Sûd on 19 January 1930. This was a good day for the excavators, who found no fewer than thirty-two ostraca, including several monthly records written by a single scribe. (O. DeM 32–47 were all found on and around this date and all belong to the one-time archive of this scribe, probably Hori.) Opinions as to what O. DeM 239 is actually about vary among a dowry, an inheritance, and a property division following a divorce. The items received by the woman Ese are listed in three columns on the recto and one on the verso. The first column is reserved for bronze items, the word "bronze" written in red ink. Apart from this, Ese also received a bed, a chair, and a coffin, which had apparently been lying in the house somewhere or had been brought into the house when she moved in, and various other items. Why was the statement about Ese's share made for another woman? Probably because this woman wanted to see what Ese had been taking with her. The terminology suggests that this was an enforced property division, in other words, a divorce, so this woman may have been the new wife or a daughter who wanted to know which property (that she would inherit) went where.

> Statement of the engraver Qen to Mrs. Qe[. . .]nakhte, so that she knows
> [all] the things that the female citizen Ese has taken.

Has taken, not received. Are we then to assume that the items taken by Ese represented her one-third share of the conjugal property, or do they also include the goods that she had brought into the house when she married Qen? And would this Qen by any chance be the same man as the engraver mentioned in O. Ashmolean Museum 90 (O. Gardiner 90) from the reign of Ramesses II? There he is seen allocating a considerable number of servants to his sons, meaning that he was not exactly poor. (The same group of servants is mentioned in O. Glasgow D.1925.83 (O. Colin Campbell 17), by the way.) The Deir al-Medina *Who's Who* does not help us here. But these servants were evidently private property.

There were also female servants who were supplied to the village by the state to assist in household chores. In fact, they are rather often listed alongside some workmen, suggesting that they bunked at some specific place together, and that their task would have been to do the cooking. But what if these were pretty servants not unwilling to have sex? In that case, some of the wives of the workmen would not have been very happy when their men were at work in one of the valleys, attended by these servants.

There is one ostracon describing a very curious case, because the sanction involved was impalement, which was not an everyday punishment. The text dates from year 66 of Ramesses II. O. Cairo CG 25237 was published in 1997 by Benedict Davies and Jaana Toivari.

Year 66, third month of the *akhet* season, day 4. On this day the arrival of the scribe Inpuemheb, Neferhotep, the [chief] of police Nakhtmin, and the chief of police [. . . and they said] to the chief workman Neferhotep: "So he says, [namely N.N. (a higher authority): 'Let] one bring the female slaves to the riverbank. What is this forced entry of the female slaves? [. . .]. I will dispute about them to Pharaoh, life, prosperity, health.'" And the chief workman Neferhotep said [to the agents]: "As far as the female slaves are concerned, my share from Penamun son of Baky, it belongs to Pharaoh, life, prosperity, health, my Good Lord, life, prosperity, health."

The female slave Pa'anmahu said <to> the agents: "Let one give me a piece of clothing for his backside." But <one of> their [superiors (?)] said: "I will not give <it> to her."

Oath of the Lord, life, prosperity, health, that the workman Baky took: "As Amun endures, as the Ruler endures, life, prosperity, health, whose manifestation is worse than death, if I am found out, the female slave having done work for me, he (I) will be struck down and put on a stick."

The fact that one of the female slaves talks back to the authorities, asking for some clothing for "his" backside, may be telling. The phrase occurs in other places, such as in O. BM EA 65936 (O. Nash 6), as described in chapter 15, "Protecting Your Daughter's Rights," where it seems to denote a wife taking proper care of her husband. The statement by the chief workman Neferhotep is also puzzling, although it is clear that he is trying to rid himself of any responsibility for the matter as quickly as possible. It may well be that what was read by the editors as 'my share' is actually 'this share,' which is also suggested by the fact that it is the workman Baky who has to take an official oath. Whatever the work allegedly done by the female slave was, it was apparently sufficient to warrant a death penalty. One wonders what was at stake here, because these female slaves were there precisely to work for the workmen, and the appropriation of her services would hardly have called for severe punishment. Was it about illicit sex with state property? Somehow it is hard to believe that the Egyptian authorities would not have foreseen scenarios such as this, and come to live with them.

If we look at some papyri from Milan, however, namely P. Milan RAN E 0.9.40126, 0.9.40127, and 0.9.40128 from the reign of Ramesses IX, which were only published very recently by Demarée, there may have been something fishy about the events in O. Cairo CG 25237 after all. The Milan texts were published without the fragments from the same papyrus kept in Turin, because until recently the papyrus collection from the Museo Egizio had been put under lock and key for an indefinite period by the person(s) responsible. Fortunately this has changed, so that we can now entertain serious thoughts about opening up the vast Turin collection of Deir al-Medina papyri online.

The Milan fragments constitute a run-of-the-mill journal of the necropolis, listing deliveries and other events, such as sex. What makes this journal interesting is that it mentions various people who would be involved in the infamous tomb robberies some years later. This is the translation from the original publication:

> Charge concerning the saying that (one) did that the scribe of the Necropolis Hori took out the owners of the tomb and he set fire in (it).
>
> Charge concerning the saying that (one) did (about) the affair of the servant-woman, to wit: the daughter of the servant-woman of Nessuseramun, she has borne (a baby) to him.
>
> Charge concerning the saying that the district scribe Wennefer did that the wife of Anhotep had sex with the three children/sons of the scribe Hori son of Pentawere and had sex with the scribe of the Necropolis Hori.
>
> Charge concerning the saying that workman Tosheri did that the deputy Khonsu had sex with a male (?) woman.

Again we get a glimpse of what ancient Egypt was like in real life. Chucking out mummies from a tomb and setting fire to it by an official scribe of The Tomb sounds like desecration, although one would like to know whether Hori did it for reasons of his own or as a state official. In either case, people clearly did not approve. The rest is all about sex. A servant girl was impregnated by her (temporary) owner; the wife of Anhotep was so infatuated with the scribal profession that she decided to try a few men associated with this office; and then someone had sex with a male (?) woman? The latter expression is not exactly the same as the expression for 'woman with a man' that occurs more often in the sources. The word used here can indeed be translated as 'male,' which raises some disconcerting questions. However, where there are people there will be sex in one way or another. Some of the workmen undoubtedly had sex with women of ill repute (although even this is just in the eye of the beholder. I once lived in a neighborhood where there were many whores—yes, that is what they are called in real life—and they were generally the nicest and wisest people I ever met, once you got to know them). We can probably safely dismiss the possibility that there were transgender persons in Deir al-Medina—meaning men born as men but identifying as women, who were then rebuilt to become women—but could it be that some men felt more like a woman than a man and acted on this, even if they still had a penis? Then again, the word translated here as 'male' was still used in an abnormal hieratic papyrus from year 6 of Taharqa (c. 685 BCE), where it stands in clear opposition with the generic word for 'woman.' So in the end this expression may simply mean 'woman with a man' after all, which was of course noted by the editor.

But we were actually talking about the property division between a husband and his wife. There is even an ostracon explaining why this division into one-third and two-thirds occurs all the time. This is O. DeM 764, a limestone ostracon of 10 × 11.5 cm blackened by fire, which was hesitatingly described as a will in the original publication. But it actually looks more like a note describing customary law.

> If there are young children, make the things as three parts: one for the children, one for the man, and one for the woman. And the one who takes care of the children, give him the two-thirds of all things, whereas the one-third is for the woman.

It is touching to see how the children come first in this otherwise rather dry note, although apparently taking care of the children meant making sure they were materially provided for (the man's task) and educated if they were boys, which rather sells short the all-important role played by the mother. The editor chose to interpret this text as a draft of a man drawing up his own will, the man and woman mentioned being some of the adult children of the testator who would take care of the younger children. In that case one would have expected these adult children to have been either mentioned by name or referred to as 'your (my) son' and 'your (my) daughter,' respectively. It looks more like an excerpt from a law book of some sort, or a note describing what people in the village normally would do if there was a divorce.

A rather enigmatic division is seen in O. Ashmolean Museum 55 (O. Gardiner 55), a limestone ostracon written on both sides. The text on the recto is largely effaced, but enough remains to see that it is a list of (household) items, including one wooden footstool and five doors (precious commodities). On the verso an anonymous speaker says they belong to his wife and children. These may be the items that were presumably divided by 'their' father and mother when they divorced and then passed on to the speaker or his wife, or so it seems.

> As far as the things that he has given are concerned, (they are) the two-thirds that were given to me when he made a division (of property) with their mother. Her share is now with her herself. As for all things, all of them that are in my house, they are for my wife and her children. After all, she brought it in . . . , me having done it to . . . to . . .

This is a very confusing text, because there are multiple ways to (try to) explain it, but all parties involved remain anonymous, so we are really in the dark. There is clearly a division of property involved between a husband and wife, but who were they? The speaker's father and mother, the speaker himself, or the father and mother of the speaker's wife? Even if he states that the property was given to him, this does not necessarily mean that it was his property. For this, one only has to remind oneself of the division of the inheritance of Naunakhte in P. DeM 23 and 25, in which Naunakhte's daughter Wasetnakhte is twice represented by her husband Nebnakhte (see chapter 7, "A Day in the Life of Menatnakhte"). This would also be the easiest explanation of the slightly curious clause, "After all, she brought it in."

The fact that the text refers to "their mother" likewise does not rule out that the division of the property took place between his own father and mother. O. Ashmolean Museum 55 is the unofficial protocol of his oral statement, and we cannot exclude the possibility that the speaker said "my mother," which the scribe automatically recorded as "their mother" because he knew the children's brothers and sisters that had been involved in the case. Finally, we can also not rule out that "their mother" was actually the speaker's first wife, and that he wanted to make sure that the two-thirds were firmly connected with his second wife. Even the use of the pronoun "he" is problematic, because it could also refer to the speaker himself. These texts can be confusing.

The people of Deir al-Medina often took an official Oath of the Lord, and almost invariably, when they got to the sanctions that would be imposed if they did not abide by their oath, they would have said: "I will be liable to a hundred blows of the stick." But this would be rendered by the scribe as: "He will be liable to a hundred blows of the stick" (e.g., O. Bodleian Library Eg. Inscr. 253 and P. Ashmolean Museum 1945.97). So in sources from Deir al-Medina the 'I' is sometimes a 'he' and vice versa. This is truly a text full of pitfalls, which is precisely one of the greatest charms Deir al-Medina has to offer us. It makes one wonder forever.

Another strange case is described in O. UC 19614, a limestone ostracon written on two sides. It is dated to year 2 of Sethnakhte (1186/85–1183/82 BCE). The reason for including it here is that—as so often—after reading it, we are left with countless questions rather than answers. The beginning of the text, which looks like the beginning of an official protocol, is clearly about a divorce.

> Year 2, third month of the *shemu* season, day 24 of King Weserkhara Setepenra (Sethnakhte), life, prosperity, health. <On this day> the throwing out of the female citizen Hel that Hesysunebef did.

We also know this couple from P. BM EA 10055 (P. Salt 124) recto col. II *l*. 3 from the reign of Siptah, where it is stated that the infamous ladykiller Paneb (see chapter 4, "Some Husband") had had sex with Hel, who was then Hesysunebef's wife, and also with other women, including Hel's daughter Webekhet. But if we can trust the date assigned to P. Salt

124 (reign of Siptah), the couple surprisingly stayed together till year 2 of Sethnakhte, the first king of Dynasty 20.

But then the text shifts to an anonymous speaker ("I"), who may be Hesysunebef himself—which would create a whole range of problems, however—or someone else who was taking care of Hel after her divorce. This may of course have been done out of the kindness of his heart, but could also be because the speaker was looking at receiving part of Hel's inheritance.

> I spent three years giving her one oipe of emmer for every single month, which makes nine sacks. She gave me a piece of *mer* cloth, saying: "Take it to the riverbank market." One wanted to buy it from me for one oipe of emmer corn and I handed it over, but it was rejected, with the words: "No good!" So I told her likewise, saying: "It was rejected." She then gave it to me.
>
> I had one sack of emmer corn taken to her through Hay son of Sawadjy. Given to her by Nubemwesekhet: one oipe. Given to her by Taâtmerut, her daughter: one oipe. Total one sack and two oipe for the *mer* cloth.

So what this anonymous man is saying here is that he took care of Mrs. Hel for three years in a row, but the connection with the cloth he received to sell on the market is unclear. Was it given to him to buy emmer corn for Hel? In any case, no buyer was interested, because the quality of the cloth was bad. In the end Hel gave the cloth to her anonymous helper, who had some emmer corn brought to her in return, at least six times more valuable than the cloth itself.

And what if this man was Hesysunebef, her former husband? In that case we would be forced to conclude that at least some marriages may have included an agreement about the payment of alimony. In the much later abnormal hieratic marital property arrangements, such as P. Louvre E 7846 and 7849, in the case of a divorce the woman would receive two deben of silver, fifty sacks of emmer corn, all or some of the property acquired during the marriage, and a share of, or even the entire property of, father and mother belonging to the children. A generous agreement, although in case of adultery by the woman she would receive nothing. And that is exactly the crime that Hel had committed, according to P. Salt 124. Who wants to pay alimony to a wife who deceived you with another man? Then again, we often do not know why the men from Deir al-Medina threw their wives out of the house. For all we know, the simple fact that the men were often away working on the royal tomb created the opportunity for women who were not sexually satisfied and wanted to do something about it. Hormones are quirky things.

Another case of alimony may be hinted at in O. Glasgow D.1925.66 (O. Colin Campbell 1), in which a man lists an incredible amount of commodities all delivered to a woman through policemen. It is equally possible, however, that the woman was a widow supported by a relative (as in the case of Naunakhte). It is clear that the man and the woman did not live together, because the items were all brought to her house and appear to be an annual income. This is what the man says he sent to her (we will skip some of the items that resist translation): *ash* liquid, bread (in many varieties), milk, fish, beans, *heqeq* fruit, a jar of (alcoholic) *seremet*, salt, cakes, beer, vegetables, and yarn. The real message comes at the end (on the verso) of this long list spanning nineteen lines (on the recto):

> It belongs to this year, but you still do not let (yourself) be satisfied with them (?).

Although this is far-fetched, because it refers to material from the Late Period, one could also suppose that in Deir al-Medina an official marriage, marked by entering the house of your father-in-law, also brought with it the obligation to support your wife materially (as one should expect). In the Late Period demotic contracts this support is called *aq hebes* 'food and clothing' (the demotic Teaching of Ankhsheshonqy, for instance, sternly warns against supplying this to the wife all at once, and it is left to the reader to decide why this was so). If this is also what we have here, we are talking about another age-old problem: women pestering their husbands because the woman next door bought new shoes and the wife did not. It must have happened at Deir al-Medina all the time, but the sources do not corroborate this. Perhaps the woman next door had indeed received more this year and had not stopped telling her neighbor about it.

14

Women Causing Trouble

part from considering things from a purely legal or philological perspective (although the first actually presupposes that the second was done correctly), it would be interesting to know how the Deir al-Medina men themselves—rather hot-blooded people who seemingly sued each other all the time over trifles—viewed their own behavior and the behavior of their women. Did they all share the same norms and values? (Probably not.) Did they, the alpha dogs in the village hierarchy (apart from the scribes and the chief workmen), come first, and their wives, sisters, daughters, and mothers only second? And would their norms and values be in line with the popular literary genre of the *sebayt* or 'teaching'?

The Maxims of Ptahhotep, for instance, named after the vizier who served under King Isesy of Dynasty 5 (twenty-fourth century BCE), contain some sound advice about the treatment of women.

> When you do well, establish your house, love your wife with zest.
> Fill her stomach, clothe her back, ointment is a remedy for her body.
> Make her heart glad as long as you live.
> She is a fertile field that is of use to its master.
> Do not dispute with her in a law court (and) keep her from power, restrain her.
> Her eye is her storm when she gazes.
> Keep her in your house.
> If you push her back, then watch the tears!
> Her vagina is one of the ways she acts.
> What she brings about is a canal to be made for her.

But that is the theory. There is one very interesting ostracon from Glasgow that seems to show that men—or at least the man in question—were not very keen on losing face in front of their friends due to the behavior of a woman, who in this particular case may well have intended to embarrass him to begin with. O. Glasgow D.1925.87 (O. Colin Campbell 21) could be described as an early case of machismo.

> The priest Weserhat says to my (his) sister Resty. I have witnessed the argumentative behavior of (the woman) Iupy toward me (when I was) among my friends. What about this giving me straw . . . at the [. . .], because I have no storehouse? (. . .) Harumph, I will take her on as well. She displayed (some) argumentative behavior (when I was) among my friends.

This translation is admittedly a totally over-the-top rendering of a very difficult text, although the gist seems to be that the writer of the letter was sitting with his friends near some building, no doubt having a beer or two, and there came the woman (or girl) Ipuy with a load of straw, depositing it right where the men were sitting, saying, "Look, I would have been happy to deliver this load at your storehouse, but you don't have one, do you?" Ouch!

Still, looking at Ptahhotep's teaching from a male point of view, a woman could apparently cause much trouble, and women knew how to use this to their advantage, which is no surprise in a village where people practically lived on top of each other and husbands could be away on duty for days on end. We must also keep in mind that the women from Deir al-Medina were human too, meaning that the village would have housed demons and angels and everything in between.

The village has left us with some copies of the Wisdom of Any, for instance, supposedly composed in Dynasty 18 at the court of Queen Nefertari, who was revered in the village as the mother of the patron god Amunhotep I. The text has a lot to say about respect for motherhood, for instance, and some of Any's maxims could have been written with Naunakhte in mind.

> Give back plentifully the bread that your mother gave you. Support her the way she supported you.

This is followed by a solid piece of advice about the afterlife of mom and dad. It just about sums up the obligations children had to their parents: be their pension plan and make sure they will be provided for in the afterlife.

> Pour out libation water for your father and mother resting in the valley of death.

And even Any had something to say about women causing trouble. This lecture was addressed to his son. He knew—as any father knows—that young people in love do stupid things.

> Push away the woman with a bad reputation in your town. Do not eye her as she walks by. Do not try to have sex with her.

One assumes that Any would have seen and met more than enough people who did not fit the bill. Still, if the Wisdom of Any was copied in the village, does this mean people read it? It would probably be part and parcel of the training of new scribes, who had to copy parts of it over and over again. But what one really would like to know is, Did they read aloud what they had just written down and *think* about it? Of course, the teachers in ancient Egypt had ways to make students pay attention. One of the maxims from the ancient Egyptian wisdom literature states that the ear of a student was on his back. Teachers were generally armed with a stick.

There is also a didactic text that appears to be a product of the village itself. This is known as the Prohibitions. It was published recently by the Danish Egyptologist Frederik Hagen (A 7, 10 and 11).

> Do not take a wife who is more powerful than you, so that you will not [...] the heart (?).
> Do not be disrespectful to a man or a woman when they are old, so that they will not [...] you when your old age has come.
> Do not satisfy (just) yourself, when your mother is in need.

The author is unknown. It could have been any scribe. The scribe Amunnakhte son of Ipuy, for instance, is known to be the author of his own teaching, which was named after him.

A definite case of tension within a marriage is described in O. UC 39619 (O. Petrie 18), which has been dated to between year 7 of Ramesses IV and year 7 of Ramesses VII. When Gardiner made a facsimile of the hieratic in 1936, large parts of the text were already illegible. This is presumably a case put before the local court. Although no reference is made to an oath in connection with a divorce, it is hard to see how the workman Amunpahapy—without doubt the same man as one of the members of the local court who listened to the statement by Naunakhte about her inheritance—and his wife would have stayed together after this.

[Year] 7, fourth month of the *shemu* season, day 11. On this day [a statement] was made by the workman Amunpahapy and the female citizen Tapa[. . .]. He said:

"As for me, the illness came to me. [. . .] I said to my sister (wife): 'Do [look after (?)] my things.' But she went out to the field and I spent one month living on my own. She received the *daiu* garment that Pharaoh, life, prosperity, health, had given me. She stole it. And she [. . .], while I was sitting there. But they are not mine. She has not done good to me. The workman Amunwa, my [. . .] son, did good to me when I was weak. His son [Nekhemmut], my [grandson]. As for all my things and likewise the burial place, any place of my [father (?) . . .] likewise [. . .] of mine, they are for Nekhemmut, my [. . .]." He made [. . .].

She took an Oath of the Lord, life, prosperity, health, saying: "I will not go near (?) the house and likewise the things [. . . of the workman] Amunpahapy. If I go near (?) the house of [the workman Amunpahapy I] will be under a hundred blows of the stick [and I will be deprived of] any property of my father."

He made her take the Oath of the Lord, life, prosperity, health, saying: "I for my part will not go near (?) the draftsman Amunhotep."

The gist seems clear. When the workman Amunpahapy was ill he expected his wife, called 'sister' as was so often the case, to take care of him, but instead she went away for a month. If we can trust the available transcription on this passage—the ink is in a dreadful condition—the suggestion is made by Amunpahapy that his wife ate with another man, which may be understood to refer to some form of cohabitation or even marriage.

The phrase could therefore also be a circumspect way to say that she had been unfaithful to him, apart from being a very neglectful wife and a thief of state property. The last detail was neatly added to show the court what kind of person she really was. It was his son Amunwa who had cared for him, presumably together with his grandson Nekhemmut, and Amunpahapy therefore decides that his inheritance will go to Nekhemmut.

His (former) wife has to swear an oath that she will not stake any claim, literally: "I will not go near (?) the house and likewise the things [. . . of the workman] Amunpahapy," and in return her (former) husband Amunpahapy will not take steps against the draftsman Amunhotep, who may have been the man his wife had eaten (slept) with. Or is this last line also part of the oath taken by his wife? The source is—as always—ambiguous. In any case, it is clear that Amunpahapy's wife had forfeited her one-third of the conjugal property because of her neglect, and this was now officially acknowledged before the court.

Some Deir al-Medina women were definitely sleeping around—although people often forget that this also requires a (married) man to sleep around with—and sometimes for good reasons. A stupid man in love, for instance. O. DeM 439 was found in the Grand Puits on 15 April 1949, together with forty other ostraca from Dynasties 19–20 (which supports the hypothesis that the site of the main administrative building was cleared out to build a Ptolemaic temple there). This was a lucky day, because in the weeks before and after, the excavators typically found nothing more than just a handful of ostraca each day. O. DeM 439 is a heated argument on limestone between a man and a woman, in which the woman warns the man about his wife sleeping around—on the verso, or the back of the text, but we have to remember that with ostraca the terms 'recto' (front) and 'verso' (back) are actually assigned by the editor, and need not represent the actual order of writing. (Many authors use 'obverse' for 'recto' and 'reverse' for 'verso,' reserving the terms 'recto' and 'verso' for papyri.)

O. DeM 439 was then sent to the man, whose name is at the bottom of the text on the recto, which also contains his answer. In view of the volatile content of the woman's message it is hoped that it was only seen by the sender and the addressee, but this would imply that the sender—a woman who had an interest in either protecting the man or damaging his wife's reputation—could write (and some undoubtedly could). She could of course also have dictated her message to a literate neighbor or relative, in which case the whole village would know about this incident within minutes. What she had to say was not particularly nice.

> As for me, did I not take you (aside) to say: "Look at the things you have done [to] your wife?" And to say: "You are blind as far as she is concerned?" You held me back because of (?) your deafness to the crime, (which is) an abomination of Montu. Look, I will make you see these sexual adventures that your wife had at your cost.

(The grammar of this text was carefully dissected by Borghouts in his full edition of O. DeM 439, in *Revue d'Egyptologie* 33 (1981), p. 11*ff*. Our translation deviates from his at several points in the text.)

For the man, this helpful letter blaming his own stupidity as the reason for his wife's adultery may have come as a nasty surprise. The crucial word is *beta*, which was rendered as 'criminal' and 'misdeed of (the god) Horus (!)' in previous editions of the text. But exactly the same word occurs in abnormal hieratic marital property arrangements from the sixth century BCE, such as P. Louvre E 7846 and 7849, where it is used to describe adultery as "the great crime *(beta)* that is (generally) found in a woman." Upon reading this note the reader probably had a fit, but he did respond.

> But this is not my wife at all. So is she my wife? When she was done saying what she had to say, she went out and left the door open.

One wonders whether the mention of the door being left open is not simply village lingo for the woman being active on the external sex market again, in much the same way as the expression used for the marriage ceremony (which according to some authors did not exist in the village), *aq er per* 'to enter the house,' may have been used used to refer to sex with another man's wife. The term does refer to sex in Egyptian love poetry, which is a jungle of seemingly innocent terms used to describe lust, temptation, and sex.

We do not know the sender or the addressee, but it is difficult to believe that the matter ended here. The marriage, however, probably did. In one case, sex before marriage appears to have prompted the local court to issue a restraining order, although from the looks of it this did not have much effect. Sex can of course be a very disruptive force in a relationship, as one unfortunate anonymous Deir al-Medina workman found out to his dismay when he stumbled on his future bride in bed with another man. He then probably went straight to the local court to complain that this should not be allowed, because he had brought or was planning to bring a "bundle" to the house of his future father-in-law. But instead of showing him some sympathy the magistrates of the court had him flogged, which may be because the accused—the workman Merysakhmet—was the son of a prominent villager.

P. DeM 27 consists of numerous fragments, but it seems that the top and bottom are almost complete. One would, however, have expected to see a dating and a list of the people who made up this court at the beginning of the text. Still, we may be sure that the chief workman Inherkha and the scribe Amunnakhte son of Ipuy acted as judges on this day.

> [As for me, I am] a follower of Amuneminet, a soldier of the crew. I brought a bundle to the house of Payom, making his daughter as a wife. As for me, I spent the night in the house of my father and (then) went and carried (it) to his house. I found the workman Merysakhmet son of Menna while he was sleeping with my wife(-to-be) in the fourth month of the *shemu* season, day 4. I went out and told the magistrates, and the magistrates gave me a hundred strokes with the stick, saying: "What is it you said?" And the chief workman Inherkha said: "What is this giving him a hundred strokes of the stick? [One person] carries a bundle and the other has sex. It is a great crime that the magistrates have committed."

Whether Inherkha—a chief workman—intended the words "great crime" as a pun is uncertain, but it is perhaps not a coincidence that the phrase *beta aâ* 'great crime' occurs in the much later abnormal hieratic marital property arrangements to refer to adultery by the wife. The adultery committed by Payom's daughter did not in fact concern the court (note that she is not even mentioned by name in the record, and as so often one wonders whether this was because she was a mere woman), so how the affair was handled at the household end we do not know, although we may be sure that some very explicit words were exchanged between the unfortunate husband-to-be, Merysakhmet, and Payom's daughter.

We do not know whether the engagement was annulled, but one would expect it. Still, her crime—if that really is what it was (she may actually have loved Merysakhmet and was not looking forward to an arranged marriage with 'our' workman)—consisted of sleeping with another man, but technically this may have happened *before* her future husband had brought the "bundle." Nonetheless, he clearly felt that he had the right to complain to the court. We may be sure, however, that she would be the talk of the town for some time to come.

The text continues on the verso, describing the next stage in the affair, because in spite of his oath not to speak to her again Merysakhmet somehow found the time to get Payom's daughter pregnant (which is of course possible without talking). Apparently the terrible sanction if he did had not been enough to scare him (or her) off, and there is no indication that he was mutilated and sent off to a border region.

This time his father, Menna, felt that Merysakhmet had gone too far, so he himself filed a complaint in court. There is probably also a reason why in another text (O. Oriental Institute Museum 12074) he refers to his son as a "wild one." This is how the case of Merysakhmet and Payom's daughter ended. Once again note how the scribe refers to Payom's daughter without mentioning her name.

> The scribe Amunnakhte made him (Merysakhmet) swear an Oath of the Lord, life, prosperity, health, saying: "As Amun endures, as the Ruler endures, life, prosperity, health. If I talk to the wife (again), his (my) nose and ears will be cut off and he (I) will be sent to the land of Kush."
>
> But he went again and he made her pregnant. The workman Menna, his father, (then) placed him before the magistrates. The scribe Amunnakhte made him swear an Oath of the Lord, life, prosperity, health, saying: "If I go to the place where the daughter of Payom is, he (I) will be assigned to cutting stones at the mountain of Elephantine. [. . .] Panefer."
>
> The magistrates placed (text ends here).

With some imagination we may view the verdict of the court as a restraining order, but Merysakhmet was indeed a wild one and had trouble reigning in his hormones. So he made Payom's daughter pregnant after all. The record does not show whether Payom's daughter did have a baby or not but, if she did and if she married the anonymous workman (or was this the Panefer mentioned at the end?), everybody in the village would know who the father was. Not the ideal start to a marriage.

Merysakhmet son of Menna would cause trouble in the village on more than one occasion. In year 4 of Ramesses IV or V he tried to appropriate part of a chapel that had been rebuilt by the workman Qenna (claiming that he had had a divine manifestion—a dream—telling him that part of this chapel was his), who very wisely sought refuge with the divine oracle. The oracle decided in favor of Qenna. The end of the whole affair is recorded in two papyri—P. Kiseleff 1–2—that are now in Würzburg, still awaiting publication even though they have been known, and displayed in the local museum, for many years. (There should be a rule saying that authors can publish a text, but that their right to do so expires after five years unless they have some results to show. Claiming texts and not doing anything with them for thirty years—yes, this happens in Egyptology—stretches the limits of scientific integrity.) But we were talking about the hot-blooded Merysakhmet.

Again, the Swiss excavations in the Valley of the Kings have added new evidence to his file. And this time Merysakhmet got the beating that he deserved, even if not all parts of this text (O. KV 18/6.882) are readily understood.

> Chisel of the left side. The scribe Amunnakhte and the chief workman Kha found that one chisel was missing. [. . .] said to me: "Make yourself scarce from here. Pairy (Merysakhmet) son of Menna took it there. And Nes[. . .] hole (?) in his head. And he spent the day there without success."
>
> One established for him a court and [. . .]: "The scribe Amunnakhte, the agent of these chisels, is in the right." He (probably Merysakhmet) remained silent and did not speak with [. . .] Anynakhte. He (Merysakhmet's father, Menna) made much noise about the crime committed by his son. Khaemipet was in the wrong [. . .] and one imposed an Oath of the Lord, life, prosperity, health, on him not to [. . .] without success. One gave Pairy (Merysakhmet) a hundred strokes, saying: "Now [. . .] the crime for you." So one said to him.

Once again a spicy case involving Merysakhmet. It seems that he had taken someone else's chisel, who was then sent after him to retrieve it, but was probably beaten with it by Merysakhmet. One supposes that one of the two men mentioned was actually this unfortunate workman, so the role of the man who was found in the wrong becomes unclear. But in the end Merysakhmet got what he deserved, probably witnessed by the men, women, and children of the village.

If passionate women were a problem in marriage, so was a frigid or loveless one, and there are cases where men and women divorce because of a severe lack of love. To quote once again the much later abnormal hieratic marital property settlements: the apparently legally justified reasons for a divorce listed by the future husband in his statement to his father-in-law when he came to collect his bride were in fact hating his wife or loving another woman more than her (e.g., P. Louvre E 7846). This clause also occurs in demotic documents.

One such case is described in O. Cairo CG 25227. It was written in Dynasty 19, or perhaps more specifically in the reign of Amunmessu. The French excavator Auguste Mariette stated that it was from Abydos, but the names mentioned in it are clearly all from Deir al-Medina, where he excavated in 1862 (meaning that the boxes containing his finds were perhaps mislabeled at some stage). The ostracon contains several cases that were brought before the local court.

On the verso there is this case about a woman—probably a wife—who refuses to have sex with her husband. There is no photograph of the text but, if we rely on the transcription from Černý's *Notebooks*, the text on the verso is not only broken, but also a bit of a mess at specific spots. The layout of the text suggests that this is a shorthand version of the protocol that was to be worked into a court record later. The proceedings on this day were supposedly aimed at the question of whether the workman Kasa had divorced his wife or not.

> [. . .] before the court, before the chief workman Neferhotep. (. . .) Cause that an Oath <of the Lord, life, prosperity, health>, is taken about the woman.
>
> [. . .] Oath of the Lord, life, prosperity, health: "As Amun endures, as the Ruler endures, [I made this wo]man as a wife, but she does not love me and she does not have sex." (. . .) [. . .] Neferhotep to Kasa: "So did you throw [her] out [or did you] stay with her?"
>
> Oath of the Lord, life, prosperity, health. He said: "As Amun endures, as the Ruler endures, I did not stay with her."

Sometimes, one would very much like to think that the question to the divine oracle on O. IFAO 199 was submitted by the workman Kasa (although most probably it was not) about his frigid (or angry) wife: "Will she give in?"

Interestingly, the rather bland statement by Kasa that his wife does not love him and that she refuses to have sex—which is how we choose to interpret it—is viewed by other authors as the exact opposite, namely the denial of illicit sex, which can be a bit confusing to non-Egyptologists. But this comes with the territory. Phrases are often ambiguous, although in this specific case it is very hard to see how one could interpret what looks like the language spoken by a workman, "She does not love. She does not have sex," differently. This is a long way away from some modern trends in describing what sex was about in Deir al-Medina. Hence one may come across statements such as this:

> On a more general level, one may ask whether male and female roles in the actual sexual interaction were strictly defined, and whether such roles belonged within the dynamics of gender hierarchy. Answers to such questions are not found in the non-literary text references, however.

There are really easier ways to say: "I do not have a clue what I do not want to say." Also, most people tend to change what role definitions they may have almost per millisecond while having sex. Would that have been so different for an ancient Egyptian woman committing adultery, with all the concomitant excitement involved? Not being caught, for instance? Authors should really not be allowed to describe (perhaps illicit) sex in Deir al-Medina as follows:

> The deviant act thus may have been committed primarily for the purpose of achieving pleasure by at least one of the interacting parties, possibly by both.

Maybe the woman was just horny or in love. Or both. In this book the verb *nek* is politely translated as 'to have sex,' although the better translation is the four-letter word, because that is what the hieratic writing implies, just as we would understand it today. The simplicity (and probably age) of the word—sounding uncannily familiar to Dutch, where the verb stem is *neuk*—just two one-letter signs, an unknown vowel, and the determinative, an erect penis, leaves little other choice. The ancient Egyptians probably became sexually active at a much earlier age than our children today. Sex was a part of everyday life. The quotes cited above are in fact one of the really serious flaws of academic writing, creating a fog of words saying nothing.

It is unknown whether the husband would always have to take a formal oath if he wanted to divorce his wife, but there are enough instances to prove that some men did. But that is strange. If a divorce required a formal act, one would expect the marriage itself to require the same. Still, the generally accepted opinion appears to be that the marriage did not come with any formal act, which is very hard to believe.

From P. BM EA 10416 (P. Salt 131) we may see that this oath to divorce a woman was actually very important and—if we understand this difficult text correctly—the expected thing to do. This text is dated to late Dynasty 20. It is about an affair between a married man and an unmarried woman, and some immediate relatives were not very amused by this. So an angry mob set out to do something about it.

> (. . .) Your people were on the move, their old and young, both men and women, in the evening. They left saying: "We will beat her up together with her people." [It] was the steward who told them: "But why are you going [to the house] of my scribe to beat up my people? She will not be there." And he resisted them and told them: "Is it your man who will be found there? My envoy told me: 'Him whom we will find we will beat up.' So please tell me." This he said to them, and they answered back at him: "He has been sleeping with that woman for eight full months until this day, although he is not (her) husband. Were he her husband, would he not have sworn this oath about this (?) woman? (. . .) Why did you receive him to sleep with him repeatedly? [Are you] looking for partners to argue with? (. . .) If the heart of that man is after you, then let [him] enter the court together with his wife and let [him] swear an oath and return to your house."

So all the adulterous man would have to do was to file for divorce in court, wrap things up financially with his former wife, and go and live happily with his new wife. So why did he not simply do this?

Before we start developing thoughts about the women of Deir al-Medina being either too passionate or not at all, however, we should remember that it takes two to tango. If some women had sex outside marriage, they may have had good reasons for doing it. Still, people would find out and partners would not be happy.

P. DeM 26 is a record of a large number of incidents and court cases that was clearly meant to be archived or be sent on to higher authorities. It looks like the report on the present local situation that a political officer at any embassy would send to his government. The provenance of P. DeM 26 is unknown, which is a shame, because both Černý and the French Egyptologist Yvan Koenig thought that it could belong to Naunakhte's papers (which would be very hard to explain, unless it was written by the old scribe Qenhirkhopshef, which it is definitely not). The text consists of two large fragments: A, measuring 22.5 × 18.5 cm, and B, measuring 16.5 × 13.5 cm; there are also some additional unplaced fragments. The dating is a mystery, with guesses ranging from Dynasty 19 and Dynasty 20 to year 16 of Ramesses III. This is strange, because the text mentions the chief workman Hay and many workmen and other officials. If the experts disagree to this extent, one should probably not venture one's own opinion, although some of the people encountered in this papyrus are clearly only known from Dynasty 20 sources.

The largest part of the text is written in black ink, but curiously the first line of the verso of fragment B is in red, whereas the other lines are all in black. The record by the scribe is succinct:

> [. . .] She said to him: "You have slept with a wife with a husband in the place of loading and branding (?)." And he said to her: "[. . . lo]aded. You should recognize it." He said: "My brand is on it." And I recog[nized it].

A text can hardly be more obscure than this (although much of the text is broken away), and the rest is more obscure still. It may refer to another case of adultery, but it was recorded by the scribe in a way that makes it hard to follow, although the crudeness of the remarks made by the man seeps through. The use of the words "loaded" and "brand" almost suggests that he had not had sex in a while, and then a woman passed by who had not either, but was willing to catch up right there and then. It would be very nice if someone would make a study of the village street language. Deir al-Medina's court records would be the place to start.

Again, there are many questions. Why this single line in red and—if this report was to be sent on to higher authorities—why would the vizier, for instance, have to know who slept with whom in the village? Of course text B is only a fragment. The parties involved were most likely mentioned in the missing part (as was the outcome of this conflict), but still, the red ink, obviously used to highlight the passage, is a mystery.

Documents such as P. DeM 26 and P. Salt 124, listing all kinds of small and large crimes and offenses, are generally great fun. For one thing, they do much to balance the picture that many people have of ancient Egypt, thinking the ancient Egyptians walked around citing the Maxims of Any all the time in between their prayers to the gods. No. These people worked, loved, hated, and died just like we do. They could be vulgar.

The next papyrus will take us to Elephantine under Ramesses V. Although it seems to fall outside the scope of this book, it is included because it shows that corruption, theft, and adultery occurred not just in the village but probably throughout Egypt. The first really useful translation of the text was by Peet—the same who provided a readable account of the famous Tomb Robberies Papyri—in the *Journal of Egyptian Archaeology* 10, which was an improvement on the first translation by the German scholar Wilhelm Spiegelberg. (Spiegelberg is mostly known for his utterly brilliant work in demotic studies, but he started his career with Deir al-Medina.) Peet had planned a transcription of the hieratic text into hieroglyphs as well, but this never saw the light of day. For this we had to wait till the publication of Gardiner's *Ramesside Administrative Documents* (1948).

The text involved is P. Turin Cat. 1887, which is better known as the Turin Indictment Papyrus. It is a mystery why nobody has ever thought of publishing a new edition of the text, which somehow tells the real story behind the stone monuments of these proud New Kingdom officials displayed in museums all over the world. Although women play a very minor role in this text, and seemingly only as victims (and very badly hurt victims at that), it is noteworthy that the scribe who wrote this text included them. He may have decided to do this to underline the lack of moral fiber of the accused.

In this papyrus, adultery and an abortion, or at the very least a consciously induced miscarriage, occur side by side with the stealing and subsequent selling of some Mnevis calves. The latter was a capital offense, one should assume, even if this happened as far south as Elephantine and not in Heliopolis in the north, home of the sacred Mnevis bull.

The reports against the priest Penanuqet aka Sed of the temple of Khnum.

Complaint (charge) about the black cow in his possession. It bore five Mnevis calves. He took them away for his own use in the field. He then let them go, took them away to the south, and sold them to the priests.

Complaint about the Great Mnevis Calf in his possession. He let it go and sold it to some Medjay of the fortress of Senmut, receiving its price from them.

Complaint about his going to Thebes and receiving some papyrus rolls. (. . .) He brought them to the south to deposit them in front of Khnum, but he (Khnum) did not acknowledge them.

Complaint about his having sex with the citizen Mutnemeh daughter of Pasekhety, who was the wife of the fisherman Djehutyemheb son of Pentaweret.

Complaint about his having sex with Tabes daughter of Shuyu, who was the wife of Ahauty (or: wife with a man?).

Complaint about the theft of a *wedjat* amulet in the temple of Khnum. He put it to use, together with its thief. (. . .)

Not exactly a role model, our Mr. Penanuqet. One assumes that the events described above had unfolded over a period of time. Apart from his criminal and sexual exploits he had also found time to insult the gods themselves.

Complaint about his entering the fortress when he had done only seven days of purification. Then the scribe of the treasury Montuherkhopshef made this priest of Khnum take an Oath of the Lord, life, prosperity, health, saying: "I will not let him enter with the god until he has completed his days of drinking natron." But he would not listen and entered with the god when he had three (more) days of drinking natron (to do).

Complaint about the appointment of the priest Bakenkhonsu by the vizier Neferrenpet to be priest of Khnum. And then this priest said to the priest Nebwenenef: "We will install another three priests and we will let the god throw out this son of Pashuty." He was examined, and it was found that he had actually said it. They made him take an Oath of the Lord, life, prosperity, health, not to enter the temple. But he bribed this priest, saying: "Let me enter with the god." Now this prophet took his bribe and let him enter with the god.

One can only assume that some investigating committee had been assembled by the higher authorities to look into the matter. This is assuming that P. Turin Cat. 1887 was found in Thebes, as one may surmise, because almost all papyri in Turin come from the collection of Bernardino Drovetti (1776–1852), which suggests a Theban provenance, although he could of course have bought papyri elsewhere in Egypt. But if the papyrus was indeed bought in Luxor, the most logical conclusion would be that this was the official report sent back to Thebes to the Great Court (did this have any jurisdiction as far south as Elephantine?), which found that there was a lot wrong in Elephantine. This investigation probably included some physical pressure on some of the people involved, such as the staff of the local treasury. This was not a case of Pandora's Box, but rather Pandora's Enema.

> Complaint about (?) Pharaoh, life, prosperity, health, sending the overseer of the treasury Khaemtir to inspect the treasury of the temple of Khnum. Now this priest (presumably still Penanuqet) had stolen 60 *daiu* garments from the treasury of the temple of Khnum. When they searched for them, they found 34 in his possession, having used up the others.
>
> Complaint about this priest cutting off the ear of Sekhatuemnefer son of (the woman) Bakesetyt, without Pharaoh, life, prosperity, health, knowing.
>
> Complaint about the sending by the vizier Neferrenpet of the retainer Pakhar the Younger and the retainer Patjauemdikhonsu, saying: "Fetch the divine father Qakhepesh (the scribe who wrote this report?)." Then the retainers found that I was doing the monthly service in the first phyle, so the retainers let me be, saying: "One will not take you during your month of service." So they said [to me]. But then this priest gave them a smooth *daiu* dress and a chair (*and much, much more*).

Apparently some priest of Khnum (one wonders who this could have been) did bribe the officials to apprehend Qakhepesh, but the papyrus is in serious disorder here. If they really did, we now know that Penanuqet's plan did in the end backfire on him seriously.

> Complaint about burning down the house of the (female) manufacturer of royal textiles Mut[ne]fer[et, who had come] to speak to him. He blinded [her]. He blinded her daughter Bakesetyt as well, and they are still blind today.

Penanuqet also stole some cows here and there and then bribed another priest to tell any detective coming to investigate that any accusation made against him was unfounded (the reconstruction by Peet makes sense). The cost: just twenty deben of copper and three *daiu* dresses. After another unclear accusation the text continues in Peet's section B, showing that even the mayor of Elephantine was an accomplice. Stealing from the temple had become routine. So much for the fear of the gods.

(. . .) [Complaint about] their stealing of [5 cloaks] and 10 smooth *rudju* dresses, totaling 15, from the temple of Anuqet, Mistress of Syene (Aswan). The scribe of the treasury Montuherkhopshef, who was mayor of Elephantine, inspected them and found these (dresses) in their possession. They had given them to Amunrekh, a workman of the Place of Truth, having received their price. This mayor accepted a bribe from them and let them go.

[Complaint about] the opening of a storehouse of the temple of Khnum which had been sealed by the agents of the granary who manage (affairs) for the temple of Amun, stealing 180 sacks of grain from it.

They then went into another storehouse, making off with some more clothing. When they were found out, the temple authorities decided to do nothing.

The scene then shifts to the deliveries of grain—taxes—by a group of farmers working for the temple of Khnum. Each year they had to supply seven hundred sacks of grain, about 56,000 liters. All went well until the trusted captain of the grain barge died in year 28 of Ramesses III. Then some priest of Khnum, whose name is not read with confidence, appointed another captain, and trouble ensued.

Now, the overseer of cattle [. . .], who was a prophet of Khnum, brought in the trader and overseer [. . .] gold barge Khnumnakhte, letting him [collect (?)] the barley here in the northern region. And he began transporting it by ship. Now in year 1 of the King of Upper Egypt Heqamâ'atra Setepenamun (Ramesses IV), life, prosperity, health, the Great God, he went off with much of the barley. So this captain of the boat [. . .], he received 40 deben that belonged to the [treas]ury of Khnum. The gold was not in the treasury of the temple of Khnum, and the barley he had taken was also not in the granary of Khnum, with him stealing [. . .] Khnum. The six crew members (?) of the ship of Khnum were in on this with his . . .

The arrears in payments to the workmen of Deir al-Medina that caused them to go on strike multiple times are now starting to fall into place. Surely the temple of Khnum would not have been the only institution that could no longer keep up with the demands of the authorities. They were being swindled out of their taxes. But it is the apparently slow and rather meek response by the people responsible for this that surprises, unless of course the administrators were all in on it (which should not be a surprise if we look at businesses and administrations in some countries today). Still, one may be sure that the royal domain would exact contributions from the temple of Khnum from time to time, and it is difficult to see how they would have been able to comply, given that the newly appointed boat captain Khnumnakhte—a man from Elephantine and no doubt a relative of one of the people involved in this whole scam—was able to get away with this. The list below is dry, but one can imagine the inspector who wrote it down having his own thoughts about the personnel of the temple of Khnum. A death sentence and subsequent execution could have helped things along. But nobody had done anything for years, so perhaps Khnumnakhte and the priest Penanuqet were simply too powerful to cross or too generous with their bribes. The new boat captain sometimes managed to deliver only twenty out of the seven hundred required sacks per year, but there were also times that he did not sail at all.

[Year 1 of King Heqamâ'atra Setepenamun (Ramesses IV), life, prosperity, health, the Great God. [Arrived (?)] at Elephantine, from the boat captain [. . .]: 100 sacks. Remainder: 600.

Year 2 of King Heqamâ'atra Setepenamun, life, prosperity, health, the Great God: 130 sacks. Remainder: 570.

Year 3 of King Heqamâ'atra Setepenamun, life, prosperity, health, the Great God: 700 sacks. He did not bring them to the granary.

Year 4 of King Heqamâ'atra Setepenamun, life, prosperity, health, the Great God: 700 sacks. Arrived in the ship The Staff, from the skipper Panekhetta: 20 sacks. Remainder: 680.

Year 5 of King Heqamâ'atra Setepenamun, life, prosperity, health, the Great God. Arrived for the divine offerings, from The Staff of Khnum: 20 sacks. Remainder: 680.

Year 6 of King Heqamâ'atra Setepenamun, life, prosperity, health, the Great God: 700 sacks. He did not bring them.

Year 1 of Pharaoh (this must be Ramesses V), life, prosperity, health: 700 sacks. He did not bring them.

Year 2 of Pharaoh, life, prosperity, health: 700 sacks. Arrived with boat captain Khnumnakhte: 186 sacks. Remainder: 514.

Year 3 of Pharaoh, life, prosperity, health: 700 sacks. Arrived with this boat captain: 120 sacks. Remainder: 580.

Total: barley for the temple of Khnum, Lord of Elephantine, which this boat captain had conspired with the scribes, the agents, and the farmers of the Temple of Khnum to embezzle and appropriate for their own use, 5,004 (sic) sacks.

As (almost) usual the figures do not match, because Khnumnakhte and his cronies had actually made off with no less than 5,724 sacks of grain in the course of the years, which is 457,920 liters, without anybody ever feeling inclined to stop them, either because they were in on it, too afraid, or perhaps too far away. What one admires most about Khnumnakhte is the fact that at times his ship came in to bring a mere twenty sacks, an amount one might expect to be delivered by a lower-middle-class tenant. Did he moor his ship, walk at leisure to the scribe's office, and then talk to the scribe in charge of the delivery with a big smirk on his face? One could also ask, How could it be otherwise? Apparently nobody could touch him.

Complaint about the demand by this boat captain of the temple of Khnum for taxes. A load of 50 sacks from (?) Rome son of Penanuqet as well as a load of 50 sacks from Pawekhed son of Patjauemabu, a total of 2, which makes 100 sacks from year 1 of King Heqamâ'atra Setepenamun, life, prosperity, health, the Great God, up to year 4 of Pharaoh, life, prosperity, health, which makes 1,000 sacks. He took them for his own use and did not bring them to the granary of Khnum.

Complaint about the burning of a barge by this boat captain of the temple of Khnum, which belonged to the temple of Khnum, with its beams and rigging. Then he gave a bribe to the agents of the temple of Khnum and they did not report him. It has not been done to this day.

So the authorities were now on to both the priest Penanuqet and the boat captain Khnumnakhte, and one gets the impression that the latter may have set fire to his boat—probably in the north and not near Elephantine—as a rather lame excuse for his not supplying the deliveries he should have made ("We had a little accident, what can you do?"). He may have been rather desperate by this time.

In between all these events Khnumnakhte had also found time to have a woman he may have impregnated suffer an abortion (which must have been an ordeal), and perhaps he had also set his eyes—and not just his eyes—on a pretty little skipper on his boat.

> Complaint about his causing a miscarriage for the female citizen Tarep[yt] . . . (. . .).
> Complaint about the sodomy (?) by this sailor Panekhetta . . . , etc.

There are more cases, but let us just finish with this sailor, who may have had sex with his captain or possibly was raped by him.

It would be interesting to know who filed this report. The long list of accusations can hardly come from a single person, that is, our scribe Qakhepesh, so he must have received information from many others, all set on destroying Penanuqet and Khnumnakhte. In any case, the Turin Indictment Papyrus goes a long way toward rectifying the image some people may have of ancient Egypt, because it describes *reality* in much the same way as the Late Period P. Rylands 9, in which the priests of Amun in al-Hiba readily resorted to arson and murder if someone touched their income.

Although the Turin Indictment Papyrus is not from Deir al-Medina, it does tell us in an indirect way why the rations for the people in the village were increasingly often late or did not arrive at all. The entire system was starting to collapse, if it had not done so already.

15

Protecting Your
Daughter's Rights

If a Deir al-Medina girl married a workman from the village, this
meant her family would remain close at hand, and from time to time
we see them flee their husbands back to the parental home. This is
certainly the case in O. Bodleian Library Eg. Inscr. 253 from year 23 of
Ramesses III. This limestone ostracon is written on both sides. It deals
with a complaint by the workman Telmontu to the chief workman Khonsu
and the scribe Amunnakhte son of Ipuy about his son-in-law, evidently in
defense of his daughter, who is not mentioned by name (again, which is a
shame, because she would have been a regular guest at the parties thrown
by members of the Naunakhte family). This raises the question of why
this daughter did not file the complaint herself. Was this not allowed,
because it was just a household issue, or would a complaint by Telmontu
simply carry more weight than a statement by his daughter? Somehow it
is not very difficult to imagine that Amunnakhte and Khonsu would have
discarded a complaint by Telmontu's daughter herself as one of those
hysterical outbursts of a woman who was supposed to run a household
and keep her mouth shut. So what do we know about what access women
had to the management of Deir al-Medina?

We do know that Telmontu was part of the local court of law that heard
Naunakhte's statement about her inheritance in P. Ashmolean Museum
1945.97 (and was related to her through marriage—his daughter Hathor
was married to her son Neferhotep). We may also assume that in the case
of O. Bodleian Library Eg. Inscr. 253 Telmontu's son-in-law Nekhemmut
was there too, and maybe even his daughter, who had been treated badly
by her husband.

Year 23, first month of the *peret* season, day 4. On this day a statement was made by Telmontu to the chief workman Khonsu and the scribe Amunnakhte son of Ipuy: "Let Nekhemmut take an Oath of the Lord, life, prosperity, health, saying: 'I will not *netja* my (his) daughter.'"

Although the word *netja* is a hapax legomenon—a word that occurs only once, or maybe more often but always in the same incomprehensible context—the determinative shows that it was something bad. Otherwise Telmontu would not have complained about it. Some authors have chosen to see *netja* as a word for 'divorce,' but that would hardly be a matter that could earn Nekhemmut a hundred blows with the stick. Divorce was, after all, relatively easy, as long as an oath was taken (probably) and the wife received proper compensation. Nekhemmut took the oath.

The Oath of the Lord, life, prosperity, health, that he took: "As Amun endures, as the Ruler endures, life, prosperity, health. If I reverse to *netja* the daughter of Telmontu, tomorrow (or) after tomorrow, he (I) will be under a hundred blows (of the stick) and forfeit anything I made with her."

(Taken before) the chief workman Khonsu, the scribe Amunnakhte, Neferher, and Khaemnun.

One may suppose that the Khaemnun mentioned here was Naunakhte's husband, which makes the whole affair even more biased from the start. How the story ended is unknown, but it is very recognizable to anyone who is the father of a daughter. You do not let them bike home alone at night and you simply want them to be happy. It is clear that the hearing committee—was this an official court case?—thought the offense committed by Nekhemmut serious enough to impose heavy sanctions if he did not abide by his oath, namely physical punishment and the loss of all the conjugal capital. From the case of Merysakhmet (see chapter 14, "Women Causing Trouble"), who was ordered by the court to stay away from a woman who was to marry another workman, *or else*, we know that these sanctions were not always carried out. Still, in what was a predominantly oral society an oath carried much weight, and most people would probably feel bound by it.

As in any marriage, the relationship between husband and wife could become strained. We can be sure that the marriage of Mrs. Takhentyshepeset was not a huge success. She was clearly worried, so she wrote a letter (or had it written) to her sister Iy. O. Prague 1826 (O. Náprstek Museum P 2027) from Dynasty 19, which contains this letter, is a red pottery sherd with eleven lines in black ink on the recto. We do not know where this ostracon was found, so it may actually not even belong to the corpus of Deir al-Medina texts. If O. Prague 1826 is really a letter, and if one of the sisters was living in Deir al-Medina, one would have to assume that the other did not, so perhaps she lived in Thebes, across the river. Otherwise it would have been easier to visit each other (women like to talk, and a letter always confines things to a short message). Still, the distance between the sisters cannot have been too great, since the letter also refers to making bread for the sender.

> Said by Takhentyshepeset to her sister Iy. In life, prosperity, health. To wit: I will have the barley brought to you. You will have it ground on my behalf and add emmer corn to it and make bread for me. The fact is that I am arguing with Merymâ'at. "I will throw you out," or so he tells me. He also argues with my mother about the required amount of barley for bread. "Your mother does not do anything for you," he tells me, saying, "You do have siblings, and they do not look after you," he says, and he is . . . with me daily. "Now look what you have done for (?) me from the moment I came to live here. Each day everyone carries bread, beer, and fish to their people. In other words, if you have something (more) to say, go down to the Black Land (the plain below). It would be good (for you) to listen."

Another case of hurt machismo? It is difficult to see why Takhentyshepeset would have to send grain to her sister Iy to make bread. To show her husband that her siblings did look after her? Why not grind the grain yourself or have it done by a state-supplied servant? There is sufficient evidence that households could have (female) servants, who sometimes seem to have been shared property that could also be leased.

But not all women doing work for others were slaves. O. Ashmolean Museum 121 (Dynasty 19) records the payments to a woman for 480 days of service. The piece with her name on has broken off, but she is referred to as "female citizen," denoting a woman free to make her own decisions. So there were female freelancers in Deir al-Medina as well. There may actually have been more than we think, weaving clothes, selling vegetables, working as wet nurses, acting as 'wise women,' and so on.

Takhentyshepeset was living with her husband Merymâ'at and her mother under one roof. But whose roof was it? Her husband seems to suggest that he came to live with her, so how could he then tell her he would throw her out of this house? The name Merymâ'at occurs in only one other source that may be (loosely) connected with Deir al-Medina, P. Ashmolean Museum 1960.1283 (P. Gardiner 8), which is dated to Dynasty 19 (reign of Merenptah). Takhentyshepeset is only known from O. Prague 1826. The name Iy occurs several times in the sources from the village (e.g., O. Cairo CG 25573), so maybe it was Iy who lived in the village, and her sister did not. Does this mean some of the houses in the village were occupied by people who were *not* on the workforce?

We likewise do not know what exactly happened in the case of the anonymous woman who pops up in O. Ashmolean Museum 1945.39 (Ramesses III), a limestone ostracon written on both sides. The text starts with an account of a payment by the workman Khnummose to Rety, and several services rendered, including construction work on the latter's house and tomb. But apparently during that time Rety's wife was staying in the house of Khnummose:

> His wife spent forty days living with me in my house. I took care of her and I gave her emmer corn, one sack and ten assorted loaves. He threw her out again and she spent twenty days in the house of Menna. I gave three oipe of emmer corn, one *inet* cloth, and . . . for . . .

One has to assume the villagers would not just take any woman into their house unless they were relatives or a new love, although this seems to be contradicted by the rest of the text. Apparently Rety had thrown his wife out while Khnummose was working on the couple's house. Khnummose then told her she could stay with him, which either means they had fallen in love and she came to live in his house (which would be a very awkward situation if he kept working on Rety's house) or she was actually Khnummose's daughter. The simple fact that Khnummose took care of her material needs supports either explanation. When the woman—who is not mentioned by name—decided to return to Rety's house he threw her out again, and she then stayed for twenty days in the house of Menna.

A woman spending her time in the houses of three different men within forty-two days or slightly more? It is difficult to believe that these would all have been her lovers (this would be known by all), so the scenario in which Khnummose took her into his home because she was his daughter is the most plausible, more plausible at least than the scenario in which Khnummose's work on the roof of her house had driven her so crazy that she decided to stay in his house as long as he was working there (it should not take forty days to fix a roof). Somehow the father-and-daughter option fits the facts best.

A certified case of dad coming to the rescue of his daughter is O. UC 39656 (O. Petrie 61) from the middle of Dynasty 19. It is a very small limestone ostracon of 8.1 × 7.1 cm, with writing on both sides. It contains a statement by the workman Horemwia to a person who seems to be his daughter, and it may have been made at the moment she married—presumably when she was collected by her future husband at his house (although in that case his statement would not have been in the best possible taste)—or when the first cracks started to appear in her marriage. Some authors say this could also be a letter. The woman, a Mrs. Tadjeseret, is only known from this source.

> The workman Horemwia to the female citizen Tadjeseret, his daughter. You are my good daughter. If the workman Baky throws you out of the house that I have made (or: that has been made). As for the house . . . Pharaoh, life, prosperity, health. You can live in the front room of my storehouse. The fact is, I am the one who made it. No man on earth can throw you out of there.

As was noted above, it would have been strange for Horemwia to make preparations for his daughter's divorce at the moment of her wedding. That is, if she was his daughter. Some authors believe that Tadjeseret was actually his daughter-in-law, and indeed *Who's Who* lists a Horemwia son of Baky, and the latter named his son after his father, as the ancient Egyptians were wont to do. All three are mentioned on a stela now kept in the Egyptian Museum in Cairo (inv. no. JdE 43565). This makes Horemwia's statement even more remarkable, certainly if it was made at the moment Tadjeseret and Baky were married. From the later abnormal hieratic marriage documents such as P. Louvre E 7846 and 7849 we know that the bridegroom made a statement about taking care of his wife, including in case of a divorce, and this would, after all, seem to be the perfect moment to assure the young bride that, whatever happened during the marriage, she would always have a roof over her head. This would imply that when a bridegroom entered the house of his future father-in-law to collect his bride, he did not do so alone, but brought some members of the family (such as his parents), which sounds like the normal thing to do.

As is to be expected, this text also has its reading problems, especially when Horemwia is talking about the house where Tadjeseret lives. It is difficult to see how we are to reconcile the often-seen translation 'the house that I have made' with the fact that the houses in the village were state property, as is implied by the mention of the king, albeit in an unclear context—unless he meant the household that he had established. From the text that follows it becomes clear that the living space that Horemwia offered his daughter-in-law in case of a divorce was built by himself (probably not in the village itself), so nobody would be able to throw her out. The question is whether O. UC 39656 is a freak text, or did a father-in-law promise this kind of protection to the wife of his son more often? One would like to know.

One person who did not even make it into the house of his father-in-law is the unfortunate man whose intentions to marry the girl of his dreams were snubbed twice on the doorstep. The story has come down to us on O. BM EA 65936 (O. Nash 6), a limestone ostracon written on one side in black ink, with some of the text struck through or added above the line (he was still confused?), in one case in red ink.

So should we imagine the situation as follows? The unfortunate man recorded his misfortune—or had it recorded by a scribe—and when the text was read back to him he started to make corrections and additions. This may be easily explained by his fragile state of mind when he made his first statement. Even if it was made some time after the incident, the recollection would have been enough to make him emotional again (yes, people find it hard to believe, but we can relate emotion and hieratic more often than we think). There he was, taking a formidable bridal gift to the woman of his dreams, only to be jilted on the doorstep, just like that.

> List of all the things that I took to her house: a smooth sheet, 1 sack of barley, four sacks of emmer corn. Total 5 sacks, a smooth *meses* garment, 2 hin of oil, 2 pairs of sandals (one left), 2 baskets, 1 cover, 1 mat, 1 headrest, 1 (hin of?) fat, 1 runner, 2 *ushabti* chests (one left), 1 *tjay* box, 165 (?) assorted

loaves, 30 loaves to celebrate, 30 complete *bery* fish, 2 sieves, 2 cups, 10 jars of beer, a quarter sack of beans, a quarter sack of perfume, a quarter sack of salt, 5 bricks of natron, 2 jasper rings, and 1 jasper *wedjat* eye made from one piece.

They threw me out. She has not made a . . . garment for my backside (?). I went once again with all my things, to live with them. Look, then she acted this way again . . .

Again this 'providing a garment for someone's (invariably the man of the house) backside.' So this expression—again village lingo?—has to mean something like 'a woman willing to take care of a man as her husband,' and this lends further support to the case of the female slave talking back to some authorities apparently sent out to investigate a case of misappropriation of her services by a workman (O. Cairo CG 25237, for which see chapter 13, "Thrown Out"). The slave and the workman may have simply fallen in love. He wanted her and she wanted him. In that case, asking for clothing from the authorities to cover his backside would have meant she consented to being his wife and wanted to see some official confirmation by the authorities, since she was state property. And the state simply said, "No way!"

We can be sure that the unfortunate man from O. BM EA 65936 did not physically carry all this stuff to his future bride's house, which was probably the house of her father, by himself. In the original statement he mentions five sacks of grain that he supposedly took there, but these were struck through by the scribe afterward. And even if he did not take four hundred liters of grain to her house, it is difficult to see how you can carry, for instance, 165 assorted loaves and ten full jugs of beer at the same time, which are only two items from the list. If he really brought all these items to her house, he would probably have needed a truck—which the ancient Egyptians did not have—or a whole range of family members to help carry it all. So this 'carrying the bundle' to the house of the future father-in-law could in fact have been a whole procession of relatives accompanying the groom to watch the ceremony. It makes more sense than assuming he went there all alone.

Still, his relatives would not have been very keen on going there a second time in the sweltering heat, carrying the bridal gift of our unfortunate would-be husband. The 165 assorted loaves he carried there the first time would by then have probably gone stale, so did he have them baked anew? Is this long list of items actually what the villagers called 'carrying the bundle' to the house of the future father-in-law? The literature does not say, although in today's language a bundle usually implies—one hesitates to suggest this to the experts—a quantity that can be carried by a single person. This list amounts to far more than that.

The much later abnormal hieratic marital property arrangements such as P. Louvre E 7846 and 7849 specifically refer to divorce as the "heavy fate" that overtakes the woman, and one has to assume that to the people of Deir al-Medina—and most certainly the women—a divorce was not exactly a laughing matter.

Except perhaps to the scribe of P. Bibl. Nat. 198, II (Late Ramesside Letters no. 46, or LRL 46 for short), believed to be none other than the famous scribe Djehutymose. The letter was written on a sheet of papyrus of 20.5 x 21.5 cm and there are three further unplaced tiny fragments. The writing is on both sides. After the usual flowery introduction invoking the usual gods, Djehutymose (the same scribe who was involved in a murder plot and apparently got away with it) comes to the point.

> So I heard you are angry. You have made me swell up with insults (or curses) because of this joke. I told the taxing-master in this letter, whereas it was Henuttawy who said to me: "Tell the taxing-master a few jokes in your letter." You are like (in) the story (?) of the wife who was blind in one eye, who lived in the house of one man for twenty years. But he found another and told her: "I am throwing you out. You are blind in one eye." So they say. And she said to him: "Is that the discovery that you have made in these twenty years that I was in your house?" That is me. That is the joke I played on you.

The letter does not end here (the ancient Egyptian humor fortunately does), but the rest is less relevant for us. It has been dated to Dynasty 20, but also to year 12 of Ramesses XI. This Henuttawy who was blamed for the incident is no doubt the woman we also know from other sources. In fact, she was partly responsible for the grain deliveries to the people of Deir al-Medina, working closely together with her husband, the scribe of The Tomb Nesamunipet. She is mentioned in P. Turin Cat. 1895 + 2006 (Turin Taxation Papyrus) from years 12 and 14 of Ramesses XI, in which we see the same scribe Djehutymose collecting grain for the people of the necropolis from various royal domains. Henuttawy is one of the three persons on the receiving end, together with the mayor of western Thebes Pawerââ and the scribe Nesamunipet.

She bore the same title as Naunakhte ('singer of Amun'). In fact, even a princess such as Nauny, the daughter of Pinodjem I, called herself "singer of Amun" in her funerary papyrus (from TT 358). As we will see below, Henuttawy may have had some trouble staying afloat in the man's world of fields, logistics, and obvious corruption, but the man who wrote the very fragmentary P. BM EA 10430 (P. Salt 248, most commonly referred to as LRL 42) evidently viewed her as competent, discussing with her his visit to the king and various agricultural matters. One assumes this man was Nesamunipet's father.

In P. Geneva D 191 (LRL 37) she writes to Nesamunipet to tell how his father won a legal case in the presence of Ramesses XI himself. The letter also mentions that things were not going as smoothly as he may have hoped, and one wonders whether this was because she was a woman (we will skip the introduction to the letter with all best wishes, etc.). Apparently the rations for the people from Deir al-Medina had been set aside (162½ sacks), but this amount would tally only if they were distributed with the right oipe measure, a smaller one than usual.

> I have heard every matter you wrote to me about. As for your talking about this issue of the 162½ sacks of emmer, of which you said: "Let the scribe Pentahutnakhte go and collect them together with the captains (the chief workmen) and not distribute them using a large oipe measure," so you said. Your letter landed with the vizier. He sent the scribe Sary together with the measurer, having them come and take along an oipe measure that was one hin larger than the oipe of the granary. I went myself and let the grain be received when I was there. They were 146¾ sacks with this (other) oipe.
>
> This young man of The Tomb and the fisher said: "150 sacks of grain is what we had measured for ourselves with the oipe of the Domain of Amun." I checked the oipe measures and said to them: "My check is with me (I have the right to check?). I will find the grain wherever it is." So I said to them.

The simple use of a different oipe by the measurer sent by the vizier immediately reduced the amount said to be delivered by nearly sixteen sacks, a nearly 10 percent deficit. And then some villager had the nerve to tell her that they had counted on receiving 150 sacks, not 146¾. One almost senses Henuttawy's indignation at the question from this snotty young man and his companion, a smelly fisherman, referring to the first as "this child of <The> Tomb," almost implying 'creature' rather than 'child.' By now, the people from Deir al-Medina were living in Medinet Habu (that is, if this story holds), where Henuttawy had her office or shared one with her husband. But when it came to their rations, the people from Deir al-Medina had grown used to arguing with the higher authorities. One wonders whether she still felt in charge of things. And this was not the end.

> You wrote to me, saying: "Collect the 80 sacks of this barge of the fisherman Itefnefer," so you said. So I went to collect them and found 72½ sacks of grain with him.
>
> I said to him: "What's with the 72½ sacks of grain?" So I said to him, "It is 80 sacks according to his (Nesamunipet's) letter."
>
> And the men said: "Three totally filled (portions) is what we have measured for ourselves, they being [2]½ sacks, making 72½ sacks of grain." So they said.
>
> I fell silent instantly, because until you come (back) Amun United with Eternity will have done all kinds of (other) bad things to me.

So Henuttawy was forced to check things after an impertinent remark by a villager probably young enough to be her son, and then snubbed by an insolent captain of a grain barge? Although these men would know who was boss here, there were of course countless ways to reduce her to a state of impotent rage while her husband was away. One is reminded of the brilliant story by the former *Rolling Stone* journalist P.J. O'Rourke, describing a visit to a South African restaurant during the apartheid regime with a company of white people. The black staff would serve the soup with a fork, and then, when ordered to bring a spoon, would reflect for a moment, take the fork to the kitchen, and return with a knife. And so on until the soup was cold.

Somehow we can almost see this young man from the village and the barge captain think: Look, you are just a woman and your husband is away, so let us see how far we can go. One wonders how many men in Henuttawy's position would have done what she did, namely try to defend herself and then fall silent, even if she ascribed her grain shortage to divine intervention (Sweeney wrote what should be the definitive article about these incidents). She could no longer bring the offerings that should have been made to Amun, and now she thought the god was angry with her.

> Look after the grain of his (?) that you had them send. There is no sack of grain for his divine offering. I myself have given 30 sacks of emmer for his [divine offer]ing from [regnal year] 2, second month of the *akhet* season, day 27 to the third month of the *akhet* seaon, day 2, from the grain that has been stored under my supervision. [. . .] for the divine offering.

Although one can understand *hetep netjer* 'divine offering' as the daily offering to the god, the same term was used in later periods to denote the economic assets of a temple in buildings, cattle, land, and so on. If Henuttawy meant the physical daily offering to the god, this would amount to five sacks (four hundred liters) per day, which one assumes to have gone to the temple personnel after the gods had taken their share through magic. It was in any case a modest amount for a god.

The next passage is slightly ambiguous. According to Henuttawy the god himself had something to do with this entire grain issue, although it is difficult to understand what the real problem was.

> Amun United with Eternity has allowed the grain to be put in a chest and apply a seal to it. Now look, you must team up with Paseny and you must speak with the overseer of the granaries about the grain for Amun United with Eternity. He (Amun) does not have it, even a single oipe, for his divine offering today. Do not abandon him, (you) two.

So it seems that Amun may have been slightly irritated with the way Henuttawy had managed her business (which is how Sweeney interpreted it, and she may well be correct), but we can also interpret the whole affair in more mundane terms, namely that Henuttawy had been requesting some grain from other temples, and that the managers of the grain reserves kept there had said: "Look, woman, you have had all these barges coming in with loads of grain. It is not our problem that you were sold short by the captains of these ships. Besides, the whole thing is now in the hands of the vizier. So take your whining elsewhere."

This hypothesis finds some support in the fact that Henuttawy tells Nesamunipet to go talk to the man in charge. Could it be that she had been snubbed by him as well? Wente's translation in his *Late Ramesside Letters* (1967) has: "You are not to abandon him (viz., Amun)," which was reiterated in his *Letters from Ancient Egypt* (1990).

Incidentally, Wente's publications are among the first successful attempts to bring to life the people from Deir al-Medina. In this respect one should also mention A.G. McDowell, *Village Life in Ancient Egypt: Laundry Lists and Love Songs* (1999), which has allowed English-speaking audiences to become acquainted with the primary sources from the village, ranging from accounts to trial records, from letters to, well, laundry lists, in sparkling, reliable translations, although the publishing house did its utmost to diminish its potential reach by selling it for $70. One other must-have (in German) is *Hieratische Ostraka und Papyri aus der Ramessidenzeit* (1973) by the Egyptian Egyptologist Schafik Allam, which remains the first useful (large) collection of translations of essential sources from Deir al-Medina. This book would have had a much larger impact if it had been in English, but somehow this has never happened, which is a shame.

Anyway, the verb *khâa* 'throw out' used by Henuttawy is actually the same as the verb used to describe a divorce. Since the "him" in this sentence is not specified, it could be either Amun or the overseer of the granaries, but it is probably safest to stick with Wente's interpretation, since *khâa* also has the meaning 'abandon.' Now that Henuttawy had taken care of business it was time to write about some personal matters, to wit, Nesamunipet's father.

Do not worry about your father. I have heard that his condition is excellent indeed. The overseer of the temple of Amun and priest Nespamedushepes wrote to me, saying: "Do not worry about him, he is fine and healthy. No bad thing has overcome him." Parawenemef has gone to court with your father in the presence of Pharaoh, life, prosperity, health, and one (the king) found him to be in the right against him. One has let the magistrates investigate his men in order to give them to him. Now Pharaoh, life, prosperity, health, has said: "Give him men as is suitable."

The priest Pawenesh of the temple of Mut (also) wrote to me, saying: "Pharaoh, life, prosperity, health, has sent off your father, and Pharaoh, life, prosperity, health, His Lord, has done all kinds of good things for him."

But the magistrates did not place [anything] good in the barge that I (Henuttawy) had sent to him full of salt and any produce (?) of the northern region. Tjema put it in (?) a ship along with his team (?) and left nothing useful for him at all. He also told me: "It was after he was sent off with the overseer of the treasury and the overseer of the granaries Menmâ'atranakhte (and) the [scribe] of the altar Hori that I came."

After some more gossip about the local people—another Nesamunipet had been appointed to an office by the king, and the vizier had written a letter with instructions about some rations—the letter breaks off.

A very odd case involving the wife and daughter of a high state official is mentioned in O. Ashmolean Museum 1945.37 + 1945.33, which was published by Černý and Gardiner in their magistral *Hieratic Ostraca*, Vol. 1 (1957), to which O. Michaelides 90 could later be added. From the facsimile that was published, it appears that this rather damaged text, describing the court proceedings, was written on a very large ostracon indeed. The hieratic is in a literary hand, with red verse points over the lines, so this is either a tale of some sort or a text that goes back to a genuine court record, almost as if to show what would happen if women were left in charge of things.

Since the text is broken at the top, we do not know the precise date (but if it is indeed a tale there would be no date anyway), although the content makes it clear that it was the reign of Ramesses II. After the break there is a list, presumably of the things that were taken from a state storehouse by these women without any official authorization. The charges were evidently made against the husband who let this all happen. Among the items stolen are more than fifty jars of wine, four cows, ten goats, thirty fat geese, and a large collection of textiles and yarn. It seems the women may have been preparing their own party to celebrate the Jubilee of Ramesses II, paid for by the state.

Look, Pharaoh, life, prosperity, health, has let (appointed?) tax officials [. . .], (namely) two men with a claim on your wife and also your daughter. [. . .] great stable of Ramesses Meryamun, life, prosperity, [health, . . .] *heb sed* Jubilee as in the list [. . .] against Pharaoh, life, prosperity, health. Look, your wife and yo[ur daughter (?)] opened the [. . .] of King Aâkheperkara (Thutmose I), that was under the authority of the controller Amunemi[pet (?) . . .].

Then there is a new list, showing that the women also had a preference for copper items and ingots (with a total of over two hundred deben), fine garments, drinks, and ointment, so someone—presumably the tax officials appointed by the king—had taken the trouble to go through the books.

> She put them in your storehouse. Now, one has a claim on her (lit. 'on her back') and one will not leave her be. The scribe Hatiay has accused your wife, saying: "What is this walking of hers into the storehouse of Pharaoh, life, prosperity, health, without (anyone) knowing? One shall take her to the Great Court before the Hereditary Prince and the great magistrates."
>
> One said to her: "What about the opening of the two magazines of the temple, without (anyone) knowing?"
>
> She said: "The places that were opened, my husband is their manager."
>
> The court said to her: "So your husband was at the temple as [its manag]er."
>
> He was replaced. And he was assigned to another exalted position of [Phar]aoh, [life, prosperity, health], to inspect the cows at the outer limit of his land. "It is not good what you have done." So one said.

With these words this court case seems to have ended, and the husband was promoted to some distant outpost.

The verso of the ostracon contains another case of theft from some storehouses. Some think this is an unrelated case, but we will side with Allam, one of the great pioneers in legal issues from Deir al-Medina, and Kitchen. In this other case, the court found much more incriminating evidence, this time also implicating the husband himself. It starts with a list, almost suggesting that the couple became greedier as time progressed and nobody was trying to stop them. The list includes 22,000 sacks of grain, 1,300 copper ingots, three hundred castrated male goats, forty cows, thirty bulls, a large amount of clothing, and—somewhat surprisingly—thirty chariots. Where did the couple (and their daughter) plan to store all this?

> [. . .] against the manager Pairy. "They did not enter the [. . .] oipe in your documents that were in your chest found in [. . .] house. The list of it was found: grain 20,000 sacks, 1,200 [. . .] and also salt 1,200 sacks. [. . .] took an Oath of the Lord, life, prosperity, health before the great magistrates of the court, saying: "If one finds [. . .] my father, in the storehouse [. . .] Jubilee, I will return (it) double. As for the remainder that has occurred with him, the things will be returned today [. . .] the four halls. The doorkeepers

of the temple of Pharaoh, life, prosperity, health, stole them, (taking) one for each of them."

Quite an unexpected turn of events. The text remains unclear, but the gist appears to be that Pairy flatly denied all accusations, incriminating others instead. The connection between the recto and verso of the text consists of the incredibly large amounts that were stolen, and the *heb sed* Jubilee of Ramesses II. With so much coming in to prepare for the upcoming Jubilee in Thebes, some people had become greedy, including some wives and daughters.

16

Two Scribes
Called Amunnakhte

The workman-carpenter-scribe Amunnakhte son of Khaemnun and
Naunakhte inherited some of his mother's possessions, including
a number of household goods. The five siblings who were allowed
to take their pick from these items took turns taking the objects of their
choice, but it is striking that Amunnakhte always came to pick first or
second in line (see chapter 7, "A Day in the Life of Menatnakhte"). He
also inherited the library of his mother's first husband and added several
items to it.

In the sources from Deir al-Medina it is sometimes difficult to distinguish
between him and the famous scribe Amunnakhte son of Ipuy, who officiated
from the reign of Ramesses III onward, or other people of the same name.
Note, for instance, O. DeM 336, in which the scribe Amunmose writes to
either the scribe Amunnakhte son of Ipuy or to 'our' Amunnakhte about
seventy-nine glazed objects, possibly *ushabti*s (in the lacuna). Since this
Amunmose was clearly a friend of the family (see chapter 8, "A Boy with a
Golden Pair of Hands"), this may actually be 'our' Amunnakhte.

We may, however, be sure that our man is meant in O. DeM 225 from
early Dynasty 20 (the same case is probably also recorded in P. DeM 26
recto *ll.* 1–8, but this is very damaged). In this text he is commissioned
by a Mrs. Iy to manufacture a coffin, probably for the burial of her late
husband. Perhaps she had first asked a man called Amuneminet to do
this, but this deal somehow never materialized, and he brought the issue
before the court—no doubt because the hut on the col between the village
and the Valley of the Kings or in the valley itself, which would be given to
Amunnakhte as compensation, had been promised to him earlier.

211

Said by the workman Amuneminet to the court of listeners, (consisting of) the scribe Pentaweret, the scribe Paser, the chief of police Pentaweret, the chief of police Montumose. What was said by the workman Amuneminet and the female citizen Iy, (the widow) of Huy, who is deceased. "She said: 'I made a coffin for my husband and I buried him.' So she said. She (then) said to the scribe Amunnakhte: 'Make a coffin for Huy (and) you take for yourself his hut.' [So she] said. She said to the scribe Amunnakhte: 'Let the coffin be [. . .]. . . . There is no [. . .].' I said to her: '[. . .].' And I [. . .]."

As usual, one quickly loses track of who said what to whom, but the gist is that Amuneminet felt wronged by Iy (the text breaks off here), so he now demanded compensation. In any case, the important thing to note here is that apparently in specific circumstances widows could dispose of (some of) the property of their late husbands as they saw fit. This was either because it was the conjugal property (with her deciding what was to be her one-third), or because her husband had put her in charge of the division of his inheritance.

Somehow it feels sad to see a grown man taking a poor widow to court about something as delicate as the burial of her husband, but in this case there seems little room for a different interpretation. Not all the people we meet are nice. Maybe Iy or even her deceased husband had actually promised Amuneminet that he could have the hut after his death, and a promise by mouth—probably supported by an oath—would have carried the same weight as any written document, especially if there had been witnesses to hear the oath. But, as so often, we do not know what happened.

If we look in *Who's Who*, we will only find a few references to our man, who is called Amunnakhte (xxvi), which is partly explained by the fact that it is so difficult to distinguish between our man and the scribe Amunnakhte son of Ipuy, such as in the so-called name stones, which generally list only a name and sometimes also a title (e.g., O. IFAO 437 and 1096).

We do know that our Amunnakhte liked to refer to himself as *sesh* 'scribe' on more than one occasion, however. The official records, such as the work journals O. DeM 41 and 47 from year 1 of Ramesses IV, refer to him without any title. There he is simply Amunnakhte son of Khaemnun. Or he sometimes occurs as in O. BM EA 50730 + 50745 from the same year, where he appears almost side by side with the scribe

Amunnakhte, as the workman Amunnakhte. But in a source such as the unpublished O. Ashmolean Museum 284, for instance, which mentions copper, woodwork, and a scribe Amunnakhte, we really cannot be sure which of the two Amunnakhtes is meant, although it is tempting to think that the mention of woodwork gives him away.

Earlier in this book O. Berlin P 12630 was construed as a letter illustrating the stinginess of the scribe Amunnakhte son of Ipuy, but what if it was addressed to our Amunnakhte? The letter is clearly about woodwork and a carpenter who had been stupid enough to deliver his products after some empty promises, also by our Amunnakhte. If this is really the case, then the woman addressed here would be our Amunnakhte's wife, who is, however, not known by name. We do know he was married, because he had at least one son, who was named Khaemnun, and there must have been many more sons and daughters. But as with his brother Maaninakhtef, women do not play a very large role in his dossier.

> (Recto) Memo from the workman Mose to the ci[tizen . . .]. To wit: the scribe Amunnakhte, your husband, has taken one coffin from me, saying: "I will give you the ox to pay for it." To this day he has not given it. I told it to Paâkhet and he said to me: "Give me a bed for it and I will bring the ox for you when it has grown up." I gave him the bed. No coffin, no bed to this day. (Verso) If you (want to) give the ox, then let it be brought. If no ox (?), then let one bring the bed and the coffin (back).

In this letter, the use of the title 'scribe' therefore either means that the sender had indeed written this letter to the wife of the senior scribe, or to the wife of our Amunnakhte son of Naunakhte, in which case he may have deemed it advisable to at least uphold decorum. After all, he was trying to get paid.

Amunnakhte seems to have been an average villager (except for the fact that he could read and write), so at times we see him attending parties, as in O. Berlin P 14328, together with his brothers Neferhotep and Maaninakhtef. He was sometimes also called upon to do his civic duty, such as attending official court meetings, or at least the taking of an Oath of the Lord by others. In O. Ashmolean Museum 137 from year 3 of Ramesses V he witnessed such an event, when one policeman promised the other to repay a loan of grain, probably after the new harvest, which often happened in Egypt. Taking a grain loan was simple, as long as one was prepared to repay it with 50 percent interest. If the loan was not paid in time, the amount to be repaid would be doubled. But the profit involved made it worthwhile, as the abnormal hieratic grain loan on Tablet MMA 35.3.318 from around 686 BCE shows:

> Regnal year 5, first month of the *shemu* season, day 2. Has said the farmer of the Domain of Amun Paterenuphis son of Pakeri to the prophet of Amun Horsiese son of Djedkhonsuiufankh: "I have received from you the 30 (sacks) of barley at interest in barley. It is I who shall give them to you in regnal year 6, fourth month of the *akhet* season, day 30, being 45 (sacks) of barley. They shall be delivered to your house, whereas I will have nothing to discuss with you."

In other words, Paterenuphis borrowed thirty sacks of barley around October 686, which he promised to pay back with 50 percent interest in June the next year. These dates are no coincidence. September and October were the usual months in which people concluded land leases, and the following June was the time of harvest. Still, Paterenuphis would have to pay about 3,600 liters of barley, when he had borrowed only 2,400. Was this really worthwhile? It would seem so. If we set the eventual yield of one sack of seed at eight hundred liters (ten sacks), Paterenuphis could expect to harvest no less than three hundred sacks (24,000 liters) of barley, so after the repayment of the loan and 10 percent taxes he would still be left with 225 sacks (18,000 liters). Not bad for half a year's work.

Just like some of his brothers, Amunnakhte worked as a carpenter alongside his regular job, and it may well be that he is the man referred to as 'the draftsman Amunnakhte' in O. DeM 232 (Ramesses III). The text lists two payments, to a carpenter for woodwork and to Amunnakhte. The fact that these payments are listed together on a single ostracon suggests that Amunnakhte and the anonymous carpenter—who may have been one of his brothers—had worked together on a single assignment. In O. DeM 553 (Ramesses III) an Amunnakhte is paid for his work on a coffin:

> What was given to the draftsman Amunnakhte in return for the large coffin [. . .]: fine linen dress 1, makes 1 *shenaty*. Barley 1 sack and 4 mats, makes 1 *shenaty*. Wood for door 1, makes 2 *shenaty*. Sleeping mat 1, 3 jugs,

makes 2 *shenaty*. Total: 5 *shenaty*, entered (as) paid. Given to him in [return for . . .]: . . . Woman's chair 1, makes 1 *shenaty*, which is also with him. Box 1, which makes 1 *shenaty*. Basket 1.

In O. Glasgow D.1925.68 (O. Colin Campbell 3) from the middle of Dynasty 20 we see him and his brother Maaninakhtef doing woodwork for the vizier, which can perhaps be interpreted as a clear recognition of their skills. The text also mentions a *sesh* 'scribe' Khaemnun. Could this actually be their own father, and if so, does this mean that Naunakhte's husband Khaemnun could also read and write—or (more probably) could this have been one of their own sons? It would be one of only two references in all the sources from Deir al-Medina, and the first hypothesis would presuppose that Naunakhte taught her husband to do this, which sounds utterly impossible. Even if the woman was the *nebet per* 'the mistress of the house,' teaching boys would be one thing, teaching your husband quite another. Maybe this Khaemnun was Amunnakhte's own son.

Amunnakhte and Maaninakhtef wrote each other letters, and in the Valley of the Kings Swiss archaeologists also found a model letter (or a draft) from Maaninakhtef to Amunnakhte (O. KV 18/3.576). In one of the letters—P. DeM 11—the former urges him to take care of their business. Unfortunately the papyrus is damaged, and it is also unknown whether they had a conflict with some Syrians or—in two out of three cases—just one woman called Kharery.

The scribe Maaninakhtef greets the scribe Amunnakhte. In life, prosperity, health and in the favor of [Pa]rahorakhty. To wit: I am here, saying to Meres[ger, Mistress of the] West and all the gods of [Thebes], to watch you, while you [. . .]. Now, what is this you being so stupid and to bring the [. . .] house of Hay? I'm not afraid of [. . .] Syrian (or Mrs. Kharery) of the West, as a person who listens [. . .] father, at this place where you are. Make sure that you give one bed to [. . .] Thebes (and a) chair. You shall let him bring them [. . .] Syrian (or Mrs. Kharery) this time. When the letter [reaches you, go to] this place where the three Syrians are [. . . and have] them brought to me . . .

Could it be that Maaninakhtef spent much of his time in Hu, trying to manage his carpenter's shop from there? In any case, we know the brothers were not confined to the village for their business, but also traded with the people from Thebes on the eastern bank of the Nile (as one would expect) and downriver in Hu.

Letters from ancient Egypt are notoriously difficult to interpret, because we often do not understand the context in which they were written. P. DeM 4 (Ramesses V) is somehow different, because it is a rather desperate letter by a friend who feels that Amunnakhte is holding a grudge against him. After the usual flowery introduction (which we will skip here), Mr. Nakhtsobek, who refers to himself as *sesh* 'scribe,' comes to the point.

> To wit: what kind of crime have I committed against you? Am I not your old bread-eating companion? Has the hour indeed come that you will turn yourself away? What must I do? Write to me about the crime that I committed [against] you [through] the policeman B[asa]. But if you will not write to me something good or bad, then [this is going to be] a bad day. It is not as if I am asking something from you at all. Any person is happy ('sweet') to be with his old bread-eating companion. Of course new things are good, but an old companion is better. When my letter reaches you, [you] must write about your situation through the policeman Basa. Instruct me about [. . .] today. Do not let <it be> said: "Do not enter your (my) house. (. . .)"

Could this by any chance be the same Nakhtsobek who at some point in time owned P. Chester Beatty I, to which he then added a colophon with his own name (see below)? And did he present this papyrus to Amunnakhte? In his brilliant essay on the owners of the Chester Beatty papyri—the scribe Qenhirkhopshef, Naunakhte, Khaemnun (possibly), Amunnakhte, and finally Maaninakhtef—Pestman reconstructed what happened to Qenhirkhopshef's library after he passed away, using P. Chester Beatty III as a case study.

During the first stage of the history of this library the papyrus contained only a Dream Book on the recto and part of the verso, which was written in the reign of Ramesses II. The papyrus then came into the possession of Qenhirkhopshef, who used the verso of the papyrus to copy the story of the Battle of Qadesh and write a model letter to the vizier Panehsy.

When the archive reached Amunnakhte, he wrote a new colophon in a rather unusual place, smack in the middle of the text on the recto, where there was an empty space (see chapter 8, "A Boy with a Golden

Pair of Hands"). It is difficult to believe that someone who so proudly added his name to this text would have been the person responsible for the mutilation of the papyrus that happened at a later date. Maaninakhtef would seem the most likely suspect. Amunnakhte did deposit several new documents in the archive, such as P. DeM 11 (a letter by Maaninakhtef) and also P. DeM 4 (see above).

It so happens that there may be two more letters (P. DeM 5 and 6) to Amunnakhte, suggesting he was not the most easygoing person who ever walked the planet. Černý, who published these letters, thought that they were indeed from Nakhtsobek to Amunnakhte, as did Pestman, but this was contested by Deborah Sweeney, in the *Journal of Egyptian Archaeology* 84. She argued that, on the basis of the way the scribe or scribes who wrote P. DeM 4–6 wrote the maculine article *pa* 'the,' the texts were actually written by three different scribes, and perhaps even four if we include the very fragmentary P. DeM 22 in this dossier (as some do). Sweeney is an expert on Deir al-Medina, but perhaps the mistake made here is the assumption that our handwriting—or Nakhtsobek's several thousand years ago—has to look exactly the same each time we write something (see below). There are so many factors influencing our handwriting that it is actually a miracle we can produce similar-looking writing most of the time. Although Sweeney did have a point in stating that the sender and the addressee are not known by name in either P. DeM 5 or 6, the tone of voice in all three letters is intimate and very direct, much more so than usual, and—this may be the decisive argument—P. DeM 4–6 were also found together (many P. DeM refer to the children of Naunakhte and Khaemnun), so why would it be different for P. DeM 5–6? Wente, in *Letters from Ancient Egypt* (1990), elegantly skirted this problem by simply listing P. DeM 4–6 in consecutive order without any commentary.

So it is time to move on to P. DeM 5, although it should be kept in mind that these numbers do not in any way need to represent the chronological order of events. We will skip the very short introduction, which this time does *not* list the gods who have to protect the addressee.

What's with you? Write and let me know the state of your heart, so that I can enter it. Now, from when I was a boy to this day I have been with you, but I do not understand your nature. Is it good for a man if he says something to his companion two times, and he does not listen to him? Like the hin measure of ointment I requested from you. You told me: "I will let it be brought to you, so that you will not be lacking." Write to me about your situation instead of (sending) the ointment. May Amun be before you. You may find something useful in them (?). It is not good at all what you have done to me repeatedly. On another note: soak some bread, and let it be brought [to me] as quickly as possible. May your health be good.

These are people who know each other very intimately. The sender cleverly reminds the addressee that they have been friends ever since they were kids, and even then he was something of an enigma. So could it be that our Amunnakhte simply resorted to silence if he was angry or hurt, knowing full well that this was a very effective way to make other people feel very uncomfortable? According to Sweeney one of the essential elements in this letter is that the sending of the ointment could have served as a token of reconciliation, in a village where gift-giving was important. This may be so, but in this letter the sender actually says: "Look, forget about the ointment, just tell me what's the matter." There may well be an underlying mechanism of gift-giving to reestablish a broken relationship in place here, but can we just this once look at this letter and simply try to understand it with our hearts? Or do we really have to suppose that the sender and the addressee would never have made amends if no ointment was transferred between the two of them? It is difficult to believe. These were, after all, friends.

P. DeM 6 raises even more questions. The recently assigned dating to Dynasty 19, and more specifically the reign of Ramesses II, is not correct, if only because the text fits so snugly into a Dynasty 20 context. The flowery intro is again skipped, although it should be noted that the gods invoked in it are not the same as the ones mentioned elsewhere.

You are with me as a brother forever, [me acting as (?)] an adult freeman (private citizen) with (?) you every day. [To wit: . . .], as for my writing to you yesterday, saying: "Let one bring me one hin of o[intment for your] bread-eating companion."

Look here, she has come, but you have not let [one bring] it. If there is none, can't you give up your clothing and let them bring what I wrote to you about? When my letter reaches you, you must let the ointment be brought about which I wrote to you. See to it immediately. Do not let the man wait, while you [. . .] run off for her to the village (Deir al-Medina).

Now look, I have intercepted her and I have not let her know that I wrote to you: "She is here." She has come to stand before (the oracle of) Nefertari, life, prosperity, health, because of a dream. Take care of her and do not do what you do day in, day out. I am the one who writes to you daily, but you do not write back. May your health be good.

"She is here" is expressed by two simple words: *su dy* 'she here.' Clear language goes a long way to help, and it has been noted before that the language of the workmen would make a wonderful dissertation that would make any Late Egyptian grammarian cry.

Clear language. Deborah Sweeney and Janet Johnson are some of the authors who make gender studies fun and interesting, and therefore relevant. They write in a clear and crisp language that readers can understand. Some of the other literature in this genre is—unfortunately— never read, because it is unintelligible. An article or book should give the reader an understanding of what life was (or could have been) like for the women in Deir al-Medina or ancient Egypt in general. The sources themselves are difficult enough to deal with in the first place, so that passages such as the following (by an author who shall remain anonymous) should perhaps be replaced with clear and crisp language:

> The generational tombs in the Western Necropolis (of Deir al-Medina) reflect an increasing awareness of the relatedness of individuals, who share a common destiny in this life and the next. This shift toward lineage- based burial might represent a different type of social awareness and responsibility, or a material response to economic pressure, i.e., limited time and resources, or perhaps an increased desire to enhance one's opportunities in living contexts through associations with dead, though related, members of the community. This last point is relevant to the competitive nature of employment in this specific village.

A Mr. Wepemnofret—or Wep for short—who was one of King Khufu's many sons, chose to have himself buried in the immediate environment of his father's pyramid in about 2650 BCE (as did other siblings), so maybe this whole 'increasing awareness of the relatedness of individuals' concept is nonsense. The Deir al-Medina women delivered children at the cost of great pain and quite often death, reared them, cared for them, worried about them, and, more often than they wished, had to bury them. The evidence for villagers practicing a cult for their forebears is overwhelming. There was very little wrong with their awareness of who was a relative and who was not. So perhaps we should rephrase things a bit:

> The generational tombs in the western necropolis may reflect either a clearly felt family bond or simply a lack of burial space. Also, being able to point to an ancestor's tomb proved that people were village people, and thus eligible for a position.

(This is actually how I make my money. Turning fuzzy stuff into something people can understand.)

But we are not finished with P. DeM 6 yet, because some crucial passages have been translated differently by previous authors. For one thing, if this is indeed a letter from Nakhtsobek to Amunnakhte, it would seem that Amunnakhte was not in the village at all, because the woman referred to in this letter ran away to the village, unless of course one accepts Wente's translation: "Do not keep the man waiting, while you (the addressee) [. . .] run off for her to the village," which seems to refer to Černý's rendering (in French). So does the notion that the bread-eating companion in P. DeM 6 is in this case actually the woman (the essential signs that would determine whether it was a man or a woman are almost erased), whereas in P. DeM 4 the same expression is used by Nakhtsobek to refer to himself. I myself have very little doubt that Nakhtsobek is once again referring to himself here, and that the whole woman thing is an entirely new subject.

So we return to the idea proposed by Sweeney that the writing of the masculine article *pa* demonstrates that P. DeM 4–6 were written by three different scribes.

In ancient Egyptian the masculine article *pa* was written from right to left in hieratic, with the sign of the duck flying (Gardiner G 40) and the vulture (Gardiner G 1). If we look at the way *pa* is written in P. DeM 4–6, it looks rather uniform in P. DeM 4 and shows some spectacular variations in P. DeM 5. The characters in P. DeM 6 are also uniformly written, but they take a slightly more cursive form in P. DeM 4. It would seem therefore that Sweeney's observation that the texts were all written by different scribes is correct. It should be noted, however, that all the other words from P. DeM 4–6 in her paleographical tables contradict this observation because they show (too) many similarities across P. DeM

4–6. In other words, the only real obstacle to identifying P. DeM 4–6 as the products of a single scribe is the masculine article *pa*. Is that enough?

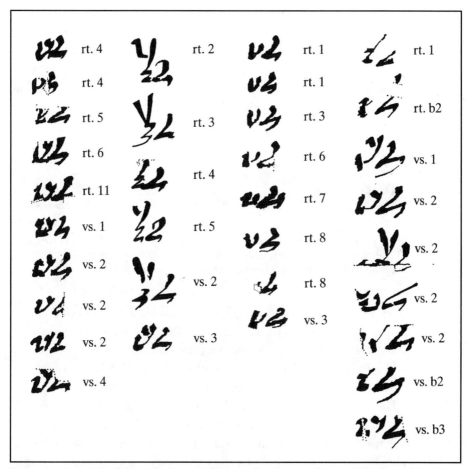

Figure 11. P. DeM 4 (left), P. DeM 5 (middle), and P. DeM 6 (right; table adapted from Sweeney, *Journal of Egyptian Archaeology* 84)

As we can see, the examples from P. DeM 4–6 show great variety, although some of these variations are easily explained by external factors such as amount of ink left on the brush, pressure exerted by the scribe when he put the brush on the papyrus, and the like. Other factors possibly involved are haste, state of mind, and concentration, but this has been commented on elsewhere (K. Donker van Heel, *Djekhy & Son: Doing Business in Ancient*

Egypt (Cairo: American University in Cairo Press, 2012), chapter 12). Still, if we look at *pa* in P. DeM 5 verso *l.* 3, we see that it is actually identical to the examples from P. DeM 4, which proves that the scribe of P. DeM 5 knew exactly how to write the form employed by the scribe of P. DeM 4.

In layman's terms: the scribe of P. DeM 5 apparently wrote *pa* in an elaborate ('Sunday') and an abbreviated ('weekday') form. This phenomenon had already been explained earlier by Jack Janssen, who noted that the famous Deir al-Medina scribe Djehutymose employed no fewer than three separate forms of *pa*.

Figure 12. Djehutymose's three ways to write *pa* (from K. Donker van Heel, in R.J. Demarée and A. Egberts, eds., *Deir el-Medina in the Third Millennium AD: A Tribute to Jac. J. Janssen* (Leiden, 2000))

Here we see another Sunday form (left), a weekday form (right), and an even more cursive weekday form (middle), showing that the use of *pa* to ascribe texts to separate scribes may not be a very reliable criterion.

The next thing that we will have to prove is, Did Nakhtsobek also employ the more cursive weekday variant as displayed by the scribe of P. DeM 6? And it turns out he did. When P. Chester Beatty I—which was to belong to 'our' Amunnakhte at some later date—came into Nakhtsobek's possession, he added a colophon ('scribe Nakhtsobek of The Tomb') in which he uses the exact form of *pa* employed by the scribe of P. DeM 6.

Figure 13. Nakhtsobek's colophon in P. Chester Beatty I (from K. Donker van Heel, in R.J. Demarée and A. Egberts, eds., *Deir el-Medina in the Third Millennium AD: A Tribute to Jac. J. Janssen* (Leiden, 2000))

So the next question is, Given that the scribe of P. DeM 5 wrote *pa* once just like Nakhtsobek did in P. DeM 4, and that Nakhtsobek did write *pa* in his colophon exactly like the scribe of P. DeM 6, should we not be allowed to propose with Černý (probably the greatest expert on New Kingdom administrative hieratic ever) that he was—or at least could very well have been—the scribe of P. DeM 4–6, all the more so because the examples of Djehutymose's writings of *pa* have already proved that a single scribe could employ three separate forms as he saw fit? In that case the writings of *pa* used by Nakhtsobek would have been as follows: Sunday form, weekday form, and cursive weekday form:

Figure 14. Nakhtsobek's three ways to write *pa* (from K. Donker van Heel, in R.J. Demarée and A. Egberts, eds., *Deir el-Medina in the Third Millennium AD: A Tribute to Jac. J. Janssen* (Leiden, 2000))

The last document to be discussed in this chapter is P. Vienna KM 3925 verso. The recto contains a magical text, unconnected with the administrative document on the verso. The writing is somehow slightly reminiscent of the scribe Amunnakhte son of Ipuy. Which is not to say that he wrote this text. Chris Eyre has shown that there may well have been 'schools' in Deir al-Medina teaching students to acquire a specific handwriting, in much the same way as Rembrandt taught his students to paint the way he did (or at least paint in a way that would not interfere with his own additions to the painting).

The verso was erased to write the present text. The content is not readily understood. The header mentions the scribe Amunmose who brought something to a number of men and women, among whom we find—if we trust the Leiden *Deir el-Medina Database*—our Amunnakhte, and also a man called Aânakhte son of Khaemnun (according to Kitchen, *Ramesside Inscriptions*), who occurs only in this papyrus, at least with a filiation. According to *Who's Who* he was also known as Minnakhte. If this really was a son of Khaemnun and Naunakhte, he did not live to see the division of his mother's inheritance. In O. DeM 398, a list of people doing work from year 3 of Ramesses IV, he appears with Amunnakhte. He is also found in O. DeM 828 + O. Vienna H. 1 (year 25 of Ramesses III), which also mentions their sister's husband Weserhat and their father Khaemnun (*ll.* 12–13; see chapter 6, "Was Husband Number Two a Demotion?").

The recent publication of the papyrus, however, suggests more. The editor reads the alleged 'Aânakhte son of Khaemnun' as 'Wasetnakhte son of Khaemnun,' which is awkward, because she was his daughter, and the correct reading should then be 'Wasetnakhte {son of} <daughter of> Khaemnun).' He also read the name 'Maaninakhtef son of Khaemnun' in column II *l.* 1. Although the passage is severely damaged, the reading seems correct, even if Kitchen had Hat[. . .] followed by the determinative one expects for the name of Maaninakhtef's father Khaemnun.

The scribe Amunmose could be the same man who was in such close contact with Maaninakhtef in some of the letters that were kept with the family archive. Then again, there were more scribes called Amunmose in Deir al-Medina, but in the future it may prove to be worthwhile to check lists such as these for just these kinds of (possible) relationships.

What makes this text interesting is that there are just names; no amounts or commodities are delivered. In a way one could say this describes our Amunnakhte perfectly well. He had at least one son, so he must have had a wife. But who was she?

17

Marriage:
The Final Step

There seems to have been no set marriage procedure or ceremony at Deir al-Medina in the sense that we know it. That would be very strange. There are indications that in Deir al-Medina a formal divorce (at least in some instances) required an official statement made in court to dissolve a marriage, and we know that people could simply decide to *hemes irem* 'sit with' someone and start a household. But there are several ostraca describing how the future son-in-law carries some gift to the house of his prospective father-in-law, hoping to marry the latter's daughter. The exact phrase is "N.N. (the groom) entered the house of N.N. (the future father-in-law) to make his daughter a wife." It so happens that later (abnormal) hieratic sources from the Third Intermediate Period and Dynasty 26 use this *exact* phrase as the introduction to a marital property arrangement setting out the property relationships and the inheritance for the offspring.

So somehow it seems very hard to understand why these scribes would have referred to this act if the entering of the house of the future father-in-law was not part of a fixed procedure or ceremony that made it clear to the outside world what was happening. And maybe there were more ways than one to set up a household, such as simply 'sitting together' with a woman, or going through the formal 'entering the house of N.N.' procedure. One might even consider that in the latter case the groom made promises about the maintenance of his future wife and the inheritance of their children, as in later times, but this we do not know. In other words, there may have been both informal and formal marriages in Deir al-Medina (an idea proposed earlier by Jack Janssen), just as I might refer to my girlfriend as 'my wife,' even if we only live together and have arranged the inheritance, with no other formalities. I have never even bothered to apply for the official guardianship over my children, because if you cannot trust the woman you love to make some sensible arrangements about the children if you were to split up, then what is the point of living?

Of course this is not where it stopped. Once inside the house, the groom-to-be would have to make a statement about the future well-being of his wife, stared down by perhaps sometimes rather sceptical in-laws and their relatives. From the later evidence we know that this statement by the groom may have been similar to the statement made by a Mr. Iturech in the abnormal hieratic P. Louvre E 7846 from 549 BCE. We have talked about this papyrus so much already that it is high time to see what it was about.

[Regnal year] 22, third month of the *shemu* season, day 5 of Pharaoh Amasis, life, prosperity, health. On this day: entering the house of the choachyte Djedher son of Amunirtais, which the choachyte Iturech son of Peteêse did, to make his daughter a wife, namely Mrs. Tsendjehuty, her mother being Ruru, his daughter of a wife, today.

The list of the things of which he said: "I will give it to her (as) a gift of a female virgin." Silver: two deben, emmer corn: fifty sacks.

He said: "As Amun lives, as Pharaoh lives, may [he] be healthy (and) may Amun give him victory. If I throw out Mrs. Tsendjehuty, her mother being Ruru, my sister who is mine, and if I cause that this heavy fate overtakes her, (because) I wish to throw her out or (because) I love other women than her, except for the great crime that is found in a woman, I will give her the two deben of silver and the fifty (sacks of) oipe emmer corn which are written above, apart from every profit (and) every accumulation that I will make with her, as well as part of my parental property that belongs to my children whom <she> has borne to me.

I will make my papyrus of a wife in regnal year 22, third month of the *shemu* season, day 5 of Pharaoh Amasis, life, prosperity, health, to replace my papyrus of a wife that I made for her in regnal year 15 of Pharaoh Amasis, life, prosperity, health, of which I have said to you (his wife): 'It is invalid.'"

Iturech's statement is followed by the signatures of the scribe and two witnesses. This is rather a long statement made by the groom in front of his father-in-law, his wife-to-be (who was in this case actually already his wife), and probably many others. The mention of the so-called gift of a female virgin only occurs in abnormal hieratic marital property arrangements and adds a spicy element to this text, because it was probably made because the couple had had children between the writing of the first marital contract in year 15 of Amasis and the present one of year 22. One should also note that in the case of a divorce his wife will receive this virgin gift only if she has not committed adultery. Granted, one could argue indefinitely over the question of whether a similar mechanism was in place in Deir al-Medina six hundred years earlier, but the essential clauses in P. Louvre E 7846—such as the one describing the groom entering the house of his father-in-law to make his daughter a wife—are in fact a one-on-one copy of the clauses known from texts that were written in New Kingdom Deir al-Medina; the Adoption Papyrus also mentions this 'entering of the house.' There are multiple legal phrases in abnormal hieratic that can be traced back to Deir al-Medina, so why not this one as well?

Somehow it is very hard to believe that the future husband would just enter the house of his father-in-law, make some vague promises about his future wife's well-being, and that was it. A daughter moving out of the house, severing her ties with her father, the *paterfamilias* (who was now no longer the first person to look to if she needed protection), and her mother, brothers, and sisters? This would have been a big thing. And all that without any ceremony of some sort? That is very hard to believe.

Luck has it that several texts have survived that provide an essential link between the evidence from Deir al-Medina and P. Louvre E 7846. P. Berlin P 3048 was written in the Libyan period. On the back of this text there are no fewer than thirty-seven texts, of which only two have been published to date. P. Berlin P 3048 verso A is also known as P. Eheverträge 1, after the seminal publication by the German demotist Erich Lüddeckens. This text is a summary of various marital property arrangements from the ninth century BCE, but again the vital clauses we know from Deir al-Medina are there.

What makes this Berlin papyrus so interesting is that it comes from the archive of the priest of Amun and overseer of the royal treasury Djedmontuiufankh, a person belonging to the absolute elite in Thebes. In fact, he seems to have used the back of P. Berlin P 3048 to jot down all these other different texts (of which P. Berlin P 3048 verso A, aka P. Eheverträge 1, is actually no. 36), varying from uncial to abnormal hieratic and anything in between, so one may well wonder whether these were all his own work. But by pushing the use of the same legal phrase to denote marriage back another three hundred years, the link with Deir al-Medina all of a sudden seems much closer, even if we cannot speak of an unbroken legal tradition going directly from Deir al-Medina to the time of Amasis via the Libyan period. So what else can the sources from Deir al-Medina reveal about marriage ceremonies?

We actually do have an undated text that may contain the remains of an oath on the occasion of a marriage (O. Varille 30), and this seems to indicate there was a ceremony of some sort, even if it would be equally possible to view it as a court record in which a man swears an oath not to mistreat his wife (again), as in O. Bodleian Library Eg. Inscr. 253.

> [. . .] daughter as a wife. If I will [. . .] act against (?) her tomorrow or the day after tomorrow [. . . or I will be under] hundred strokes of the stick, (and be) deprived of any accumulation [. . .] them with her. It will be given to her [. . .] as well. And she [. . .].

So this procedure probably did not just stop at the future son-in-law presenting his father-in-law with gifts, as in O. Berlin P 12406 from Dynasty 20, and then simply herding off his daughter to their new home. There is every indication that the members of the prominent families in the village—the chief workmen and scribes, for instance—had a tendency to intermarry. It is difficult to imagine that this would happen without at least some pomp and ceremony for the outside world to see, including hanging a bloodstained sheet from the roof the next morning.

Perhaps the marriage between Naunakhte (twelve or slightly older) and the scribe Qenhirkhopshef (fifty-something) did involve some such ceremony as well. But in that case how would her mother—about whom we know nothing except that she may have been called Henutshenu—have felt? Glad to be rid of her or very, very anxious, because her daughter was about to be taken away by a man who could well have been her grandfather?

There are no indications that Naunakhte's first marriage was an unhappy one. She inherited from her husband Qenhirkhopshef (which suggests that he may have adopted her to secure her rights to his inheritance) and named her eldest son from her second marriage after him. People do not do that if they hate each other. Although Naunakhte will forever remain something of an elusive figure in the numerous sources we have from Deir al-Medina, apart from her famous statement in court, we do have a clearer picture of the people in her life. The sources mentioning her two husbands and her children allowed us to reconstruct at least part of her life and to get an intimate look over her shoulder after more than 3,000 years. Naunakhte may not longer be with us, but it is hoped that this book may serve as her very own *peret er kheru*. Meeting her has been both vexing and fun, which is the perfect description of our better halves. Nothing has really changed in this respect.

Indexes

Deities
Rulers and officials (selection)
Members of Naunakhte's second family
Place names and local landmarks
Sources
General

Deities

Amun 5, 29, 50, 57, 59, 60, 61, 62, 79,
  80, 81, 84, 90, 102, 109, 110, 113,
  120, 123, 129, 138, 149, 150, 167,
  182, 184, 191, 194, 196, 203, 205,
  206, 214, 218, 226, 227
Amun-Ra 36, 152
Amunrasonter 45, 64, 110, 113, 115,
  117
  of the Good Encounter 57, 152,
  153, 156
  of the Holy Eight 53
  United with Eternity 204, 205
Amunhotep I 5, 46, 50, 52, 71, 72, 83,
  84, 132, 135, 176
Anuqet 47, 191
Bes 23, 45
Hathor 5, 6, 14, 23, 29, 32, 35, 40,
  111, 113, 116, 137, 138, 151, 153,
  156
Isis 147
Khnum 189, 190, 191, 192,193
Khonsu 115
Min 23

Mnevis 188, 189
Montu 80, 180
Mut 115, 133, 206
Nefertari 5, 71, 176, 219
Osiris 40, 81, 82, 147
Ptah 36
Qadesh 23
Rahorakhty 40, 115, 215
Reshep 23
Sakhmet-Hathor 137
Sehaqeq 39, 40
Sobek-Ra 46
Taweret 23, 50, 51, 146, 147

Rulers and officials (selection)

Aâkheperkara 207
Akhenaten 7
Amasis 54, 226, 227, 228
Amunmessu 29, 31, 34, 43, 56, 67, 184
Amunnakhte son of Ipuy (scribe) 33,
  52, 53, 73, 75, 84, 87, 88, 95, 114,
  120, 121, 129, 133, 134, 135, 142,
  143, 144, 177, 181, 182, 183, 195,
  196, 211, 212, 213, 223

Members of Naunakhte's second family

Place names and local landmarks

Sources

O. DeM 232 214
O. DeM 239 166
O. DeM 303 45
O. DeM 336 211
O. DeM 389 26
O. DeM 398 223
O. DeM 418 110, 149
O. DeM 439 179, 180
O. DeM 534 33
O. DeM 553 214
O. DeM 562 45
O. DeM 567 61
O. DeM 569 87
O. DeM 570 13, 138
O. DeM 571 20
O. DeM 582 78
O. DeM 586 46
O. DeM 642 50
O. DeM 643 49
O. DeM 676 30
O. DeM 698 25
O. DeM 764 169
O. DeM 828 + O. Vienna H. 1 87, 224
O. DeM 918 33, 83
O. DeM 919 55
O. DeM 952 42
O. DeM 956 111
O. DeM 973 77
O. DeM 999 *see* O. Cairo CG 25555 +
    O. DeM 999
O. DeM 1057 40
O. DeM 10004 129
O. DeM 10082 132
O. DeM 10084 111
O. DeM 10166 146
O. DeM 10253 130
O. Florence 2621 76
O. Gardiner 55 170
O. Gardiner 90 166
O. Gardiner 157 165
O. Gardiner 300 39
O. Gardiner AG 19 61, 165
O. Glasgow D.1925.66 173
O. Glasgow D.1925.68 108, 215
O. Glasgow D.1925.78 132
O. Glasgow D.1925.83 166
O. Glasgow D.1925.87 176

O. Heidelberg inv. no. 567 69
O. IFAO 199 184
O. IFAO 437 212
O. IFAO 628 87
O. IFAO 1005 50
O. IFAO 1079 33
O. IFAO 1096 212
O. IFAO 1253 104
O. IFAO 1262 74
O. IFAO 1322 *see* O. Cairo CG 25705
    + O. IFAO 1322 + O. Varille 38
O. KV 18/2.415 116
O. KV 18/3.576 116, 215
O. KV 18/3.584 15
O. KV 18/5.757 116
O. KV 18/6.882 183
O. KV 18/6.951 116
O. Leipzig 42 39
O. Leipzig 5152 39
O. Louvre E 27679 27
O. Louvre N 696 124
O. Louvre inv. no. 698 80
O. Michaelides 79 114
O. Michaelides 90 207
O. Munich 1638 108
O. Náprstek Museum P 2027 197
O. Náprstek Museum P 3809 49
O. Nash 1 12, 50, 55, 58, 60, 63
O. Nash 2 58, 60
O. Nash 5 128
O. Nash 6 167, 200
O. Nicholson Museum R. 97 70
O. Oriental Institute Museum 12073
    133
O. Oriental Institute Museum 12074
    182
O. Oriental Institute Museum 13512
    12
O. Petrie 6 109
O. Petrie 16 27, 51
O. Petrie 18 178
O. Petrie 21 135
O. Petrie 61 199
O. Prague 1826 197, 198
O. Prague H 10 49
O. Strasbourg H. 42 *see* O. DeM 40 +
    O. Strasbourg H. 42

P. Turin Cat. 1879 + 1899 + 1969 15
P. Turin Cat. 1880 17, 70, 95, 119,
  123, 124
P. Turin Cat. 1885 142, 143
P. Turin Cat. 1887 188, 190
P. Turin Cat. 1891 8
P. Turin Cat. 1895 + 2006 202
P. Turin Cat. 1899 *see* P. Turin Cat.
  1879 + 1899 + 1969
P. Turin Cat. 1966 122, 123
P. Turin Cat. 1969 *see* P. Turin Cat.
  1879 + 1899 + 1969
P. Turin Cat. 2006 *see* P. Turin Cat.
  1895 + 2006
P. Turin Cat. 2021 *see* P. Geneva D
  409 + P. Turin Cat. 2021
P. Turin Cat. 2074 *see* P. Milan E
  0.9.40127 + P. Turin Cat. 2074
P. Turin Cat. 2087 82
P. Turin CGT 54063 *see* P. Geneva
  MAH 15274 + P. Turin CGT 54063
P. Vienna KM 3925 223
Prohibitions 177
Raum 43 116
Setne and Tabubu 147
St. BM EA 144 25, 43, 51
St. BM EA 278 84, 90, 153, 154, 155,
  156
St. Cairo JdE 43565 199
St. Oriental Institute Museum 14315
  36
St. Szépmüvészeti Museum inv. no.
  51.232 74
St. Turin N. 50050 56
St. Turin N. 50066 23
Stato Civile 124, 129, 139, 149, 151
Tablet MMA 35.3.318 214
Teaching of Amenemhat 22
Teaching of Ankhsheshonqy 173
Tomb Robberies Papyri 188
TT 1 164
TT 7 22
TT 100 163
TT 210 30
TT 212 22
TT 220 36
TT 250 22

TT 321 73
TT 358 203
TT 1126 22, 43
TT 1159 A 131
Turin Indictment Papyrus 188, 194
Turin Judiciary Papyrus 63
Turin Strike Papyrus 17, 18, 70, 95,
  119, 120, 121
Turin Taxation Papyrus 202
Ushabti BM EA 33940 22
Wisdom of Any 176, 177

General

abnormal hieratic 80, 81, 122, 160,
  169, 172, 180, 181, 184, 199, 202,
  214, 225, 226, 227, 228
abortion 188, 194
absence record 25, 26, 29, 31, 34, 41,
  42, 43, 109
account 5, 25, 29, 34, 49, 50, 77, 87,
  100, 104, 107, 108, 109, 119, 140,
  141, 142, 146, 147, 150, 152, 198,
  206
accusation 31, 32, 36, 50, 52, 53, 54,
  55, 56, 57, 58, 59, 60, 61, 62, 63, 64,
  71, 74, 84, 86, 121, 122, 129, 133,
  134, 135, 156, 161, 175, 181, 182,
  188, 189, 190, 191, 193, 194, 195,
  196, 208, 209
administration 11, 13, 26, 31, 48, 192
administrative center (main office) 5,
  11, 13, 14, 15, 16, 56, 58, 68, 79, 86,
  87, 106, 136, 179
adoption 2, 22, 24, 27, 32, 33, 36, 37,
  49, 55, 92, 161, 228
adultery 3, 49, 53, 62, 122, 159, 172,
  179, 180, 181, 182, 185, 186, 187,
  188, 227
afterlife 7, 37, 45, 71, 75, 80, 177
age 1, 5, 21, 42, 43, 67, 70, 76, 88, 90,
  91, 92, 93, 94, 95, 102, 103, 113,
  128, 138, 139, 160, 162, 177
agriculture 13, 78, 79, 80, 81, 82, 83,
  189, 203, 205, 214
akh iqer (en) Ra 74
alimony 172, 173
Allam, Schafik 206, 208

Amarna heresy 38
Amarna kings 38
Amarna Period 7
archive (library) of Qenhirkhopshef
    2, 21, 38, 39, 46, 48, 50, 91, 96, 101,
    106, 108, 109, 110, 115, 116, 211,
    216, 217, 224
arrears in salaries 13, 71, 192, 194
Ashmolean Museum 89
Ayrton, Edward 116

baby 41, 42, 168, 182
Baines, John 75
beer 31, 45, 58, 110, 132, 141, 142,
    146, 147, 173, 176, 197, 201
Belmore, Earl of 153
Belzoni, Giovanni 153
Bierbrier, Morris 42
birth 7, 22, 23, 24, 41, 42, 100, 137,
    147, 148, 168, 219
Borghouts, Joris 40, 180
bribe 33, 36, 135, 189, 190, 191, 192,
    193
Bruyère, Bernard 16, 22, 23, 127, 131,
    153
burial 7, 29, 30, 42, 51, 71, 131, 211,
    212, 219, 220
Burkard, Günter 13, 14, 15, 19, 106

camp of workmen
in Valley of the Kings 116
on col 28, 37, 93, 153, 211
Canaanites 164
Carter, Howard 34, 142
Carter-Carnarvon excavations 35
Catalogue Général 12
Černý, Jaroslav 12, 22, 37, 43, 46, 98,
    99, 102, 116, 133, 139, 140, 141,
    142, 145, 149, 151, 153, 155, 159,
    184, 187, 207, 217, 220, 223
chapel 5, 6, 36, 37, 46, 50, 73, 183
checkpoint 12, 14, 15, 17, 18, 19, 20,
    82
chief of police 17, 57, 68, 70, 71, 76,
    82, 83, 132, 133, 134, 167, 212
chisel 13, 56, 57, 58, 59, 60, 71, 95,
    128, 183

choachyte 27, 81, 82, 226
circumcision 147, 148
claim 12, 13, 27, 48, 51, 53, 54, 72, 73,
    76, 121, 124, 128, 133, 162, 179,
    207, 208
coffin 14, 30, 51, 75, 76, 77, 80, 87,
    109, 110, 127, 131, 134, 144, 150,
    166, 211, 212, 213, 214
copper 13, 57, 58, 60, 62, 82, 85, 95,
    102, 107, 119, 120, 127, 128, 132,
    133, 134, 148, 149, 150, 151, 152,
    191, 207, 208, 213
Coptic church 6
Coptic period 6
Coptic settlement 5
copy (of document) 22, 38, 99, 125,
    164, 177, 216
court of law
    court record 2, 5, 57, 93, 95, 101,
    171, 184, 187, 207, 228
    Great Court of Thebes 164, 190,
    208
    in Medinet Habu 160, 161, 162,
    163, 164
    in Ramesseum 62
    in royal residence 206
    local court (*qenbet*) 1, 2, 13, 27, 33,
    49, 50, 51, 52, 53, 54, 55, 56, 57, 58,
    59, 60, 61, 62, 63, 67, 70, 71, 74, 78,
    79, 84, 85, 86, 87, 89, 90, 91, 94, 95,
    96, 101, 102, 111, 120, 123, 124,
    127, 128, 129, 133, 134, 135, 160,
    178, 179, 180, 181, 182, 183, 184,
    186, 187, 195, 196, 211, 212, 213,
    225, 229
cousin marriage *see* marriage
crime 33, 50, 55, 56, 58, 59, 62, 75, 83,
    172, 180, 181, 183, 188, 216, 226
cult 23
    forefather cult 24
    cult guild 47
    mortuary cult 27, 74, 81, 82, 220
customary law *see* law
damnatio memoriae 7

Davies, Benedict 3, 4, 105, 121, 124,
    138, 167

195, 199, 200, 201, 202, 225, 226, 227, 228
infertility 24, 44, 161
inheritance 1, 2, 3, 27, 28, 37, 43, 46, 48, 49, 51, 54, 55, 72, 82, 85, 89, 86, 90, 91, 92, 93, 94, 98, 99, 100, 101, 102, 103, 104, 109, 120, 124, 127, 128, 129, 139, 143, 144, 148, 149, 152, 161, 162, 166, 170, 172, 178, 179, 195, 211, 212, 223, 225, 226, 228
heir 93, 99

Janssen, Jack 15, 41, 140, 141, 142, 145, 222, 225
Journal of Egyptian Archaeology 19, 39, 99, 140, 143, 154, 188, 217, 221
joint (marital) property *see* property

Kitchen, Kenneth 77, 208, 223, 224
Koenig, Yvan 187
Kushite period 82

Late Period 13, 26, 39, 78, 80, 173, 194
Late Ramesside Letters (1967) 206
law 2, 54, 61, 62, 134, 163, 164, 170
customary law 54, 78, 122, 169
of Pharaoh 28, 162
lease 78, 80, 81, 82, 131, 132, 197, 214
Letters from Ancient Egypt (1990) 44, 206, 217
Libyan period 227, 228
Libyans 164
lit clos 23
literacy 2, 5, 21, 22, 83, 91, 108, 114, 115, 129, 130, 141, 152, 179, 213, 215
loan 47, 104, 133, 213, 214
logistics 8, 15, 44, 68, 70, 203
Louvre 27, 81
Lüddeckens, Erich 227

machismo 176, 197
magic 7, 29, 31, 39, 40, 56, 80, 205, 223
Manning, Joe 134

Mariette, Auguste 184
market *see* riverbank
marriage 2, 12, 21, 24, 30, 40, 43, 46, 48, 50, 52, 62, 67, 68, 78, 85, 90, 93, 95, 103, 104, 119, 120, 121, 122, 124, 129, 137, 138, 148, 151, 152, 160, 161, 164, 165, 166, 172, 173, 178, 179, 180, 182, 184, 186, 195, 196, 199, 213, 225–29
carrying the bundle 181, 182, 201, 202
cousin marriage 128
marital property arrangement *see* property
materfamilias 90, 138, 155
McDowell, Andrea 206
menstruation 12, 138, 148
Middle Kingdom 6, 38
migraine 29, 31, 39, 44
mobility 11, 12, 13, 17, 82, 133
Möller, Georg 15, 69, 106
Monastery of St. Mark 18
Monastery of the Town 3–5
mortuary foundation 32, 81, 121, 160
Mrs. Tsenhor (2014) 89
mummy 7, 72, 168
murder 62, 63, 64, 194, 202
Museo Egizio 23, 159, 168

necropolis 9, 12, 17, 19, 72, 82, 121, 152, 203, 219, 220
necropolis (work) journal 5, 6, 34, 61, 68, 70, 105, 108, 109, 144, 168, 212
New Kingdom 1, 3, 5, 12, 31, 81, 84, 122, 138, 161, 188, 223, 227
Newberry, Percy 39

Oath of the Lord 49, 57, 58, 59, 60, 62, 75, 78, 86, 96, 102, 120, 121, 122, 123, 124, 128, 134, 160, 167, 168, 171, 178, 179, 182, 183, 184, 186, 189, 196, 208, 212, 213, 228
oracle 50, 51, 52, 53, 54, 72, 73, 74, 83, 84, 85, 86, 135, 136, 152, 183, 184, 219
Oriental Institute Chicago 36